CONTESTING CHILDHOOD

Autobiography, Trauma, and Memory

KATE DOUGLAS

RUTGERS UNIVERSITY PRESS

NEW BRUNSWICK, NEW JERSEY, AND LONDON

Library of Congress Cataloging-in-Publication Data

Douglas, Kate., 1974–

Contesting childhood : autobiography, trauma, and memory / Kate Douglas.

    p.   cm. — (The Rutgers series in childhood studies)

Includes bibliographical references and index.

ISBN 978–0–8135–4663–6 (hardcover : alk. paper) — ISBN 978–0–8135–4664–3 (pbk. : alk. paper)

1. Autobiographical memory.   2. Memory—Social aspects.   3. Collective memory. 4. Psychic trauma.   I. Title.

BF378.S65D68 2010

305.2309—dc22

2009008096

A British Cataloging-in-Publication record for this book is available from the British Library.

Visit our Web site: http://rutgerspress.rutgers.edu

Manufactured in the United States of America

Typesetting: BookType

CONTENTS

ACKNOWLEDGMENTS

This research was undertaken with the support of grants and awards from the University of Queensland and from Flinders University of South Australia. For permission to reproduce book covers, my sincere thanks to Doubleday, Fourth Estate, Fremantle Press, Granta, Hale and Iremonger, HarperCollins, Headline, Penguin, Picador, and Random House.

Earlier versions of two chapters have appeared elsewhere: chapter 3 in *Biography* 24.4 (2001) and chapter 6 in Andrea O'Reilly and Elizabeth Podeneiks, eds., *Textual Mothers, Maternal Texts: Representations of Mothering in Contemporary Women's Literature: Fiction, Poetry and Life Writing* (Waterloo, ON: Wilfred Laurier Press, 2009). I presented earlier versions of chapters at conferences at the University of Queensland, the University of Adelaide, and the University of Sydney and at the International Auto/ Biography Association conference in Mainz, Germany, in 2006. I am grateful to all who offered helpful comments on these discussion papers.

This project began during my time as a postgraduate candidate at the University of Queensland, under the tutelage of Professor Gillian Whitlock, whose intellect and generosity have informed my thinking at every stage. My thanks go first to Gillian, my mentor, friend, and collaborator, who has had such an invaluable influence upon all aspects of my career. Second, I want to thank all who read this manuscript in its various stages of development: Tom Couser—whose work and advice have been particularly influential—Susanna Egan, Jude Seaboyer, Sidonie Smith, and Joanne Tompkins. I appreciate the rigor you each brought to this the manuscript, the time you took to offer insightful comments, and the encouragement you offered. I benefited greatly from drawing on the wealth of expertise offered by people whose own work in the field I admire so much.

Thanks to friends and colleagues near and far who have listened to my rambles, offering feedback, encouragement, and/or conversation along the way: Brodie Beales, Kylie Cardell, Shannon Dowling, Anna Johnston, Susan Luckman, Tasha Mayne, Kelly McWilliam, Catriona Mills, Laurie McNeill, Anna Poletti, Sue Sheridan, and Sue Williams. Current and former graduate students have offered fruitful challenges and encouraged me to think more about the genres I am working with: Tully Barnett, Sharyn Kaesehagan, Hannah Kent, Threasa Meads, and Ianto Ware.

Thanks to my colleagues in the International Auto/Biography Association (IABA), as well as those working in the disciplines of trauma and memory studies, whose work has had a profound impact upon mine: Paul John Eakin, Leigh Gilmore, Craig Howes, Margaretta Jolly, Rosanne Kennedy, Nancy K. Miller, Susannah Radstone, Julie Rak, and Julia Watson.

Thanks to Karen Douglas, Eileen Douglas, and David Douglas for their unwavering belief and encouragement over the years. Thanks to Robbie Sutton and Jamie and Rose Douglas-Sutton, simply for being you.

My thanks to Leslie Mitchner, Myra Bluebond-Langner, Marlie Wasserman, Marilyn Campbell, Rachel Friedman, India Cooper, Nicholas Humez, and all others at Rutgers University Press who were involved in the editing and preparation of this manuscript. Their dedication and professionalism propelled the project forward.

Finally, but most importantly, I would like to acknowledge the support of my family—Danni, Ella, and Josh Spencer—and to dedicate this book to them with love. Thanks for believing in me and the project, and for providing distractions when necessary.

CONTESTING CHILDHOOD

INTRODUCTION

CONSTRUCTING CHILDHOOD, CONTESTING CHILDHOOD

Childhood—a temporary state—becomes an emblem for our anxieties about the passing of time, the destruction of historical formations, or conversely, a vehicle for our hopes for the future. The innocent child is caught somewhere over the rainbow—between nostalgia and utopian optimism, between the past and the future.

—Chris Jenks, *Childhood*

The most notable and perhaps most infamous publishing trend of the 1990s was the autobiography of childhood—a piece of autobiographical writing concerned with the narration of childhood experiences. Autobiographers such as Mary Karr, Frank McCourt, and James McBride burst onto the American literary scene in the mid-1990s, paving the way for a plethora of similarly styled texts to follow. These autobiographies were distinctive for their depiction of challenging, often traumatic childhoods—characterized by abuse, poverty, discrimination, and identity struggles.

A search on Amazon.com reveals that over a thousand autobiographies of childhood have been published in roughly the past fifteen years—and this only considers mainstream forms of publication. This literary trend shows no signs of abating; the form is merely shifting to consider new voices and representations of childhood. Many autobiographies and biographies of childhood have been published in the United States and beyond during the 2000s, ranging from narratives about child abuse or family dysfunction, such as the autobiographies of Dave Pelzer, to "bad girl" autobiographies of fraught adolescences such as Koren Zailckas's *Smashed: Growing Up a Drunk Girl*. The genre has spawned autobiographies about childhood health and illness such as Judith Moore's *Fat Girl* and biographies of crimes against children such as *Girl in the Cellar*—a biography of the kidnapped Austrian girl Natascha Kampusch, who was found in 2006 at age eighteen after being held captive for over eight years. The childhood autobiography has extended beyond the book industry to documentaries concerned with racial or class inequalities suffered by children—such as the Academy Award–winning *Born into Brothels: Calcutta's Red Light Kids* and Michael Apted's continuing *Up!* series. Most recently, autobiographies of childhood have emerged in online media forms—such as personal Web pages, blogs, and social networking sites like Facebook and MySpace, which are heavily populated by adolescents sharing stories about their lives. These online declarations of social life, tastes, and accomplishments have allowed children and adolescents to exert greater control over cultural representations of young lives.

Collectively, these cultural texts reflect the ways in which childhood is imagined and constructed via life-writing forms within contemporary culture. They reveal the cultural spaces that are available to host and circulate these narratives—and the limits of their representations. These texts also reflect the cultural investments that have affected childhood during the 1990s and 2000s and continue to do so—examining why particular representations of childhood exist in repetition whereas others emerge radically from the margins, challenging perceptions of childhoods past.

Contesting Childhood links autobiography studies and studies of childhood to explore the ways in which one particular cultural site, in this instance auto-biography, has constructed childhood—has contested its meanings, histories, and representations. This book imagines autobiography as a cultural micro-cosm, a rich case study to promote a better understanding of the myriad ways in which constructions of childhood are contested every day within culture, and the implications of these contestations. I use the term "autobiography" to refer to a published life-narrative monograph in which the author and protagonist are the same person. Many of the texts I discuss will be popularly referred to as "memoir," and, while I acknowledge the important differences between the two terms, and their different history and politics, I agree with Susanna Egan, who suggests that arguing over terms does not necessarily advance the common cause of studies into life writing. Egan writes:

> We are politically and theoretically short-sighted when we quarrel with a term as comprehensive and as flexible as "autobiography." I recognize that each alternative term has been introduced either as a form of resis-tance to the exclusionary practices of traditional humanism, and part of a valuable reshaping of the field, or in what I think of as a mistaken understanding that this or that curious item that has caught our attention does not really belong. With the field of autobiography studies radically reshaped over the past twenty years, my concern now is that we reach for

new horizons not as separate or contested territories but as significant features of the landscape, protecting ourselves from anxiety about what does or does not belong by acknowledging the flexibility of a word that admits so many variations. (*Mirror Talk* 14)

I will use the term "autobiography" interchangeably with "memoir," "life writing," and "life narrative." These terms are, for the purpose of this study, functionally interchangeable. "Autobiography of childhood" is used as a practical, umbrella term that does not deny the diversity within the genre but rather seeks to open up the conceptual and theoretical overlaps between the different concepts.

Autobiography and the Politics of Childhood

Autobiographies of childhood most commonly take the form of an adult author writing about events from his or her childhood. Although some of these autobiographies have been written by established writers of literary fiction such as J. M. Coetzee and Hilary Mantel, a large proportion of the autobiographies of childhood published during the 1990s and 2000s represent the writer's first full-length publication—as in the cases of James McBride and Dave Pelzer. The autobiography of childhood is a diverse subgenre of autobiography, occupied by writers of literary and popular autobiography, by academics, celebrities, therapists, and social activists, to give just a few examples.

Autobiographies of childhood have been widely read and have gained popularity and notoriety primarily through their representations of traumatic childhoods—particularly autobiographical depictions of child abuse. The association between autobiography and childhood trauma has brought the genre both acclaim and infamy. At best, autobiographies of childhood have been praised for bringing child abuse to public attention and becoming tools for advocacy; at worst, these books have been criticized for being exploitative, unethical, and even voyeuristic in their representation of child subjects.

Such responses are perhaps not surprising when considering the cultural contexts within which these texts appear. Autobiographies of childhood have emerged at a cultural and historical moment of intense socio-cultural interest in the child figure. The United Nations Convention on the Rights of the Child (which became effective in 1990) has solicited a deeper cultural awareness of children's rights globally—and has encouraged an acknowledgement of, and commitment to, universal children's rights based on international legal principles. At the heart of the convention is an assertion of the child as an individual with human rights equal to adult individuals'. Children are not to be considered the rightful property of parents or guardians. Opposition to the convention (from the United States and United Kingdom, for example) principally revolved around conflicts between the convention and existing national laws—particularly relating to the treatment of juvenile offenders and to the perception that the convention might confuse or undermine the rights of parents to discipline their children.[1]

In the 1990s and 2000s the child has been, and continues to be, highly visible at all levels of Western cultural life from art and literature though advertising, popular television programs, and films. Further, as Henry Jenkins argues, the child figure has been, and continues to be, important in a range of political and ideological battles; in fact, he contends, "almost every major political battle of the twentieth century has been fought on the backs of children" (*Children's Culture Reader* 2).

Jenkins's assertion is well supported by a cursory glance at political events of the 1990s and 2000s. A number of "flash points" relating to Western childhoods have marked the late twentieth century and the early twenty-first as a time when childhood was "in crisis." Henry A. Giroux uses the term "flash points" to describe moments of social crisis, which can be seen to challenge or consolidate specific aspects of cultural memory that surround childhood ("Stealing Innocence" 269). High-profile events such as school shootings (particularly Columbine) and child abductions and murders (for instance, JonBenét Ramsey, James Bulger, and Madeleine McCann) place childhood, and more particularly the relationship that societies have with childhood, under deep scrutiny. Such events provoke collective debate (usually led by the media) wherein our various investments in, and preconceptions of, childhood are brought into sharp focus.

Consider two high-profile child murder cases: JonBenét Ramsey in the United States and James Bulger in the United Kingdom. JonBenét Ramsey was a six-year-old girl who was

found strangled in her wealthy parents' Boulder, Colorado home the day after Christmas, 1996. Throughout the first half of 1997, the press displayed a fixation on the case. Major media networks, newspapers, and tabloids besieged the public with images of JonBenet, dubbed as the slain little beauty queen, posing coquettishly in a tight dress, wearing bright red lipstick, her hair highlighted blonde. The JonBenet Ramsay [*sic*] case revealed once again that the media gravitate toward victims that fit the dominant culture's image of itself. Children who are white, blonde, and middle-class are not only invested with more humanity, they become emblematic of the social order. (Giroux, "Stealing Innocence" 268)

As Giroux contends, the murder of JonBenét Ramsey captured public attention because it shattered the assumption "that the primary threat to innocence lies outside the family" (269). In the "stranger danger" era, people were being asked to consider the plethora of diverse and complex relationships that exist within contemporary Western families. Ramsey's death also provoked pointed questions about childhood maturation and the apparent dangers of allowing children to grow up too soon, a point I return to in chapter 2.

In line with this, contemporary autobiographies of childhood have commonly placed the family under intense scrutiny. When child abuse occurs, the most common site is the family—whether biological, adoptive, or foster care—or agents of the family such as babysitters, family friends, or trusted family connections such as clergy (consider the autobiographies of Andrea Ashworth, Constance Briscoe, Augusten Burroughs, Duncan Fairhurst, Antwone Fisher, Donna Ford, Rosalie Fraser, Mary Karr, and Dave Pelzer, to name just a few examples).

Across the Atlantic just three years prior to the death of JonBenét Ramsey, similar questions were being raised about childhood and the family being in a state of crisis—apparently a result of the decline of traditional family values. James Bulger was three years old when he was abducted and killed by two ten-year-old boys (Jon Venables and Robert Thompson) in Liverpool, England, in 1993. The Bulger murder represented a watershed in the perception of childhood in the United Kingdom and beyond. That two children perpetrated the murder proved, at least as far as the media was concerned, that society had "gone too far" and that childhood and families were well and truly in moral decline. Phil Scraton explains, "At the very moment when informed analysis and understanding of the complexities [of childhood] was most needed, the political agenda was set to condemn, demonize and punish" ("Introduction" viii). The fact that

children are capable of violence, of rape, muggings and even murder, is an idea that clearly falls outside traditional formulations of childhood. As people privately struggled to make sense of the events of 1993, newspaper headlines echoed their confusion, a confusion engendered by children revealed in a new role as suspects in a hitherto adult crime[:] "it is supposed to be the age of innocence so how could these 10 year olds turn into killers?" (Jenks 127–128)

The unitary idea of "the child" as innocent was revealed as illusory (125). Perhaps predictably, though, the dominant paradigm for thinking about childhood (innocence) was replaced by an all-encompassing binary: that children are either innocent or evil and, moreover, that "innocent" children are under constant threat from "evil" children. According to media reports the incident was representative of the broader "subjugation of innocence and . . . potential for evil in all children" (Scraton, "Introduction" viii). Childhood was seen to be in "crisis" (Davis and Bourhill 28; Scraton, "Introduction" ix).

Many scholars, however, saw the Bulger murder as evidence of, and providing the impetus to discuss, the plurality of childhoods existing in Britain and beyond—the complexities of childhood that are too often ignored. Chris Jenks explains that "what the British public seemed to have to come to terms with in 1993 was that childhood could no longer be envisioned unproblematically as a once-upon-a-time with a happy and predictable ending" (118). The Bulger murder "sharpened a theoretical focus on the plurality of childhoods, a plurality evidenced not only cross-culturally but also within cultures" (121). Furthermore, this traumatic incident also disassembled the "traditional binary opposition between the categories of 'child' and 'adult'" (127–128), particularly in terms of expectations of the behavior and capabilities of children or adults, respectively.

Cultural flash points leave a significant impression upon how people see their everyday lives, driving public debates and impacting heavily upon cultural representations of childhood—within news media, documentary, and literature. Certain ideological positions relating to childhood are legitimized at these cultural moments.

Autobiographies of childhood circulate within this milieu and within contemporary debates about childhood. When authors write about their childhoods, the personal is inevitably political. As Bain Attwood argues, political and cultural environments "enable, even demand, that particular narratives reach and be accepted by a large number of people" (189). Thus a turn to traumatic autobiographies of childhood indicates a culture preoccupied with trauma, with childhood, and with their intersection. Further, in representing childhoods past, these autobiographies reveal more about the present than they do about the past. These texts are deeply imbued with the preoccupations of the present—children's rights, children's futures, education, violence against and by children, socialization, and childhood sexuality, to name just a few pertinent examples. Individual lives become emblematic of wider social concerns about childhood.

This book has two aims: first, to examine autobiographies of childhood as a cultural phenomenon, collectively revealing more about contemporary social, political, and cultural concerns and preoccupations about childhood than they do about the past. I consider autobiographies of childhood as tools of cultural memory. Cultural memory is the innumerable ways in which so-called individual memory is socially and culturally shaped—for example, by institutions, cultural myths, and traditions. Cultural memory also encompasses challenges to official or historical memory—for instance, facilitating the emergence of new or counter-memory.[2] I consider the ways in which autobiographies of childhood function to both "corrupt" and "protect" childhood (to appropriate Jenkins's terms). To what extent do autobiographies of childhood confirm, distill, or challenge dominant histories of Western childhoods or established paradigms for representing childhood? I am interested in what is being written in autobiographies of childhood and the limits of these representations. Who is authorized to write about childhood, and how are readers positioned to read about childhood via autobiography?

Second, I aim to explore some of the ways in which autobiographies of childhood have become politically important, even politically influential, texts. How are these autobiographical representations of childhood involved in the reshaping of childhood within cultural memory and the public sphere? For example, these texts have generated activism for children's rights. Autobiographies of childhood are commonly listed on health and welfare agency Web sites as therapeutic tools or tools for social action.[3] As well as bringing particular experiences of childhood to public attention, autobiographers of childhood have commonly made or confirmed their authors as advocates for children's rights. Autobiographer Kathleen O'Malley writes about the abuse she endured in an industrial school run by the Sisters of Mercy in Ireland in the 1950s in her autobiography *Childhood Interrupted*. O'Malley now works with survivors and has publicly campaigned for an apology from the National Society for the Prevention of Cruelty to Children (NSPCC), the Irish government, and the religious organizations that failed to protect her as a child. In short, autobiographies of childhood have had tangible social impact: They have formed part of a network of cultural texts that have impacted upon social justice initiatives for children.

Autobiographies of childhood respond to and are sanctioned by their contemporary contexts, but they are also authorized by literature and history. The autobiography of childhood form has a rich history, which provides a further context for reading those published in the late twentieth and early twenty-first centuries—particularly the latter—as a means of "writing back" to paradigmatic historical representations of childhood. Of particular significance has been the gradual shift that the genre has made from primarily being a space for the exploration of an artist's development to being a space for exploring and celebrating the independent cultural function of childhood and for highlighting the experiences of the traumatized child.

Childhood, History, and Autobiography

There is a long and well-documented literary context for writing about childhood, particularly in European literature. However, as Valerie Sanders notes, with the exception of Augustine's *Confessions*, childhood was given little attention in European life writing until the eighteenth century—arguably coinciding with more general cultural shifts in the perception of childhood. One school of thought suggests that during the sixteenth, seventeenth, and eighteenth centuries, people increasingly saw childhood as a separate developmental stage to adulthood, worthy of consideration in itself. Artistic and literary depictions of childhood increasingly represented children as physically and socially distinctive from adults. However, gender and class inequalities prevailed and shaped these perceptions and representations of childhood. The eighteenth-century interest in autobiographies of childhood extended to boyhoods but rarely girlhoods, and to saints rather than ordinary people (Sanders 203–204).[4]

In the nineteenth century, Romantic poets used childhood experience as a means for reflecting on human development. Retrospective narratives of childhood—such as William Wordsworth's *The Prelude*—explain the development of the artist's mind, the loss of innocence, and the rise to experience. Another significant form was the *bildungsroman,* or novel of personal development. Novelists such as Charles Dickens, Charlotte Brontë, and Thomas Hardy used fictional forms to explore the (often difficult) physical, social, psychological, and/or spiritual development of the protagonist from childhood to adulthood. Though the bildungsroman was most commonly a fictional narrative, its style heavily influenced future autobiographical writings.[5] The bildungsroman also marked a significant development in the autobiography of childhood form. It overtly addressed the tensions experienced by the protagonist as he or she searched for his or her place in the social order—the conflicts that occur between childhood and adulthood. Novels such as Dickens's *Great Expectations* and Brontë's *Jane Eyre* were directly concerned with the rights of the child through—for example—their representations of child mortality, class and gender inequality, and benevolence.

Childhood would seem to be an essential and inevitable part of all life writing—after all, how can a person represent his or her life or development without representing where it began? However, in the twentieth and twenty-first centuries, the representation of childhood within autobiography has come to be more significant than this. Childhood has assumed a crucial place in autobiographical writing rather than an inevitable one. Childhood is recognizable synecdoche for history—a means for explaining and interpreting the past, revising and correcting the mistakes of history. Concurrently, childhood continues to be a symbol of the future and its potential—a means for sanctioning an autobiographical narrative and for drawing attention to its politics.

Representations of childhood have featured commonly and increasingly in autobiographical writings in the twentieth century—from the memoirs of Virginia Woolf to the diary of Anne Frank through to the academic and activist writings of Christa Wolf, Annette Kuhn, and Richard Rodriguez—all of whom are concerned with the relationship between the child and the social world. Twentieth-century autobiographers sought to understand childhood developmentally and socially—to understand their experiences of the world—but also to explore how experiences of childhood impact upon adult life. For example, in *Hunger of Memory: The Education of Richard Rodriguez*, Rodriguez explores the alienation he felt as a Mexican immigrant child in the United States. Rodriguez's alienation and identity struggles, stemming from his experiences of language, education, masculinity, sexuality, and family life, are explored both as he experienced them as a child (thus sanctioning the experiences of the child as an autobiographical subject) and as they affected him as an adult (thus exploring the impact of childhood experiences on the adult). Disclosing his own experiences of childhood also allows Rodriguez to make (controversial) political statements in his autobiography, for example, advocating assimilation for migrant children.

Rodriguez's approach is emblematic of many autobiographies of childhood produced in the late twentieth and early twenty-first centuries. Autobiographers have commonly used their autobiography as a platform for exploring social history, particularly the difficulties faced by children in the social world. The mid-1990s saw the publication of three notable autobiographies of childhood: Mary Karr's *The Liars' Club*, Frank McCourt's *Angela's Ashes*, and James McBride's *The Color of Water*. These three autobiographies are commonly thought to have been the catalysts for the boom that followed. What is distinctive about this grouping is that each of the texts represents a lower-socio-economic experience of childhood, and each depicts trauma. Each represents a rags-to-riches journey from a poor childhood and unconventional family life to adult success. Karr's *Liars' Club* represents the effects of adult dysfunction—alcoholism, violence, mental illness, neglect, and rape—on the children that witness this dysfunction and inevitably become implicated within it. Karr's autobiography was widely praised for its wit and lack of self-pity. McBride's *Color of Water* was also praised for its lack of self-pity, but most notably this autobiography was commended for its exploration of racial identities and its celebration of McBride's resilient mother. *Angela's Ashes*—McCourt's autobiography of his poor, miserable Irish childhood—became one of the literary success stories of the 1990s. McCourt's autobiography is presented as an accessible, "real-life," rags-to-riches narrative reconstruction of childhood from a child's perspective, addressing issues such as poverty, alcoholism, domestic violence, and infant mortality.

Despite this developing corpus of texts, there are only a handful of scholarly studies devoted to analyzing autobiographies of childhood, and most predate the boom period of autobiography. In the 1980s and early 1990s Richard N. Coe, David McCooey, and Joy Hooten recognized the centrality of childhood in autobiographical writing. These studies focus on mostly pre- or early twentieth-century European and Australia "literary" autobiography and attempt to generalize about this form by finding common preoccupations and literary styles.[6] In these studies, autobiographies represent childhood as a mythic stage—a site for the recovery of Edenic memories. McCooey suggests that this standard was commonly employed in nineteenth- and twentieth-century autobiographies as a means to stress a "fall"—a move from childhood to adulthood that entails the loss of sexual or some other form of "innocence" ("Australian Autobiographies" 136). Within such texts, the child was not necessarily of interest in itself and was beyond history.[7] References to childhood illustrate the growth of the artist and the particular debts owed by the adult self to childhood. The pains of childhood are largely due to childhood development, the death of a family member, or the anguish of artistry. The primary trauma associated with childhood is its loss, the inevitable move away from mythic childhood innocence into the adult world.

As autobiographical representations of childhood altered, so did scholarly approaches to the genre. The previous models for reading autobiographies of childhood, which focused on universal notions of childhood innocence and/or the development of the artist, proved to be largely inadequate for reading the increasingly diverse representations that emerged in twentieth-century autobiography. For example, studies by Rosamund Dalziell and others represent a shift in thinking about autobiographies of childhood—toward an examination of autobiographies of childhood that focus on childhood trauma. Dalziell, writing about twentieth-century Australian autobiographies of childhood, suggests that these autobiographies illustrate the particular spaces that have opened up for the expression of shame experienced in childhood: "Accounts of personal errors and failures, of deception and lying, of humiliating punishments by parents or schoolteachers, of other children's mockery for some perceived difference, of embarrassing sexual experiences in adolescence, or shame about parents, self, status, race or ethnicity, class or gender can be seen to permeate Australian autobiography of the early twentieth century" (*Shameful Autobiographies* 9). Also in Australian autobiography, Gillian Whitlock notes the inadequacy of Western models of childhoods for analyzing Indigenous Australian autobiography. Whitlock argues, "To put the narration of [an Indigenous] childhood in [Sally Morgan's] *Auntie Rita* alongside that of Jill Ker Conway's *The Road from Coorain*, for example, is to turn aside from the fact that childhood as it is traditionally understood in Western biographic writing as a time of innocence is non-existent in Aboriginal autobiography" ("From Biography to Autobiography" 246). Similarly, Nellie Y. McKay points out that African American childhoods, and the childhoods of other minority groups, cannot be represented according to notions of the universal, innocent child. For McKay autobiographies can provide alternative representations to challenge universal notions of childhood that have circulated for too long (107). And Rocio G. Davis, in *Begin Here*, her study of Asian North American memoirs, explores how these minority memoirs become tools of cultural memory—challenging the dominant experiences of national identity and rewriting the ascendant childhood scripts they have inherited.

Contesting Childhood builds on these late twentieth-century studies of twentieth- and twenty-first-century autobiographies, by focusing on the cultural memory work that autobiographies of childhood do: engaging with dominant discourses, institutions, and histories to offer alternative narratives of childhood. Reading a diverse assortment of autobiographies of childhood involves reading across childhoods, analyzing autobiographies from different moments and histories, looking at how various narratives, tropes, sites, figures, and moments are used polemically. This approach promotes an understanding of how particular autobiographical narratives become authoritative at particular cultural moments.

Writing Autobiographically about Childhood at the Turn of the Millennium

This book examines the cultural work of autobiographies of childhood produced from the mid-1990s to the early 2000s—at the turn of the century, and in this instance it is also the turn of the millennium. Such endings and beginnings are commonly associated with catharsis. It is significant that such a quantity of autobiographies of childhood emerged at the turn of the millennium. To what extent do these autobiographies of childhood signal a catharsis, a renegotiation of childhood experiences and histories, and an evaluation of the relationships and identities associated with childhood?

My focus on this period is also in recognition of critical movements in autobiography scholarship in the late 1990s and early 2000s. The choice of this time frame is significant in that it traces what most theorists suggest has been the most significant boom period of autobiographical production to date. Leigh Gilmore writes:

> In the midst of a much-remarked-upon economic boom another pocket of extraordinary vitality emerged in the United States. As the Dow soared high in a climate of speculation, memoir boomed. Signs of growth abounded: book reviewers ritualistically cited memoir's ubiquity, more publishers expanded their lists to include memoir, more first books were marketed as memoir. . . . This memoir boom did not prominently feature elder statesmen reporting on how their public lives neatly paralleled historical events. Instead, memoir in the '90s was dominated by the comparatively young whose private lives were emblematic of unofficial histories ("Limit-Cases" 128).

Significantly, Gilmore comments on the genre being marked by new voices challenging established histories ("Limit-Cases" 128). Autobiographies of childhood have emerged at a time when intense critical attention was being placed upon the cultural work of autobiography. Countless scholars, media commentators, and book-trade practitioners agree that the late twentieth century and early twenty-first century has been the "first-person era." Review publications have abounded with discussions of the significance of these autobiographical trends, focusing on what they imply about autobiography's readerships.[8] Such critical attention has resulted in autobiography becoming one of the most talked-about literary forms. The genre has become a site where a range of literary-cultural politics are fought out, raising an array of new ideological concerns, particularly in relation to self-disclosure, memory, and representation. Autobiographical research during this period has been preoccupied with autobiographical writing and social justice, the "right" to represent oneself and others, subjectivity, and the politics and didacticism of autobiography.

This period has also been a boom period for writing about childhood, for example, in the disciplines of cultural studies, sociology, education, and psychology, as William Corsaro contends:

As recently as ten years ago there was a near absence of studies on children in mainstream sociology . . . [yet there has recently been] a large and growing number of monographs, edited volumes, and journal articles which address theoretical issues and report empirical findings related to the sociological study of children and childhood. Childhood socialisation has been given expanded coverage in basic introductory texts in sociology and social psychology, and new journals and sections of national and international associations devoted to the sociology of childhood have been established. (7)[9]

Children feature prominently in all forms of contemporary cultural representation, for example, as characters in television, film, and literature and in magazine and television advertising featuring children's toys and care products. Alongside nostalgic images of playful innocence is a diverse range of traumatic images of childhood in the media, such as "street kids," child prostitutes, and drug addicts, and apocalyptic notions of youth disorder. Children are both victims and perpetrators of violent crime; they are refugees and victims of disasters, poverty, and neglect. Children are "stolen," abused, murdered. Children are most commonly represented according to the binaries of innocence and experience. The child becomes a malleable scapegoat for a wide range of fears related to the future of social life and the preservation of identities in a rapidly changing world.

In *Contesting Childhood* I use these cultural contexts as a foundation for examining a sample of autobiographies of childhood written during the 1990s and early 2000s. Of the thousands that have been penned, I have selected a small number of case studies that I hope will illuminate how the subgenre has developed. I have chosen a varied selection of autobiographies written by a diverse range of authors—from experienced to first-time authors, from literary through popular autobiographies. Some of the texts I have chosen are famous, even infamous, examples of the genre. Others are less well known but equally intriguing for what they reveal about the form.

The texts I have chosen are predominantly from Australia, the United Kingdom, and the United States; however, the texts represent a broad cultural mix of autobiographies from within these countries (for example, exploring issues of race, culture, gender, class, and sexuality). These countries have been prolific producers of autobiographies of childhood and have shaped a diverse output of autobiographies. Autobiographies of childhood from the United States and the United Kingdom have been largely responsible for shaping the genre as it exists in other countries—for example, enabling particular narratives of childhood and disabling others.

Concentrating on autobiographies of childhood from particular countries allows for a focused, contextual study of autobiographies of childhood, which interprets these texts in light of socio-political events that have influenced their production and circulation.

By contextualizing these autobiographies within specific socio-political locations and moments I am able to explore how autobiographies of childhood result from, and engage with, contemporary cultural "flash points," or moments of social crisis. I am interested in the ways in which autobiographies of childhood engage with cultural memory: with master narratives of childhood that circulate within these countries. I do not offer the examples I use in this book as representative of global trends in autobiographical writings about childhood; rather, I am interested in looking specifically at examples from particular countries as a means of illuminating the ways in which they become part of the cultural production of Western childhood/s. I hope that this specialized and focused approach will enrich rather than limit the conclusions I am able to draw in this book.

I use different methodologies to read these autobiographies. One is close textual readings of primary sources—of the autobiographies themselves; I also examine their cultural production by looking at contextual evidence such as reviews and promotional material. I read this primary and secondary material in light of theoretical material on childhood, autobiography, and memory. I examine patterns and trends in autobiographical writings about childhood as others have done; however, this is not the primary aim of this book.[10] I am interested in the socio-cultural impact of these texts—particularly the ways in which they engage with cultural memory and respond to cultural constructions of childhood. Autobiographies of childhood written between 1990 and 2007 most commonly represent childhoods between 1940 and the 1980s. How can these pasts be represented? What contemporary preoccupations, even agendas regarding childhood, do they reveal? In investigating the memory work that these autobiographies of childhood are engaged in, I propose that nostalgia and trauma have become two of the dominant memory practices affecting how autobiographies of childhood are written, circulated, and read in contemporary Western contexts. Nostalgic and traumatic memories exist in an interdependent productive tension within autobiographies of childhood.

I am interested in, and thus devote chapter-length discussions to, the constructed relationships between the child and the adult author—who must compose his or her childhood self; the child and the adult parent—both of whom the author is mandated to represent ethically in the autobiography;

and the child and the reader—who is positioned to receive the narrative and respond in particular ways. Collectively, these relationships, which are constructed within autobiographies of childhood, mirror society's relationship to children.

Chapters 1, 2, and 3 broadly contextualize this project. These chapters consider autobiographical scholarship (including memory studies), the literary industries that circulate these texts, and the sociology of childhood as the three main foundations for analyzing autobiographies of childhood. Chapter 1 locates the production of autobiographies of childhood within the socio-political contexts in which these autobiographies have emerged, from the mid-1990s to 2007. Autobiographies of childhood have emerged at a time of deepening awareness of, and commitment to, the rights of the child. Autobiographies always reveal more about the present than about the past, and also reveal something of an imagined future. Texts such as Mary Karr's *The Liars' Club* and Lorna Sage's *Bad Blood* are products of cultural memory and engage in significant memory work.

In chapter 2 I argue that the literary-cultural and economic contexts within which these texts appear are crucial to an understanding of how these autobiographies are produced and read. In particular, these contexts reveal the extent to which autobiographies of childhood mobilize, and depend upon, the trope of the "innocent" child for cultural and commercial currency. In autobiographies of childhood, childhoods are produced and sold (by writers, publishers, and booksellers) and bought and consumed (by readers). Autobiographies of childhood pledge to offer experiences and stories of childhood for adult consumption, allowing adults to fantasize about their collective pasts and futures.

Autobiographies of childhood construct a relationship between the autobiographical child and the adult reader. In chapter 3 I explore the impact of the adult autobiographical author in the production and reception of autobiographies of childhood. The adult autobiographer constructs the child self, bringing the child back to life a generation on. To write an autobiography of childhood is to inhabit and/or challenge the identities that are available for articulating childhood experiences at a particular cultural moment. What relationship is constructed between the adult autobiographical author and the child self the author represents? What links are made between childhood and adulthood both inside and outside the text (for example, within the text's representations and in promotional material and author interviews about the autobiography)? And what tropes or templates emerge for representing this relationship, for example, the resilient child and the recovered, forgiving adult? I read these textual constructions of the child subject to adult autobiographer, through Frank McCourt's *Angela's Ashes* and Andrea Ashworth's *Once in a House on Fire*, in light of therapeutic discourse, psychoanalysis, and trauma theory.

Chapters 4 and 5 look at two particular scripts for remembering childhood: trauma and nostalgia, as well as the overlaps and interstitial spaces of these modes of remembering. In chapter 4 I isolate nostalgia as a case study. Nostalgia most commonly describes a longing for the past, a wish to return to the past, or a wish to return to a lost place or time. I am interested in the continued prevalence of nostalgic representations of childhood within autobiographies of childhood, especially considering the emergence, even dominance, of traumatic autobiographies of childhood within the genre.

In looking at nostalgic memories of childhood in chapter 4 and traumatic childhoods in chapter 5, I am not suggesting that they are binary opposites or that they are exclusive categorizations—quite the contrary. Rather, I am interested in their interrelationship, their coexistence within similar social contexts, and the ways in which these two memory modes, which might traditionally be thought of as polar opposites, complicate, overlap, and fuel each other. Via Thomas Keneally's *Homebush Boy* and Robert Drewe's *The Shark Net*, I explore how the child figure is conducive to representations of nostalgia and examine how the child is implicated or employed within nostalgic cultural memory.

In chapter 5 I examine a selection of traumatic autobiographies of childhoods and ask how these texts have found their cultural moment. Linking back to the socio-political contexts of the childhoods explored in chapter 1 of this book, I ask what social "work" traumatic autobiographies of childhood do. I look closely at the ways in which traumatic childhoods are represented—for instance, in Jenny Diski's *Skating to Antarctica*—examining what cultural spaces are available for the articulation of, for example, child sexual abuse. What are the ethical issues affecting the representation of child abuse? And how are readers positioned to interpret these traumatic descriptions of pain and physical injury?

Chapters 6 and 7 explore ethical questions affecting the construction and circulation of autobiographies of childhood. In chapter 6 I isolate two key ethical issues surrounding autobiographies of childhood. Following on from the previous chapter's discussion of the limits of representing child abuse, I discuss the ethical responsibilities that the adult author has in representing the child subject and in authenticating and publicly disclosing childhood traumas. I explore the pressures and limits associated with writing about childhood within autobiographical forms—for example, in relation to judgment, forgiveness, privacy, disclosure, and truth.

Second, I ask how abusive parents are represented in autobiographies of childhood, through a discussion of Augusten Burroughs's *Running with Scissors* and Dave Pelzer's *A Child Called "It": One Child's Courage to Survive.* Autobiographies of childhood are necessarily relational; they become "auto/biographies" conveying the life narratives of both the author and the author's parent/s. They are also what G. Thomas Couser refers to as "intimate life writing—that done within families or couples." Couser writes, "The closer the relationship between writer and subject . . . the higher the ethical stakes" (*Vulnerable Subjects* xii). Who is the auto/biographer responsible to in constructing a life narrative, or, as Couser asks, "What are the author's responsibilities to those whose lives are used as 'material'?" (*Vulnerable Subjects* 34) And do the stakes shift if the author is writing about abuse? I compare and contrast these auto/biographical depictions of abusive parents and suggest the different ideological concerns and ethical dilemmas that underlie these different auto/biographical projects. In these auto/biographies we can see the tension between the weight of traumatic life writing, or the need to write, and the ethical and cultural responsibilities that relational auto/biography, and more particularly writing about children and their parents, summons.

Readers shape autobiographies of childhood as much as any of the other contexts I have discussed in this book. They play a crucial role in interpreting and inscribing meanings upon these childhoods. Readers of autobiographies of childhood may be "professional readers"—researchers engaged in scholarship, reviewers, or media critics—or "recreational readers" responding to these texts in reading groups or in online discussion forums.

Whereas in chapter 6 I discuss the ethical responsibilities that authors have to their child subjects, in chapter 7 I discuss the ethical responsibilities that readers have to child subjects of autobiographies. I link up and advance the discussion from chapter 5 on traumatic narratives in asking: Why have so many readers responded to traumatic narratives of childhood, for example, those depicting child abuse or bereavement? Looking at a range of examples, I explore the reception of traumatic autobiographical texts, predominantly by analyzing online reader responses to these autobiographies (on bookseller Web sites). I analyze these responses focusing on the concepts of testimony and witnessing.

At a time when the autobiographical genre is dominated by adults speaking about and on behalf of children, *Contesting Childhood* concludes with an attempt to allow children to speak for themselves—to author their own lives. I discuss the available spaces for children (perhaps more specifically, adolescents) to author their own life narratives—paving the way for future research in this area. I am inevitably drawn into a discussion of online media, as providing the most accessible means for young people to author their own life narratives. Hundreds of thousands of young people are presenting their life narratives every day via Internet technologies. I discuss these spaces very generally, before briefly exploring social networking as a case study of the challenges facing would-be adolescent autobiographers.

I offer social networking as a mode of early twenty-first-century life writing that has redefined the ways and means in which young people present their life narratives. However, I am particularly interested in looking at sites like Facebook and MySpace as sites for young people to circulate their lives and/or have their lives received by others. Through social networking, the narratives of young adults are available for public consumption in unprecedented ways. However, instead of echoing the backlash against this trend, I argue that this life-writing phenomenon presents a unique opportunity to theorize on young people's life writing—an undertheorized life-writing form—and to explore the ethics of writing and receiving these life-narrative texts.

Comparatively, these narratives, along with the wealth of examples of adults writing about their childhoods retrospectively, become a powerful means for thinking about the intersection of autobiography, memory, and the socio-cultural construction of childhood in contemporary Western cultures and societies.

CHAPTER 1

CREATING CHILDHOOD

AUTOBIOGRAPHY AND CULTURAL MEMORY

To contest the past is also, of course, to pose questions about the present, and what the past means in the present. Our understanding of the past has strategic, political and ethical consequences. Contests over the meaning of the past are also contests over the meaning of the present and over ways of taking the past forward.

—Katharine Hodgkin and Susannah Radstone,
Contested Pasts: The Politics of Memory

It's only looking back that I believe the clear light of truth should have filled us, like the legendary grace that carries a broken body past all manner of monsters.

—Mary Karr, *The Liars' Club*

The autobiography of British feminist academic Lorna Sage—*Bad Blood: A Memoir*—was published in 2000, shortly before her death from emphysema at age fifty-seven in 2001. In *Bad Blood*, Sage recounts growing up in Shropshire in the 1940s and 1950s. Despite her adult success as a literary critic and author, in *Bad Blood* Sage writes exclusively about her childhood. The autobiography focuses in particular on Sage's unplanned teenage pregnancy and her struggle to rise above class and gender discrimination to gain a university education. Sage does not remember her childhood as a golden age of happiness, innocence, and prosperity—quite the contrary. She writes of a time when children, particularly girls, were isolated from knowledge, education, and careers.

Sage presents us with a paradigm for thinking about the cultural function of autobiographies of childhood—texts that rehistoricize and politicize childhood—asking readers to witness the difficulties, even traumas, of being a child of a particular historical time and place. In other parts of the literary world during the same period, autobiographers were penning their autobiographies with a similar focus upon cultural, racial, class, or gender inequalities and their effects on the author's experience of childhood. These autobiographies include Stolen Generations narratives in Australia, narratives of institutional abuse from Ireland, traumatic postcolonial African autobiographies, and the plethora of narratives recounting abuse within the family circulating in the United States and the United Kingdom.

A profitable, influential, and infamous literary trend, autobiographies of childhood inevitably do more than simply represent an author's individual memories. These texts reflect broader moods and preoccupations about childhood. They provide insight into what it is possible to say about childhood in the current era—reflecting and prescribing ways of thinking about and representing the child.

In this chapter I consider the relationship between autobiographies of childhood and cultural memory. Autobiographies of childhood have emerged at a time when memory has entered a range of discourses—from science to philosophy and social science—in an extraordinary way. Michael Lambek and Paul Antze write, "We live in a time when memory has entered public discourse to an unprecedented degree. Memory is invoked to heal, to blame, to legitimate. It has become a major idiom in the construction of identity, both individual and collective and a site of struggle as well as identification" (vii). Kerwin Lee Klein has described memory as an "industry" (127), while Paula Hamilton writes, "Social scientists particularly have been concerned with the process of remembering both individually and collectively and the relationship of memories to place and identity" (10). Autobiographies of childhood are products of, and confrontations with, "cultural memory"—the collective ways in which the past is remembered, constructed, and made intelligible within culture. These autobiographies are memory texts born from individual, group and collective memory. I consider the cultural and memory "work" that autobiographies of childhood attempt to do—how these texts are influenced by, and in turn influence, what can be remembered about childhoods past and how these memories can be articulated within autobiography. How do contemporary contexts and paradigms for thinking about childhood underscore these autobiographical representations?

In reviewing exemplars, I consider the statements these texts make (in their writing and in their reception) about childhood: past and present. In looking at Karr's *Liars' Club* and Sage's *Bad Blood*, alongside two Stolen Generations autobiographies—Rosalie Fraser's *Shadow Child* and Donna Meehan's *It Is No Secret*—I identify a particular paradigm for thinking about childhood that is illuminated within autobiographies of childhood: the rehistoricized, politicized, female child who, from her position within the text, asks that the reader witness her trauma and reconsider what can be remembered and written about childhoods past and present.

Memory, Autobiography, and Childhood

Memory drives autobiography, and, in turn, autobiographies influence perceptions of the ways in which memory functions. Memory necessarily forms the backbone of autobiographical writing about childhood. Autobiographies are about the past; the adults who write them are removed from their childhood by time and, usually, place. To write about childhood the author must remember and reconstruct something of his or her experiences of childhood into narrative. The difficulties inherent within this process are well documented and have become axioms of life-writing scholarship. As Lambek and Antze argue, although memory is part of our commonsense world, it is fraught with "ambiguities and complexities" (xi). These ambiguities around memory are further complicated by the schools of thought we invest in. For example, the disciplines of psychoanalysis/psychology, history, sociology, and anthropology each make different investments in memory—its neurological and cultural functions. For an adult writing an autobiography of childhood, childhood memories are at best fragile and fragmented and at worst impossible to retrieve. In short, the notion that individual childhood memories exist and are accessible to the autobiographer has been hotly contested within both popular and scholarly responses to these texts.[1]

Autobiographies are laden with memory loss, memory gaps, false memory, and a plethora of other memory-related controversies. Autobiography is a genre weighed down by public suspicion, and memory, along with truth, remains a key stake in authorizing autobiographies of childhood. For example, book reviewers and reader comments on Web sites such as Amazon.com consistently ask how autobiographers manage to remember their childhoods from so long ago. Moreover, television talk shows throughout the 1990s and 2000s frequently focused upon psychological memory disorders, and newspaper literary pages were preoccupied with "autobiography hoaxes."

Autobiographical genres have been affected by numerous high-profile hoaxes during the 1990s and 2000s. *A Rock and a Hard Place: One Boy's Triumphant Story* by Anthony Godby Johnson was released in 1993. The book, which details Godby Johnson's abusive childhood and his subsequent battle with AIDS, is suspected to be a hoax written by his supposed adoptive mother, Vicki Johnson. Helen Demidenko (also known as Helen Dale and Helen Darville) posed as a Ukrainian immigrant in promoting her supposedly autobiographical novel *The Hand That Signed the Paper* (1993). Binjamin Wilkomirski, in his autobiography of childhood *Fragments* (1995), constructed a false identity as a Holocaust survivor. Norma Khouri wrote *Forbidden Love* (2003), claiming to tell the true story of the honor killing of her friend Dalia in Jordan. Khouri's claims were exposed as false by the Australian journalist Malcolm Knox. In *A Million Little Pieces* (2003), James Frey writes candidly and graphically of his criminal past and of his alcohol and drug addictions. Like Khouri's, the veracity of Frey's story was challenged by investigative journalists. Frey was accused of embellishing the truth—changing facts and making exaggerated claims about his past. White Anglo-American Margaret Seltzer wrote a fraudulent autobiography as Margaret B. Jones, *Love and Consequences: A Memoir of Hope and Survival*, recounting her experiences as a biracial (Native American/white American) girl growing up in Los Angeles amid drug and gang cultures.

The climate for writing autobiographically has shifted greatly because of these controversies. Though still arguably one of the darlings of the publishing industry, autobiography has been branded a "difficult" genre; all highly successful autobiographies are now held up to intense scrutiny. Witness the recent controversy of Ishmael Beah's *A Long Way Gone: Memoirs of a Boy Soldier* (2007). Beah's story of his time as a child soldier in the government army during the civil war in Sierra Leone was challenged by the *Australian* newspaper, which disputed the veracity of some of the dates he presented. In doing so, it raised more general questions about the credibility of Beah's autobiography.

Such scrutiny of autobiography is highly problematic on many levels. It fails to recognize the long-held belief (within autobiographical genres) of the constructedness of *all* autobiographical writing. There is no such thing as pure autobiography—autobiography that holds a mirror up to a person's childhood and reflects back the events as they happened. There is an obvious difference between organic memory loss and/or traumatic memory loss and the deliberate and strategic imposture of an author like Seltzer. Criticizing an autobiography such as Beah's also fails to consider the impact that trauma might have had upon his memory and his ability to tell his story faithfully.

This problematization of memory leads to a range of questions about the cultural and social spaces that are available for remembering and writing about childhood. Though much media attention has been given to the apparent sensationalism of contemporary autobiographies of childhood, less focus has been given to these writings as cultural memory practices—as narratives that are propelled by particular political and cultural conditions that extend beyond their recent autobiographical intertexts.

Cultural memory becomes a useful concept here, for considering how autobiographies of childhood function as acts of memory.[2] Cultural memory reflects the ways in which people collectively remember the past and imagine the future. Cultural memory explains the relationship between memory and the individual who is bound within a culture or cultures. According to Marita Sturken, it "represents the many shifting histories and shared memories that exist between a sanctioned narrative of history and personal memory" (119). Individuals are socialized—for example, by history books, festivals, and popular culture—to accept certain views of the past and to incorporate these views into their own lives via collective memory. However, cultural memory is in a state of constant flux; as interpretations of the past change, so does cultural memory. Societies are obsessed by remembering, and individuals and cultural groups are constantly offering counter-memories and histories that challenge existing cultural memory and may, in turn, become part of cultural memory.

Exploring the tenets of cultural memory reveals my preoccupation with the myriad ways in which memories of childhood are mediated or shaped through social institutions and cultural practices, rather than psychological explanations of how childhood memories might be accessed and articulated within autobiography. Individuals cannot simply draw memories of childhood from their conscience and write about them within autobiography. Memory is mediated by the various cultural texts and discourses that invite us to remember our childhoods on a daily basis: family photographs; newspaper articles on missing children; nostalgic advertisements for children's products refashioned for contemporary audiences; enduring childhood songs, games, and fairy tales; and collectables such as classic toys. There is a range of culturally available templates for remembering and/or documenting our own childhoods or the childhoods or our children. We are intrinsically aware of what we are supposed to remember and document, of which stories and events are culturally valuable, of what is speakable and unspeakable (at any given time) about our childhoods. We document firsts—first word, first step, first tooth, first day of school. We celebrate occasions that shape our self-fashioned and socially constructed identities: birthdays, graduations, marriages, anniversaries.

For those who were born during the era of the instant camera, photographs provide a direct means for accessing particular people and events from our childhood—for reviving childhood memories. Those who do not have access to childhood photographs and mementos may have difficulty accessing their childhood selves. In more recent times, technology has expanded the opportunities for documenting childhoods: from "baby blogs" through to online photo albums and universal family newsletters. The reliance on photography as a means of accessing childhood memories often results in an overinvestment in happy childhood memories, as these are the ones most commonly recorded in childhood photography—a point I return to in chapter 2. Children are increasingly taking responsibility for documenting their own lives, particularly as they become old enough to access the templates needed for documentation. Through diaries (traditionally in hard copy but increasingly now in online spaces), photography, instant messaging, and creative and social networking sites, children tell stories about themselves using the available memory tools.

What stories do we tell about childhoods within autobiography, and why? Like Lambek and Antze, I see memory as a "practice, not as the pregiven object of our gaze but as the act of gazing and the objects it generates. Memories are produced out of experience and, in turn, reshape it" (xii). In the section that follows, I want to look at the ways in which autobiographies of childhoods reveal particular preoccupations relating to childhoods present.

Portrait of the Artist as a Young Woman: Mary Karr's *The Liars' Club* and Lorna Sage's *Bad Blood*

Commended and reviled for being one of the catalysts of the mid-1990s "memoir craze"—a period of unprecedented interest in so-called true-to-life autobiography, award-winning U.S. author Mary Karr has written two autobiographies alongside collections of poetry and numerous academic and review articles. Karr is part of an unprecedented wave in late twentieth-century women's autobiography committed to using life-writing forms to write about events from the private sphere—recounting details of everyday family life. Karr's best-known work is *The Liars' Club*. This autobiography, which spent over a year on the *New York Times* bestseller list, is a harrowing yet often affectionate and humorous recounting of her turbulent Texan childhood. The majority of Karr's narrative takes place between 1961 and 1963, when Karr was between seven and nine years old.

Karr recalls the trepidation with which she approached the release of *The Liars' Club*:

When I set out on a book tour to promote the memoir about my less than perfect Texas clan, I did so with soul-sucking dread. Surely we'd be held up as grotesques, my beloveds and I, real moral circus freaks. Instead I shoved into bookstores where sometimes hundreds of people stood claiming to identify with my story, which fact stunned me. Maybe these people's family lives differed in terms of surface pyrotechnics—houses set fire to and fortunes squandered. But the feelings didn't. After eight weeks of travel, I ginned up this working definition for a dysfunctional family: any family with more than one person in it. ("The Family Sideshow")

Karr's assumptions about the relevance of her autobiography seem modest. However, *The Liars' Club* was published in 1995 and, as I have suggested, is credited with being one of the pioneering texts of the memoir boom. Unlike her adherents, Karr could not have anticipated the appetite for texts like *The Liars' Club*—an autobiography that opened up literary spaces and language for the narration of working-class childhoods amid alcoholism, mental illness, poverty and sexual abuse. As Karr concedes, "Maybe coming-of-age memoirs are being bought and read by the boatload precisely because they offer some window into other people's whacked-out families, with which nearly everyone born in the fractured baby-boom era can identify" ("The Family Sideshow").

Karr writes affectionately of living in a "Dangerous," "Not Right" family—a result of the volatile relationship between her "Liar" father and "Nervous" feminist mother (who always refers to God as female and who "didn't date, she married") (10). They live in (the fictional) Leechfield, "one of the ten ugliest towns on the planet" (34). In *The Liars' Club* Karr describes a colorful community of characters including an unlovable, rotting grandmother, a suicidal schoolteacher, and murderous neighbors. Karr's young narrator, like most children, longs to be in a different family. After a terrible argument between her parents, during which the seven-year-old Karr's birthday dinner (a lasagna) was smashed on the kitchen floor, Karr recalls blowing out birthday candles on her cake: "I squinted my eyes as hard as I could and wished silently to go and live some other where forever, with a brand new family like on *Leave It to Beaver*. Then I sucked up as much air as I could get and blew the whole house dark" (137). However, despite these longings, and in spite of the many failings of her mother and father, Karr writes with deep devotion, loyalty, and love when speaking about them.

Writing in the first person, Karr employs a naïve child narrator, complete with childish local idiom ("The world smelled not unlike a wicked fart in a close room") (34). This approach allows Karr to extend beyond the conventions and limitations of retrospective adult narrators writing about childhoods long past. For example, Karr's narrator remains nonjudgmental about what goes on around her—in particular, reserving judgment on her flawed parents as only a child would do. The narrator's unapologetically (and realistically) fragmented memory imposes limits upon what the reader can know about events of the past. For Karr, "when the truth would be unbearable the mind often just blanks it out. But some ghost of an event may stay in your head" (9). For instance, Karr writes of her mother's failed attempt to kill herself, her father, her, and her sister by running their car off a bridge. The event sticks in her mind because it occurred on her birthday, following the lasagna-smashing argument between her parents:

> I don't remember our family driving across the Orange Bridge to get to the Bridge City café that evening. Nor do I remember eating the barbecued crabs, which is a shame, since I love those crabs for their sweet grease and liquid-smoke taste. I don't remember how much Mother drank in that bayou café, where you could walk to the end of the dock after dinner and toss your leftover hush puppies to hungry alligators.
>
> My memory comes back into focus when we're drawing close to the Orange Bridge on the way home. (137)

Karr vividly recounts the events that follow: as the car lurches closer to the edge of the bridge, as her sister attempts to cover her in the backseat, and as their parents fight over the steering wheel, a fight that culminates in Karr's father knocking her mother out cold. There is little commentary on this event other than this. The family returns to "normal," to quote Karr, shortly after.

In a similar vein, Karr is sexually assaulted twice in her childhood (once by a neighborhood boy, once by a babysitter) but chooses not to make these events a focal point in the narrative. The potency of these events lies in Karr's lack of judgment; she chooses instead to focus on her childhood responses to these events. Karr explains this approach in an interview: "Can I tell about the boy who raped me without investigating who may have raped him as a child (data that would certainly spin the moral compass a few degrees at least)?" ("How My Old Friends") Late in the text, when Karr describes being sexually assaulted by a babysitter, she initially does so in a matter-of-fact fashion:

> More signs scrolled past, and days so gray and grainy that not one stands unblurred from any other, till I get sick one day and the grown man who allegedly comes to care for me winds up putting his dick in my eight-

year-old mouth. In fact, the whole blank winter sort of gathers around
that incident like a storm cloud getting dense and heavy. (239)

However, this seemingly unemotional description functions as a prelude
to a portrait of a frightened and traumatized child. Through this incident,
Karr reflects upon her childhood vulnerability and powerlessness—for
instance, how she saw herself as complicit in her sexual assault: "Maybe
grown-ups know I know words like Hard-on from looking at me" (242).
Here Karr relies on the reader to provide a moral compass—to disagree with
the child's view that she was in any way responsible for the sexual assaults
inflicted upon her. The second assault brings back traumatic memories of
the previous assault:

> His hand fishes into that zipper and farther, into the shadow of his shorts.
> The seriousness of that reaching keeps me even from breathing regular.
> I'm also afraid to make him mad somehow, and even more afraid that
> any move I make or any word I speak will seem like welcome. So I sit still
> and pretend not to be home inside myself. I worry worry worry though
> about what's about to happen.
>
> I think of that old neighbor boy laying me down on the cement sack
> in the Carters' garage, him on top of me bucking. Probably I don't even
> have a cherry from that. I didn't hear it pop inside me, because I was so
> busy thinking for him to hurry before I got in trouble. Whether I have a
> cherry or not, though, I can feel how marked I am inside for being hurt
> that way. (243)

Karr uses autobiography to defend the child and to speak on her behalf—
both to address her individual pain and to offer broader (feminist)
commentary on the misconceptions surrounding girlhood sexual abuse.

The sequel to *The Liars' Club*, *Cherry*, is a narrative of youthful intro-
spection in the late 1960s and early 1970s, depicting Karr's adolescence in
Leechfield, Texas, up to her eventual move to Los Angeles, which concludes
this autobiography.[3] *Cherry* focuses on the central character, constructed as
Karr's adolescent self, rather than on her family, who play a much smaller
part than they did in *The Liars' Club*. *Cherry* uses first-person and second-
person narrators to construct this self. In doing so, Karr uses her skills in
poetic experimentation to search for a fitting autobiographical voice. Karr's
second autobiography is more light and humorous than its predecessor,
though its subject matter embraces nostalgic references to lost time, comic

representations of characters and places, and contemptuous evocations of a narrow-minded society.

In taking this approach *Cherry* gives rebellious girlhood, and more particularly girlhood sexuality, a voice and language to articulate its experiences. *The Liars' Club* and *Cherry* depict the development of young girls, experiences of abuse and neglect, alcoholism, mental illness, and familial eccentricities. These autobiographies assert the contradictory but necessary forces of blame and forgiveness that coexist in much autobiographical writing about childhood. *Cherry* explores girlhood "firsts" and friendships, as well as the protagonist's drug use, disaffection, suicide attempt, juvenile crime, and need to escape from adolescent spaces and traumas. The exploration of her development and escape via books makes *Cherry* read like a portrait of the artist as a young woman. Karr's adolescent narrator is a girl from a working-class background who desires something more. In her self-representation of adolescence, Karr presents her multiple identities—from surfing hippie to poet—thus asserting the many possibilities for female adolescents. Her autobiographies are concerned with the (external and internal) restrictions placed upon young women, particularly those growing up in small towns.

Male writers have traditionally dominated coming-of-age autobiography, and the experiences of girlhood, such as those depicted by Karr, were not archetypes in women's autobiography prior to the last two decades. Thus, Karr's texts are part of the broader project of women's autobiography that seeks to open up cultural spaces for the representation of adverse childhoods and adolescence. Karr's autobiographies are not bound by conventions of language; *The Liars' Club* and *Cherry* make dexterous use of adolescent and local idioms, particularly sexual vernacular. Her writing merges her working-class influences with her literary perspectives, and the subject matter she deals with is not sanitized.

Through her writing Karr emerges as deeply committed to implementing and celebrating a voice that is unapologetically autobiographical—subjective, personal, and stirring. Her coverage of the movements between childhood, adolescence, and adulthood is unsentimental and yet asserts the significance in seemingly insignificant events, objects, and relationships. There is a candor in her writing that works to extend the limits of contemporary women's autobiography. Indeed, Karr's brash and fragmented take on childhood paved the way for other autobiographies of childhood by American women recounting personal experience of a difficult childhood and adolescence—such as Koren Zailckas's *Smashed: Growing Up a Drunk Girl* and Lauren Slater's experimental, renegade autobiography *Lying: A Metaphorical Memoir*. In Slater's text, for example, the boundaries of autobiography—of truth and lying—come under close scrutiny. Slater emphasizes the fragility of memory in exploring the delicate relationship between illness, gender, and autobiographical narration. For Slater, narration is valuable in itself. The stories we tell about our childhood (which inevitably inhabit the large space between truth and fabrication) present a means by which the self can be constructed into history. Since this act of remembering and writing can never be truly reliable, it is the act of telling, the art of telling, that is important. Again, this telling reveals more about contemporary preoccupations with memory, and more particularly the relationship between childhood memories and the adult self, than it does about the actual past as it happened.

Like Karr and others in the United States, late twentieth-century British autobiographers worked within and against dominant histories to insert alternative accounts of childhood into cultural memory. Michael Erben suggests that one of the preoccupations of late twentieth-century British autobiography was the experiences of women from working-class backgrounds, citing autobiographies such as Carolyn Steedman's *Landscape for a Good Woman*, Gillian Rose's *Love's Work*, and Ann Oakley's *Man and Wife* (48). This interest in the lives of working-class women is probably a result of movements toward more equitable education initiatives in Britain, for, as Steedman notes, "from the 1950s onwards in Britain, state school children were taught creative writing in line with beliefs about the psychological benefits of writing the self, particularly for working-class children" ("Enforced" 27). Steedman suggests that "creative writing flourished in conjunction with new practices of self-narration outside the school: adult education, the development of the worker-writers' and community publishing movement (and thus an astonishing flowering of working-class autobiography in the 1970s)" (28).

Sage's *Bad Blood*, like Karr's autobiographies, highlights the experiences of a working-class girlhood, explicitly suggesting autobiography can write experiences into history in a way that had previously been impossible. Indeed, Sage's childhood is retrievable because of particular contemporary ideologies of the child. It is these ideologies of childhood, especially mythologies of "lost" contemporary childhoods (as opposed to idealized "golden" childhoods of the past), that encourage the telling of these narratives now. [4] Autobiography is an accessible medium for feminist public intellectuals (such as Karr and Sage) to explore the ways in which their unconventional girlhoods shaped the woman they each became.

Sage, like Karr, does not present her childhood as an ideal yesteryear alternative to contemporary crises of childhood. She experienced an unhappy home life that was rife with feuding and secrecy, and her narrator explicitly debunks her family's presentation of "happy families" as an illusion:

> They always closed ranks and pretended that everything was solid, normal and natural. Here we have the family of the period: self-made and going places. Only when you look more closely can you see that this housewife is pathologically scared of food, hates home, is really a child dreaming of pretty things and treats; and this businessman will never accumulate capital, he's still a boy soldier, going over the top again and again. Their obsessions had met, fallen in love and married; they completed and sustained each other. (186)

This autobiographical construction functions as a more general reminder that families did break down in the so-called golden age, but these experiences were often silenced. Autobiographies of childhood have become a means for breaking silences (for example, about the family) that may have been enforced upon children during their infancy and youth.

Bad Blood is an academic's memoir, a subgenre of autobiography that has boomed in the past decade. Gillian Whitlock suggests that academic memoir "is frequently shaped in order to naturalize and confirm the professional identity and vocation of the narrating subject and to produce a pedigree of sorts. That is to say, it can work to invent continuities between past and present" (*Disciplining* 340). This is an important consideration when reading Sage, who is very much concerned with understanding how her past shaped her present career. Sage's retrospective all-knowing adult narrator rediscovers rather than relives her childhood, shamefully mocking both her own ignorance and that of the adults who imposed this ignorance upon her. This allows her to employ a sociological (rather than therapeutic) stance in explaining the inequality suffered by working-class rural children in England during the 1940s and 1950s. Sage implicates her own story within broader social changes that enabled social mobility. For example, Sage's narrative explains how working-class children were mocked at school, citing a particular incident involving her teacher:

> One day he lined up his class and went down the line saying with gloomy satisfaction 'You'll be a muck-shoveller, you'll be a muck-shoveller . . . ' and so on, only missing out the homework trio. As things turned out he was mistaken—by the time my Hanmer generation grew up there were very few jobs on the land, the old mixed labour-intensive farming had

finally collapsed, farmers had gone over to machinery, and the children
he'd consigned to near-illiteracy and innumeracy had to re-educate
themselves and move on. Which they did, despite all the school had done
to inculcate ignorance. Back there and then in our childhoods, though,
in the late Forties, Mr Palmer seemed omniscient. (21)

The adult narrator imagines how adults must have perceived her and
her schoolmates. The tone of this admission is shame: "I think that we
all forget the pain of being a child at school for the first time, the sheer
ineptitude, as though you'll never learn to mark out your own space. It's
doubly shaming—shaming to *remember* as well, to feel so sorry for your
scabby little self back there in small people's purgatory" (23). Though this
statement works to debunk the cultural memory of childhood as an Edenic
time, to refute this particular cultural memory, this representation renders
childhood inferior to adulthood. In this instance, autobiography provides
a means for addressing childhood shame, though this is not necessarily
productive for the autobiographer.

The shame she suffered as a child renders the adult narrator unable to
represent her child self as having any agency. It is only as an adult, with autobiography as a weapon, that Sage can address the wrongs of her childhood,
to critique the naïve feelings that were instilled within her because she was
young and female. She writes, "Like all the girls back then I knew that being
too clever was much worse than being too tall" (219). Though this exploration
of child naïveté is often achieved by narrating humorous incidents whereby
both adults and children are derided for their lack of awareness—such as the
visit by the "lady from Ponds"—the overall effect is that the child self seems
wholly disempowered by Sage's representation (202).[5] Sage does not attempt
to recapture the child voice, just its experience. For Sage, adult ownership of
childhood shame becomes a means for writing childhoods into cultural space
and for asserting particular memories of cultural moments.

In contrast, Karr reinstates a knowing child into her past, and in doing
so asserts the intelligence of children. For instance, Karr's narrator recounts
the shrewd ways in which her and her sister would manage their mother's
drinking:

The big game for me once she'd started drinking was to gauge which way
her mood was running that I might steer her away from the related type
of trouble. Hiding her car keys would keep her off the roads and, ergo,
out of a wreck, for instance. Or I'd tie up the phone by having a running

chat with the busy signal (seven-year-olds don't yet have any phone life
to speak of), so she couldn't dial up any teachers or neighbors she was
liable to bad-mouth. (127)

This creates the impression of a child with a fast-developing intellect and
cunning survival strategies. Karr's child narrator is actively inquisitive, sharply
intelligent, yet remains at the mercy of adults. For example, when her mother
is institutionalized, the young Mary questions her father's not explaining it to
her and her sister: "Maybe our own silence on the subject—Lecia's and mine,
for we didn't bring it up either—was meant to protect him somehow, so as not
to worry him overmuch. If we failed by not telling him all about it, he sure as
shit failed us by not knowing how to ask" (158). Such narrative constructions
achieve more than merely suggesting that a child is capable of intelligent
comprehension and feeling. It is the child who is right, but remains powerless.
The child becomes a moral marker for the reader to emulate.

Both Karr and Sage set out to inscribe an adverse history of childhood into
the mythology of the golden age. They are shaped by a personally felt need to
"write back" to these myths as accomplished, educated adults and to acknowledge their origins as lower class and rural. These feminist critiques contribute
to rights-of-the-(girl)-child debates. For example, these autobiographies
assert a girl's right to education. Sage's narrative explores the system of education she experienced as a child in rural Britain in the 1950s. Girls wanting
an education were seen as delinquent. The narrator explains that while her
primary school "had been designed to produce domestic servants and farm
labourers, and functional illiteracy was still part of the expectation, almost
part of the curriculum" (19), the high school she attended "was designed to
produce solid, disciplined, well-groomed girls who'd marry local traders and
solicitors like their fathers" (143–144).

Sage's narrator represents her childhood as on the cusp of significant social
change. She describes how "unheard of" it was for children at her school
to pass the eleven-plus exams: "The world was changing, education was
changing, and the notion that school should reflect your ready-made place in
the scheme of things and put you firmly back where you came from was going
out of fashion even in Hanmer" (20). This consolidates the impression that
many contemporary autobiographies of childhood seek to make: that their
childhood was a socially consequential one.

Female adolescent sexuality is an important theme within *Bad Blood*. Sage
writes of finding herself pregnant at sixteen without knowing she had actually
had sex: "How could I have got it wrong?" (238). This revelation, which some
reviewers remain skeptical about, works as an illustration of the dangers of

enforcing children's ignorance. Writing about this experience allows Sage to (ironically) document this event, which was publicly erased at the time:

> My parents' plan was that I should go to a Church Home for Unmar-
> ried Mothers, where you repented on your knees (scrubbed floors, said
> prayers), had your baby (which was promptly adopted by proper married
> people) and returned home humble and hollow-eyed. Everyone would
> magnanimously pretend that nothing had happened. (237)

This acknowledgment of youthful sexuality asserts a space for the adolescent self as a radical pacesetter, concerned about the rights of women and children. Sage defies expectations and attends university, despite being refused a grant because she was a mother:

> You were supposed to choose between boys and books, because for
> girls sex was entirely preoccupying. . . . On this logic County Education
> Committees would stop a girl's university grant if she cohabited, married
> or became pregnant because it was a waste of public money, although
> it had probably been a waste of public money all along (many people
> thought) because the girls would marry when they got their degrees, have
> families and only work part-time, if that, at jobs they were overqualified
> for. (232–233)

Sage ends her autobiography by looking to the future via her daughter: "She's the real future, she tells the world that we broke the rules and got away with it, for better and for worse, we're part of the shape of things to come" (278). This statement is a call to action whereby the reader is encouraged to see and respond to social change positively.

Collectively the narratives of Sage and Karr force a reexamination of childhoods (in this instance, girlhoods) past in light of present preoccupations relating to gender and class inequality. The examples that follow demonstrate another way in which the autobiography of childhood has been taken up—to reveal racial and cultural inequalities from the past that preoccupy the present.

Stolen Childhoods: Rosalie Fraser's *Shadow Child* and Donna Meehan's *It Is No Secret*

Fraser's *Shadow Child*, a Stolen Generations autobiography, relates her experiences living with a foster family in the 1960s and 1970s after being removed from her parents' care as a child. Though the narrator recounts the abuse she suffered at the hands of her foster mother, Mrs. Kelly, *Shadow Child* links the direct forms of (physical, sexual, and emotional) abuse that she suffered to the cultural abuse and neglect leveled at her and her siblings by the welfare institutions that were responsible for them. Fraser endures horrific physical and sexual abuse from her foster mother. The narrator uses the term "the Welfare" to describe the various systems that, while claiming to have her interests and protection in mind, offered no protection and seemingly had no interest in her.

Fraser's *Shadow Child* and Donna Meehan's *It Is No Secret* offer a bold challenge to dominant paradigms for representing mid-twentieth-century Australian childhoods. The mid-twentieth century, from the end of World War II to the prosperous 1960s, has been represented and re-represented within Western cultures as a golden age. In Australia, for instance, the dominant cultural memory represented in autobiographies has emerged from white childhoods in a settler culture: postwar suburban prosperity, the portrait of the artist, and innocent children "coming of age."[6] During this time, cultural memory constructed an era of cultural (and racial) homogeneity, which was unchallenged by alternative histories. Bain Attwood describes the destruction of communal memory that this cultural dominance entailed:

> In the postwar era of assimilation, new and old Australians were urged to abandon both their communities and their communal memory—to forget the past and enter into the future—and there were few Australians who wanted to hear their histories. Australian history was a grand narrative of modernity and progress, and had no place for a "dying race" or "a primitive culture." (188)

The cultural memory that surrounds the postwar era is the span of "living memories" for many turn-of-the-millennium consumers of autobiography, for this is the era when they were children. The tendency to view this particular era through "rose-colored glasses"—which produces a penchant to bemoan the loss of family values or the breakdown of the traditional family unit in contemporary Australia—has been a characteristic of late twentieth-century conservative politics. The past is imagined and remembered in ways that influence political agendas in the present, and, in turn, contemporary politics sanction particular representations of the past. An example of this is Geoffrey Blainey's reference to "black armband history," which privileges consensus-based representations of Australian social history (10).[7]

Yet, as Chris Healy argues, memories that are within "the reach of lived experience" are never as solidly entrenched as those, for instance, from the nineteenth century (7).[8] As a consequence, cultural memory can be refused and replaced. For example, multicultural autobiographies of childhood entered cultural memory as post–World War II child immigrants became adults in the late twentieth century. The publication of autobiographies such as Amirah Inglis's *Amirah: An Un-Australian Childhood* and Andrew Riemer's *Inside Outside* and the presentation of television miniseries such as *The Leaving of Liverpool* brought minority histories of childhood into mainstream consciousness.[9] There have been a number of autobiographies of childhood recounting the experiences of displaced children—Alan Gill's *Orphans of the Empire* and Geoffrey Sherington's *Fairbridge: Empire and Child Migration* are two notable examples published during the late 1990s. The publication of these autobiographies collectively reveals a growing preoccupation with childhood history in Australia, and the potential for autobiographical writing to do memory work—to reshape history through individual experiences. These experiences can only now be read, as those who experienced the childhood are old enough to write about it, and the cultural climate is ready to receive these stories. It is the recognizable figure of the child—the child in need of a hearing and requiring protection—that provides the common denominator of these stories.

Indigenous autobiographies of childhood entered the Australian public consciousness through the growing acknowledgement of the Stolen Generations, and these narratives have, in turn, contributed to the broader dissemination of Indigenous life narratives. Indeed, the Stolen Generations brought the traumatic child to public attention in Australia in an unprecedented way. The Human Rights and Equal Opportunity Commission (HREOC) report (1997) recorded over a thousand testimonies, reaching the conclusion that from 1910 to 1970 between one in three and one in ten Indigenous children were removed from their families and communities (Whitlock, "In the Second Person").[10] These children were raised in institutions or white foster homes. The Australian government's policy of assimilation led to the cultural genocide of Indigenous Australians. How, then, could Stolen Generations narratives enter mainstream consciousness? A range of discourses had to be engaged in memory work. As Attwood writes, "There is nothing inevitable about this metamorphosis: this is not simply a case of 'the return of the repressed' or the oppressed, a necessary surfacing of a hitherto silenced or submerged history; instead it might better be understood as a matter of 'narrative accrual' or 'narrative coalescence'" (183). The HREOC report was, as Whitlock argues, "the culmination of three decades of political struggle by activists to return the control of Aboriginal children to Aboriginal families. . . . Narratives by and about stolen children are embedded in many of the autobiographies by Aboriginal Australians that circulated since the 1980s" ("In the Second Person" 202). Stolen Generations narratives are significant because of the ways in which they come to constitute a collective memory around Indigenous childhood and identity. The narratives encourage Indigenous Australians to recognize a shared pain and to be empowered to share this trauma via writing and reading autobiographical narratives.[11] These narratives have become fundamental to Reconciliation as well as the central site for Indigenous collective memory. They are sanctioned as histories, becoming a privileged mode of political activity.

The autobiography of childhood is effective in this context, mediating between Stolen Generations narratives, traditional forms of autobiography, alternative histories, and sociological interest in the child. In utilizing the autobiographical form for Stolen Generations narratives, autobiographies such as Fraser's *Shadow Child* and Meehan's *It Is No Secret* appeal to the collective memory of the Stolen Generations by offering counter-histories to the predominant white histories. These autobiographies also work to dispel socially constructed myths of idealized Australian childhoods. By appealing to both Indigenous and white Australian readerships, these narratives become part of the process of instating a new cultural memory about a particular era of Australian history. Both Fraser and Meehan explicitly locate their experiences within historical time and space, for example, by naming particular Australian institutions and bureaucracies as racist. Writing about the 1960s, the autobiographical narrator of *It Is No Secret* remembers being teased by both teachers and students at school: "I couldn't claim Aboriginality, but was always stigmatized by it, always treated like a second class citizen" (Meehan 53). The narrator explicitly relates these childhood traumas to government policy: "This was during the government's 'Keep Australia White' campaign. . . . Could anyone blame a child for not wanting to go to school in these circumstances?" (54) Fraser similarly names the social institutions responsible for her being forcibly removed from her culture:

> When I look back, I see that my life as a child with my natural family really ended two years and three months after I was born. The date was 13 March 1961, the place was Beverley, in Western Australia. On that day, my brothers and sisters Terry aged eight, Stuart aged six, Karen aged four-and-a-half, Beverley aged eight months, and myself, were all made Wards of the State through action taken by the Child Welfare Department of Western Australia. (9–10)

The narrator later reflects on the ease with which her foster mother, Mrs. Kelly, was able to fool "the Welfare" into believing that she was providing a good foster home for her foster children:

> The only time we had a nice room and our own bed was when the Welfare came to see us. So nice, in fact that great lengths were taken to make sure another bed was borrowed for the day, and dolls that belonged to my foster mother's own daughters were placed on our so-called beds for the grand occasion. How dumb those officers were, not to see through the facade. (27)[12]

Shadow Child seeks to expose the official version of her life, imposed upon her by welfare institutions and her foster mother, as false. The narrator reveals how as a child she was forced to lie about the abuse being perpetrated upon her. *Shadow Child* functions as a silence-breaker: The writing of this autobiography works to replace official histories with personal testimony and to vehemently assert this counter-history as "truth." This deconstruction of official sources of knowledge, along with the assertion of autobiography as authentic knowledge, suggests that this autobiographical text cannot be any less reliable than these other "official" sources. It is an empowering revelation for the narrator when she and her sister can construct their child-hood narrative:

> Bev and I decided that no one—not the Welfare, not the hospital, nor our foster parents, nor the others associated with our pain and the crimes done to us—should be allowed to get away with what happened to us as children. As far as we could see, no one had ever cared about us. They just left us to rot. Especially the Welfare, whose so-called caring hands were safely in their pockets. (23)

The narrator uses the autobiography as an opportunity to publicly inscribe the blame for her removal on welfare institutions, not her parents:

> The Welfare. I blamed them for a lot. They could have helped get Mum and Dad on their feet; they could have supplied bedding and clothing as they did while we were in foster care; they could have helped Dad out with his bills. . . . No, Dad, I do not blame you, but I left my thoughts in this book, so people could see the struggles I have had in my mind, due to my childhood. (228)

Steedman explains how writing about childhood involves interpreting the past through the agency of social information; this interpretation can only be made when people gain a sense of the social world and their place in it ("Stories" 243). In this instance the presence of an adult narrator allows the narrative to make connections between her childhood and adulthood and to appeal directly to contemporary consciousness of issues such as Reconciliation and the Stolen Generations.[13]

The narrator of *Shadow Child* makes a passionate appeal regarding the authenticity of her narrative in asserting the validity of her memories. For example, though the narrator makes no apology for the lost memories and chronological gaps at the beginning of her narrative, she asserts that

> from the time I was three years of age I can remember everything vividly. Maybe it was because I became the big sister from that day on—maybe it was because the oldest got the worst. It just seems as though I woke up one morning with an absolutely clear head, and I can remember our life from that day onwards. (15)

Such statements are a recurrent feature of *Shadow Child*, as is the suggestion that constant, painful trauma is the memory trigger for this narrative: "All I have to do is close my eyes, and through a kind of dizziness my mind just plays the scene, as though I were watching television, and takes me back to what seems like yesterday" (18). The narrator's assertion that her memories are the result of "a clear head" is later clarified by the reference to other sources of knowledge that helped her construct this autobiography; these sources include her own memories, those of her siblings, and the Welfare records she was able to access, excerpts of which are inserted into *Shadow Child*.

One of the most significant aspects of the narrative structure of this autobiography is the extent to which it seeks (perhaps needs) to qualify its memory claims. This again demonstrates the implicit conflict with contemporary autobiographical practice—postmodern skepticism regarding memory combines with autobiographical market forces demanding authenticity. Yet *Shadow Child* and the declarations it makes about memory also reveal something of the imperatives of Indigenous autobiography. *Shadow Child* affirms the power of collective counter-memory and the political importance of testing the boundaries of non-Indigenous autobiography and memory. As Lambek and Antze argue, memory is "part of our commonsense world" (xi), and it is to the reader's common sense that autobiographies such as *Shadow Child* often appeal.

Fraser's and Meehan's identification of themselves as "stolen," Meehan's recognition of being a "second class citizen," and Fraser's understanding of her childhood "ending" at age two occur alongside the naming of government institutions and policies. This is powerful because these institutions and historical moments are living memories for many Australians, although for the dominant group their practices have until very recently been understood as benevolent. Attwood argues that such naming can have the effect of creating a historical event, replacing previous namings (189–190).[14] Autobiographies of childhood are juxtaposed with official histories such as government policies and documentation, in these instances, to offer a counter-discourse to them. In the 1990s autobiographical accounts came to be recognized and widely accepted as legitimate alternative histories of the Australian state.

The autobiographies of Fraser and Meehan are exemplary of the role of the autobiography of childhood: as history, as advocate, and as representative narrative. Fraser's *Shadow Child* and Meehan's *It Is No Secret* utilize what has become an established, recognizable cultural form, and the interest this form has generated, to draw attention to the experiences of the Stolen Generations. But Fraser and Meehan adapt the conventions of this form. For example, both of these autobiographies are concerned with a longer period than other autobiographies of childhood in this study. This is a crucial change, because it allows these autobiographers to explain the effects of childhood on their adult lives. It also permits these texts to draw direct reference to their contemporary consciousness (such as Meehan's discussion of how painful "National Sorry Day" was for her).

Another way these Indigenous autobiographies of childhood have affected this autobiographical form is in their language and structure. The narratives are structured as an intimate conversation between narrator and reader that is highly emotive and personal. Meehan and Fraser identify the insecurities they had about being writers of an autobiography.[15] In doing so they position themselves not as writers or autobiographers but as "everyday" people who *had* to write. In the "dedication" section of *Shadow Child* Fraser documents her "need to write" and in the final chapter recommends the act of writing "to anyone who has problems" (270). Such author/reader constructions mark a particular therapeutic space for these Indigenous autobiographies of childhood distinct from that of "high" (or literary) modes of autobiography.

Both Indigenous and non-Indigenous readers are directly addressed within the narratives of *It Is No Secret* and *Shadow Child*. Meehan and Fraser take the position of advocates for Indigenous Australians, using autobiography to generate a cultural memory of Stolen Generations childhoods. The narrator of *It Is No Secret* overtly offers her text as a regenerative force, and she appeals directly to the reader:

> For our people who are still searching for their families I pray that you find the answers your heart needs to know. For the thousands who were institutionalised and unloved in your childhood and ignored and unwanted when you returned home, we weep with you. (Meehan 292)

In *It Is No Secret* Meehan represents herself not as a unique individual but rather as a communal autobiographer. Joy Hooten argues that this is a particularly common feature in Indigenous women's autobiography, when "the individual story, sharp and even unresolved as it may be, is perceived as describing a general experience; it is both unrepeatable autograph and cultural archetype" (*Stories* 315). This is one of the central tensions of auto-biographies of childhood—the adult autobiographer speaks for the child, but the autobiography can also be employed to speak for others beyond the self. This is an issue I return to throughout this study. As Sidonie Smith and Julia Watson argue, "Acts of personal remembering are fundamentally social and collective" (*Reading Autobiography* 21). However, the explicitness with which Meehan's and Fraser's autobiographies adopt "representativeness" is another way in which these Indigenous autobiographies use the autobio-graphical form with intent.

Communal memory is important to Indigenous life writing; it is "a social, political position understood to be shared" (Hamilton 16). In *It Is No Secret* the naming of places, people, and experiences unique to Meehan might imply the specificity of this narrative. Yet throughout the autobiography Meehan is positioned as one of a community of people who suffered a similar experience. For example, Meehan describes the feelings of other children as if they are her own memories. Similarly, she relays the emotions and opinions of members of her community. *Shadow Child* employs a similar approach of writing a broader history of the Stolen Generations stemming from the personal experiences of the narrator:

> Up to the 1960s, many children who were stolen from their parents were either put in government settlements, or missions run by religious institutions, or placed in foster homes. Many of us were abused in these places—and that I cannot understand. Are we to believe that we were ripped from our parents because the government genuinely intended to ensure we would have a better life? No, not in my experience. They had

no right to take us away from our parents and put us in situations that would jeopardise our lives, our education and our very being. (266)

In this example, communal representation is affirmed through Fraser's claim to communal memory. The stolen child, the individual autobiographical subject, becomes metonymic of the Stolen Generations.

It Is No Secret assumes a currency of social myths about Indigeneity among its non-Indigenous readership. For example, the narrator suggests, "people probably think that just because we live in the city and eat the same foods as they do and speak the same language and dress the same way that I have assimilated" (291). The narrative directly rebuts this myth, moving from the events of Meehan's childhood to contemporary Australian racist myths of Aboriginality. Fraser's autobiography adopts a similar approach:

The government, through the Welfare, has always controlled my life in some shape or form. They did so all through my childhood and even now they control my life, because of what they have done to me—and not just to me, but to all the Aboriginal people in Australia. The non-Aboriginal people of Australia may sometimes wonder why Aboriginal people seem so dependent on government handouts. Well, for 200 years, what else did we have? Our independence was taken away, our dignity was destroyed and our country stolen from us, along with the murder of untold thousands of our people. What else was left? (267)

Such direct, powerful statements call upon non-Indigenous readers to witness these experiences and acknowledge white Australia's racist past. The child figure provides a recognizable symbol for this acknowledgment, allowing Meehan's and Fraser's narratives to use the autobiography of childhood to write histories for the Indigenous child.

In this chapter I have looked at some of the ways autobiographical writers are engaged in what Hamilton would describe as the " 'recovery' of memory—to facilitate the production of more and more inclusive histories—and to bring into the public domain the many conflicting interpretations of the past" (10). For these autobiographers, writing about discrimination, poverty, or abuse stems from a need to "write back" to mythologies of childhood that have been prevalent in the twentieth and twenty-first centuries. In particular, these autobiographies contest the notion that the mid-twentieth century was a "golden age" for children that existed in stark contrast to contemporary crises of childhood. Autobiographies of childhood at the turn of the millennium have become a location for the reconstruction of mid-twentieth-century childhoods—offering more diverse and inclusive representations of childhood experience.

The work of autobiography as a cultural memory practice has enabled autobiographies of childhood to "successfully '[unsettle] the past,' leaving . . . questions unanswered about what else has been strategically 'forgotten'" (Hamilton 14). Autobiographers such as Karr, Sage, Fraser, and Meehan respond to the cultural politicization of the child by "creating new emphases" (Gilmore, *Limits* 16). Whitlock predicts that further changes in autobiographies of childhoods will occur as a consequence of future socio-political shifts: "The more autobiographical writing is used by those who have not been authoritative or dominant, then the more likely it is that childhood narratives will be a record of the incursions of history and conflict rather than a pre-adolescent idyllic phase" (*Autographs* xxvi).

However, it is important to acknowledge that just as these writings about childhood are propelled by past mythologies of childhood, autobiographies of childhood are significantly enabled by contemporary discourses for representing childhood. Thus autobiographies of childhood function as rewriting of past childhoods as much as they reveal modern preoccupations about childhood—and autobiography joins the plethora of mediators on contemporary childhoods.

The following chapters work to consolidate and complicate these issues. I propose that different types of autobiographical writing about childhood, reflecting different memory modes, have emerged within the socio-political contexts outlined in this chapter. For example, at the millennium, and as a consequence of the same cultural flash points identified here, autobiographies remain a site for the consolidation of nostalgic memory, of particular myths of childhood from previous social eras that circulate as cultural memory now. I explore these tensions in cultural memory and their pertinence to autobiographies of childhood throughout this study.

CHAPTER 2

CONSUMING CHILDHOOD

BUYING AND SELLING THE
AUTOBIOGRAPHICAL CHILD

A dominant modern discourse of childhood continues to mark out "the child" as innately innocent, confirming its cultural identity as a passive and unknowing dependent, and therefore as a member of a social group utterly disempowered—but for good, altruistic reasons.

—Chris Jenks, *Childhood*

If you perused the autobiography or nonfiction section of any bookshop during the 1990s and 2000s, you would inevitably meet the child's gaze. An autobiography of childhood characteristically contains a photograph of the child on its cover. Often smiling, sometimes frowning, the child is commonly attractive but often shackled with a hairstyle and clothes that are unfashionable—underlining the child's place in history. The child gazes down upon you from the well-stocked bookstore shelves, imploring you to pick the book up and share in this story of childhood.

In chapter 1 I explored the ways in which the autobiographical child has become a socio-cultural, even political, construct upon which memory struggles are contested. I offer this as one explanation for the voluminous production and consumption of autobiographies of childhood. In this chapter I offer a further context for interpreting autobiographies of childhood: the autobiography's initial, visual presentation, which manifests in its cover image. The consumption of the autobiography's cover image involves the consumption of the child who adorns the book's cover and whose story lies within its pages. The cover image—its construction and containment of the child image—is crucial to an understanding of how the autobiography is produced and read. I am interested in the ways in which an autobiography of childhood's photographic cover, imbued with meaning by the conventions of autobiographical writing (and what it promises to the reader), intersects with other photographic images of children that are circulating concurrently in the public domain. How do these photographs engage with cultural memory to tell stories about childhoods past and present?

Within autobiography, childhoods are commodified. Childhoods are produced and sold (by writers, publishers, and booksellers) and bought and consumed (by readers). Autobiographies of childhood pledge to offer experiences and stories of childhood for adult consumption, allowing adults to fantasize about their collective pasts and futures. Childhood lives are presented as available, desirable, and consumable for adult readerships.

As I have previously argued, within autobiographies of childhood, the child figure is ideologically mobilized to tell stories about childhood—to confirm or challenge particular childhood histories. In doing so, however, autobiographies are inevitably bound by existing cultural templates for representing childhood within Western culture. Within this discussion I offer an analysis of a number of book covers of autobiographies of childhoods (which are reproduced in this text) to suggest how and why the child image gives meaning to the autobiographical text, projecting particular representations of childhood, and creating relationships between reader and text, and between the text and cultural history. I interrogate the trope of childhood innocence and explore its utility within the circulation and reception of contemporary autobiography—for example, by looking also at the jacket copy and the ways in which it fleshes out and complicates the image presented on the cover. I read these representations of childhood in light of the theories of childhood introduced in chapter 1 and also consider visual culture theories on childhood and family photography.

Judging a Book by Its Cover: Childhood Photography

Book covers are often the first meeting place between reader and book and play a key role in mobilizing certain interpretations.[1] One of the autobiographical genre's most arresting and persistent features is its use of photographs on its covers and within its pages. A passing glance at the shelves of any bookshop instantly reveals where the fiction section ends and the nonfiction shelves begin.[2] Fictional books tend to use artistic images for their covers, whereas nonfictional texts such as autobiographies and biographies commonly signal their subject/s on their covers. In autobiography the cover functions as another part of "the autobiographical pact," to use Philippe Lejeune's term, with a photograph providing as significant a guide to interpreting the text *as* autobiography as the author's name. For example, cover photographs on autobiographies commonly assert that the person in the photograph is the same person whose story will be contained in its pages. The photograph and the autobiography combine to make a potent assertion of the truth of the text. Photographs, like autobiographical writing, are commonly associated with truth and authenticity—a means for accessing the past and for constructing stories about personal and collective histories. Photographs are "part of the material with which we make sense of our wider world. They are objects which take their place amongst the other objects which are part of our personal and collective past, part of the detailed and concrete existence with which we gain some control over our surroundings" (Holland, "History, Memory" 10). Add to this powerful mix the figure of the child—which has long been a cultural symbol of authenticity—and we can begin to witness the cultural significance of these cover images.

In chapter 1 I suggested how cultural memory surrounding Western childhoods focuses on the child figure as lacking agency, and thus as an object of adult concern. When myths of childhood innocence "[transform] culture into nature," to use Henry Jenkins's term, they force children outside the political domain; this removes their agency, giving it to the adult consumer of this image (*Children's Culture Reader* 15). I am interested, then, in how these cover images represent the autobiographical child—in particular, how they respond to the trope of the innocent child. How does this photographic response intersect with the representations of childhood made within the pages of the autobiography?

Pictures of childhood are, as Anne Higonnet proposes in her exceptional study of childhood photography, "at once the most common, the most sacred and the most controversial images of our time" (7). Almost half of all advertisement photographs depict children, and billions of amateur photographs are taken of children each year (9). From advertisements through school photographs and child beauty pageants—these images circulate to create dialogue on, and meanings for, childhood. Higonnet rightly contends that in the "highly visual" contemporary era, pictures play a leading role in our perception and understanding of childhoods—past, present, and future. Childhood photography has become a contested space where many of the debates affecting childhood in the late twentieth and early twenty-first century have been fought (8).

As suggested in chapter 1, the turn of the millennium witnessed significant flash points, or moments of crises, in relation to Western childhoods. Notions of childhood "innocence," while shifting and often contested, have retained a strong influence in contemporary cultural representations and interpretations of childhood. For example, within public photographs of children, such as those in advertisements for children's products or services, certain visual strategies work to position the photographed child as innocent. However, this appearance of innocence is heavily dependent on the adult spectator responding to particular visual tropes. For example, Stephen Kline notes that in advertising for children's products in the nineteenth and twentieth centuries, images of children commonly played on adult anxieties about childhood. A picture of an ill child within a print advertisement persuaded consumers to buy manufactured medicines. Such advertisements stress "a therapeutic ethos with an emphasis on well-being, self-help and betterment" nostalgically aimed at restoring a child's "natural" state of innocence and purity (102–103). Advertisements for specialized breakfast foods emphasized childhood as a natural and pure state, urging consumers to consider children's unique nutritional needs. Kline writes:

> Advertising repeatedly articulated the need for parents to become aware of the unique needs, vulnerabilities and sensitivities of their child. Most particularly, this idea was expressed through a madonna-and-child motif: the concerned mother and the frail and innocent child were coupled in the image of a bond rooted in a deep emotional concern for the child's well-being. (103)

Another common (and perhaps contrary) trope in public photographic representations of children is the child who has lost (or may lose) his or her innocence. The child may be constructed as damaged and thus demands the viewer's attention and sympathy. Chris Jenks discusses how pictures of children are employed to evoke sympathy for charities and welfare campaigns. However, Jenks suggests that these photographs commonly depict children as disempowered victims who have lost any semblance of childhood innocence as we traditionally know it:

> Charity adverts for overseas development and aid, for example, manipulate images of children's compliant part in their own deprivation, emphasizing that children are the least complicit in causality yet the most affected. Similarly, it is as a passive victim of abuse, neglect and poverty that "the child" is often displayed for the British public through mass media and Government rhetoric. (124)

In these instances, those consuming the image are asked to take action to restore the child's innocence. Whether innocent or experienced, healthy or unwell, children in publicly displayed photographs are most commonly conventionally attractive. They meet the spectators' gaze, directly engaging them and imploring them to take action—whether to buy a product or to donate money to a charity.

The notion that childhood is "in crisis"—that children face the constant threat of (predominantly) sexual predators, violence, drugs, and poverty—has pervaded twentieth-century media and popular culture representations of childhood. Higonnet discusses the role that visual cultures have played in unsettling the innocent child and in representing the child in crisis. For example, Higonnet argues that the trend toward viewing certain photographs of children as sexualized accelerated in the late 1970s. In the 2000s it is not uncommon for children to be eroticized in visual media—from fashion photography through mainstream cinema and television programs. Higonnet cites the photography of Robert Mapplethorpe and mass-media commercial photographs such as Calvin Klein's 1995 jeans advertising campaign as two examples of scandals surrounding the sexualization of children in photographs. Such representations are always fraught with controversy because, as Higonnet contends, when "we look at troubling images of children we not only see abstract meanings, but dread real consequences" (11). A representative example of this is the case of JonBenét Ramsey, as discussed in chapter 1. A handful of photographs brought the murdered child into popular consciousness. As these photographs of the heavily made-up child beauty queen circulated in the popular press, spectators responded with retrospective projections of fear. It was easy for media spectators to view JonBenét Ramsey's eroticization as a precursor to her murder. Such an association confirmed popular fears regarding the dangers of objectifying children, and the risks of children maturing too soon.

Thus, "troubling images" of children, to appropriate Higonnet's term, have diverse manifestations within visual cultures—from overtly troubling images of child abuse or poverty to images (such as those of JonBenét Ramsey) that subvert accepted conventions of how children should appear. I have suggested that in the late twentieth and early twenty-first centuries, images of childhood innocence have been pervasive alongside images depicting childhood in crisis. I am not suggesting that such representations exist in binary opposition, nor am I suggesting that such depictions are mutually exclusive or objectively self-defining. These images are open for interpretation, and we interpret these images of childhood in light of the values and social codes of our time. These diverse images of childhood exist in a productive tension. The juxtaposition of the child in crisis as seen in welfare advertisements with the natural, healthy child advertising children's products accentuates the innocent child as ideal, while constructing a fine line between the healthy, happy, innocent child and the traumatized child. One could easily become the other at short notice; we become acutely aware of how much these different children have in common—for instance, a tender age, an engaging physical beauty, a diminutive stature, and an entreating stare.

Consider the media representations of JonBenét Ramsey and Madeleine McCann, the four-year-old British child who disappeared while holidaying with her family in Portugal in 2007. The photographic images of both girls as shown by the media functioned to construct them as conventionally innocent. However, the juxtaposition of these images alongside narratives of crime and images of distressed parents (who were, in each case, also murder suspects) had the dual effect of constructing both Ramsey and McCann as innocent children who became victims of trauma. This representation is one that media spectators have eagerly digested—reflecting a dual, conflicting investment in the innocent and traumatic representations of childhood.

The child, however culturally drawn, is at once symbolic of the past, present, and future—reflecting society's deep engagement with, even dependency on, particular ideas about childhood. Patricia Holland suggests that the pervasiveness of the child image in contemporary culture reflects the rich investment society has in its children, who, according to Holland, represent the future:

> The engaging smile, the mischievous grin, the pout, the tear, the expression of joys forgotten to adulthood—we greet these beguiling pictures with a special sort of pleasure as they circulate in the public spaces of our decaying inner cities, our spruced-up country towns, and our suburban parades. Childhood lends itself to spectacular presentation. (*What Is a Child?* 8)

Holland's assessment reveals something of the investment that adults make in childhood; the child represents "joys forgotten to adulthood." However, these joys are obviously not quite "forgotten" if the adult responds to them. They are recognizable because they offer something to the adult that the adult desires. Within these images, childhood represents much more than simply the future that Holland suggests.

Adults (particularly those who have children) invest in children—emotionally, economically, spiritually, socially, and so on. Children are commonly thought to be growing up faster, but they are living with their parents longer. Television programs and advertisements offer a steady stream of idealized templates for parent-child relationships—focusing on the importance of affection and nurturing between parents and young children, and emphasizing mutual love and responsibility during adolescence and young adulthood. A plethora of expectations result from these cultural investments, ideas, and images (and these expectations may manifest implicitly or explicitly within adults). When adults respond to children, their responses are inevitably affected by a sense of how things should be (for example, in light of dominant cultural representations) and by expectations for the future—as these adults may one day be dependent on their children. And inevitably, adults will make comparisons between contemporary childhood and their own childhoods—a means for making up for past wrongs or for replicating past joys.

Thus, just as the child is symbolic of an idealized present and an idealized future, the contemporary child is also imbued with adult desires from the past. Jenks explains:

> Late modern society has re-adopted the child. The child, in the setting of what are now conceptualized as post-modern cultural configurations, has become the site or the relocation of discourses concerning stability, interrogation and the social bond. The child is now envisioned as a form of "nostalgia," a longing for times past, not a futurity. Children are now seen not so much as "promise" but as primary and unequivocal sources of love, but also as partners in the most fundamental, unchosen, unnegotiated form of relationship. The trust that was previously anticipated from marriage, partnership, friendship, class solidarity and so on, is now invested more generally in the child. This can be witnessed empirically in a number of ways: through the affectual prolongation of adolescence; the disputed territory that children constitute during divorce; the uprating of children's status through the modern advances in children's rights (like the 1989 Children Act in the UK); the modern iconography of the child in Third World aid politics and in Western campaigns against addiction and criminality. (107)

Each of these desires is embedded with nostalgic longings. Nostalgia, as discussed in chapter 1, is more than simply a longing for a past that cannot be recovered. Nostalgia is also a desire for an idealized past that never was. It can denote a reconstruction of the past, and of the present (and future) in light of a (perceived) past. Thus, nostalgia is a useful concept for thinking about the ways in which child images are constructed to tell stories and reflect desires about the past and present, and in offering particular futures. And these investments in childhood and the child's image become complementary in photography; photographs at once reflect the past, are viewed in the present, and affect future constructions of childhood.

Telling Stories about Childhood:
Autobiographies and Cover Photography

Photographic constructions of childhood may reflect (or attempt to construct) the desires of those who create, circulate, and consume them, but to what extent is the child actually accessible to those consuming the child's image? In his essay "The Dark Continent of Childhood," Jean Baudrillard discusses the extent to which the child is becoming a "clone" or a "performance," where particular images are becoming repetitious or pastiche and the individual child becomes embedded or lost (103). Baudrillard's assessment seems founded, for example, when considering the increasingly blurred boundaries between private and public photography. Public photographs of children often take on the appearance of private photographs, as if they could have been taken straight from the family album. Private and public photographic representations of childhood exist in a cyclical relationship. Just as public photographs mimic private photographs, private family photographs are heavily performative and respond to existing photographic narratives and templates. Private photographs are constructed according to particular

Figure 1. Cover image,
Once in a House on Fire.
Reprinted by permission
of Picador.
© *1998 Andrea Ashworth.*

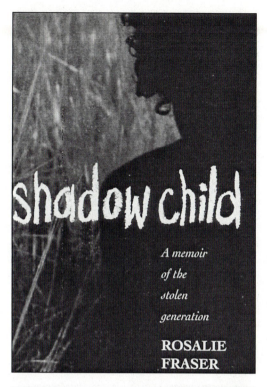

Figure 2. Cover image,
Shadow Child.
Reprinted by permission
of Hale and Iremonger.
©1 998 Rosalie Fraser.

Figure 3. Cover image,
Skating to Antarctica.
Reprinted by permission
of Granta Books.
© 1997 Jenny Diski.

Figure 4. Cover image,
Out of Darkness.
Reprinted by permission
of Fremantle Press.
© 1998 Ivor Knight.

Figure 5. Cover image,
A Saucepan in the Sky.
Reprinted by permission
of Hale and Iremonger.
© 2001 Brian Nicholls.

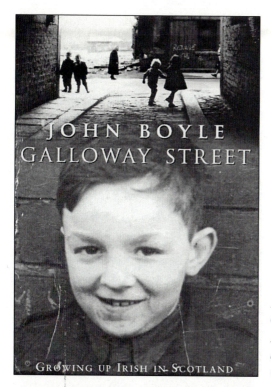

Figure 6. Cover image,
Galloway Street.
Reprinted by permission
of Random House.
© *2001 John Boyle.*

Figure 7. Cover
image, The Shark Net
(paperback). Reprinted
by permission of Penguin.
© *2000 Robert Drewe.*

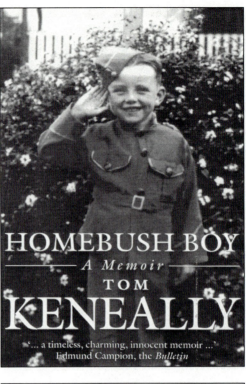

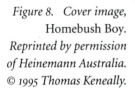

Figure 8. Cover image,
Homebush Boy.
Reprinted by permission
of Heinemann Australia.
© 1995 Thomas Keneally.

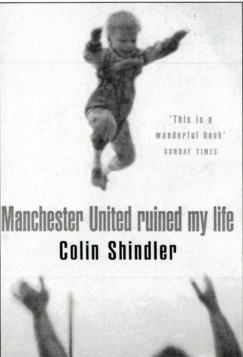

Figure 9. Cover image,
Manchester United
Ruined My Life. *Reprinted*
by permission of Headline.
© Colin Shindler 1998.

It is no Secret
the story of a stolen child
DONNA MEEHAN

Figure 10. Cover image,
It Is No Secret.
Reprinted by permission of
Random House Australia.
© 2000 Donna Meehan.

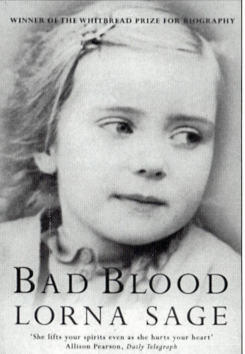

WINNER OF THE WHITBREAD PRIZE FOR BIOGRAPHY

BAD BLOOD
LORNA SAGE

'She lifts your spirits even as she hurts your heart'
Allison Pearson, *Daily Telegraph*

Figure 11. Cover image,
Bad Blood.
Reprinted by permission
of Publishers Ltd.
© 2001 Lorna Sage.

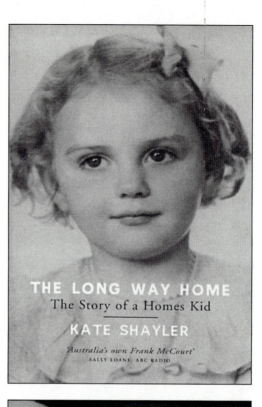

THE LONG WAY HOME
The Story of a Homes Kid

KATE SHAYLER

'Australia's own Frank McCourt'
SALLY LOANE, ABC RADIO

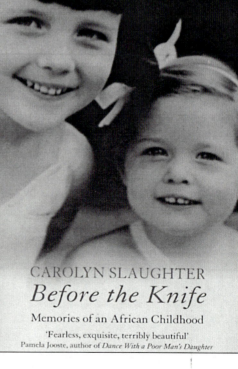

CAROLYN SLAUGHTER
Before the Knife
Memories of an African Childhood

'Fearless, exquisite, terribly beautiful'
Pamela Jooste, author of *Dance With a Poor Man's Daughter*

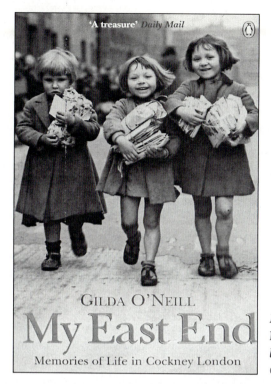

Figure 14. Cover image, My East End. Reprinted by permission of Penguin. © 1999 Gilda O'Neill.

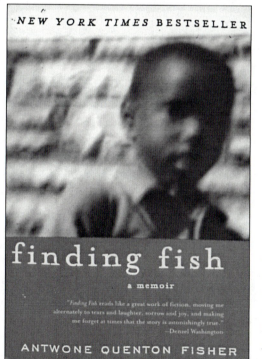

Figure 15. Cover image, Finding Fish: A Memoir. Reprinted by permission of HarperCollins Publishers. © 2001 Antwone Quenton Fisher and Mim Eichler Rivas.

social customs—for instance, recording special occasions and happy events. The repetition of childhood images within culture, from advertising through to personal albums, reveals the ways in which particular, dominant images of childhood—for example, childhood innocence—develop and circulate to tell stories about childhood.[3]

Autobiographies of childhood are a cultural site where a private photograph of a child becomes public. The public display of these personal photographs, as Holland suggests, "poses a series of challenges to different pasts, as memory interweaves with private fantasy and public history ("History, Memory" 14).[4] These texts traverse and negotiate the cultural memory of childhood, engaging with dominant memory modes for representing childhood such as trauma and nostalgia. These texts are not simple reflections of established ideas of childhood; rather, they are part of how memories and mythologies of childhood are produced, circulated, and interrogated. They do this from the front cover to the final page.

The strongest allusions in the cover photographs of autobiographies of childhood are to innocence. Whether the autobiography is in the nostalgic mode or is one that recounts traumatic memories, the child is most commonly objectified as vulnerable, inexperienced, and in need of protection. Of the cover photographs I sample in this chapter, each includes a child photograph on the cover, a compelling sign of the text's subject. Apart from two, Fraser's *Shadow Child* and Ashworth's *Once in a House on Fire*, each appears to be a reproduction of an actual family photograph. Ashworth's (see fig. 1) and Fraser's (fig. 2) are artist's images of childhood.[5]

When photographs appear on the covers of autobiographies, it is usually presumed (as I do), and yet not always confirmed, that the photograph is of the author-autobiographer subject. Given this embedded assumption, the photograph becomes a gesture of authenticity. The child perhaps bears more than a passing resemblance to the author (whose photograph may also be printed upon the book jacket). This provides the first interpretive clue to reading the text: The autobiography is to be read in terms of this photograph. These photographs are commonly dated as belonging to a particular era by the style or quality of the photograph or by the fashions. The selection and arrangement of the image tells a story and constructs the childhood within history.

The layout of the covers is also important in constructing meaning for the childhood within. The photograph of the child is prominently positioned. The autobiographer's name is written above, below, or superimposed upon the photograph. This also functions as a marker that the child and the autobiographer are the same person. The presence of the childish figure playing or posing neatly for a photograph becomes a point of reference to which the adult autobiographer can be compared. The book title is placed alongside the photograph and the author's name. This juxtaposition of the author's name and the book title confirms the ownership of the story by both the named adult and the child in the photograph.

In her study of media representations of children, Holland identifies particular photographic tropes. Many of these tropes recur in the cover imagery of autobiographies of childhood: "the energetic boy" (figs. 6, 7, 8, 9), "the dependent child in need of protection" (figs. 1, 4, 5, 9, 10, 11, 12, 13), and "the playful child" (figs. 6, 7, 8, 9) (*What Is a Child?* 12). Three of Holland's categorizations—"the ignorant child in need of education," "the violent child on the streets," and "the seductive girl"—are noticeably, and perhaps not surprisingly, absent from the covers of autobiographies of childhood, since such images connote experience rather than innocence. While autobiographies of childhood are often concerned with representing adverse experiences, and traumatic autobiographies sometimes convey this on their covers, cover images are designed to seduce the reader into purchasing the text, so they rarely confront the consumer with distressing pictures. This is a point I return to further on.

These cover photographs engage with the trope of childhood innocence via the child image used. One of the markers of childhood innocence on the covers of these autobiographies is the happy child, reminiscent of Holland's "playful child" (figs. 6, 7, 8, 10, 11, 12, 13, 14). The smiling child is emotive and attractive. He or she invokes sympathy or recognition, potentially reminding consumers of themselves, of someone they know from their own family albums, or of times of happiness.[6] The representation of the happy child again suggests innocence but also points to the familiarity (and thus accessibility) of such representations, suggesting the consumer's ability to read and know the meaning of this image.

Autobiography's accessibility is an important marketing strategy, and the visual images on the covers become symbols of truthfulness and authenticity. As Timothy Dow Adams suggests, no amount of appeals to logic regarding "the obvious distortions of photographs" can convince consumers to question the popular idea that photographs represent reality (4). Most consumers of photography will have experienced the "constructedness" of photographic posing, particularly evident in the family photograph. As Pierre Bourdieu proposes, "the 'natural' is a cultural ideal which must be created before it can be captured" ("Social Definition" 166). Though most photographs of children involve posing, smiles appear "casual" and "natural"; "it seems as if we are catching the children unawares, as is the adult's right," Holland suggests

(*What Is a Child?* 125). Children are contained or frozen in such images, and the images become metonymic of their story.

The majority of the child figures on the covers of autobiographies of childhood can be categorized as "the playful child" (for example, fig. 9), smiling directly at the camera/observer (fig. 6) or looking serenely, though not unhappily, away (figs. 11 and 12). Though close-up images of attractive, angelic child faces are often used to emotive effect (figs. 11 and 12), the child's image is sometimes engulfed by the page to emphasize the vulnerability of the figure (fig. 5). Colin Shindler's *Manchester United Ruined My Life* contains a photograph of a young child being playfully tossed in the air with outstretched adult hands below him. This is the playful child depicted with a hint of danger—the child in need of protection.

Such images encourage an empathetic, maternal or paternal relationship between viewer and child. As Holland argues, the "expressiveness" of children in photographs, through smiling or playing, "invites our expressiveness. They are a signal for a release of emotions" (*What Is a Child?* 18). Such a response mirrors maternal or paternal conventions. The children in the book-cover photographs are constructed as being cared for (fig. 9) or as needing to be cared for, because of their diminutive posture in an adult world (fig. 5) or because their beauty must be preserved (fig. 12).

Yet it is important to remember that the child in the photograph no longer exists—the pictured child has since grown up. Thus, contemporary consumers must activate meanings for these images. While the photographs may be new to them, the images are not. As previously argued, these images will be interpreted within the "symbolic system" in which they occur, amid a range of existing photographic images of children.[7] For example, these photographs coexist with other images of the child circulating within culture at the turn of the millennium: missing person photographs, for instance, and advertisements for children's charities or for children's products. It is unavoidable that intertextuality shapes our approach to childhood images. Childhood memories are evoked by contemporary knowledge. When we consume images, like those on the covers of autobiographies, our reactions may have "little or nothing to do with what is actually in the picture"—they are generated "in an intertext of discourses that shift between the past and present, spectator and image, and between all these cultural contexts, historical moments" (Kuhn 18–19). Thus, as suggested in chapter 1, direct and indirect parallels can be drawn between the rise of the autobiography of childhood and particular cultural "flash points" or socio-historical events affecting children. We read the cover images of these texts in light of our own reflections on what we think childhood is and projections of what we want childhood to be.

Selecting these texts from crowded bookshelves allows readers to reflect upon childhoods past, present, and future and to address their concerns, even absolve their shame or responsibility, regarding contemporary "crises" of childhood such as school shootings or child sexual abuse. To respond empathically to these texts is to be a good citizen—a compassionate witness to the needs of a child. In reading the text, the reader will become (directly or indirectly) an advocate for the child.[8]

Consuming autobiographies of childhood has become in itself a gesture of social activism. When consumers hold the material object in their hands, they are informed (often by the "jacket copy" or "blurb" as well as the photograph)[9] that they are consuming a text of socio-political consequence. Consumers make statements about themselves through what they consume. In consuming childhood autobiographies, readers are able to align themselves with the lives they consume, particularly to offer ideological support to the autobiographical subject and designate their own ideological or political stance—a point I will begin discussing here but will return to in more depth in chapter 7.

Autobiographies of childhood are commonly categorized and marketed by the jacket copy according to their sociological worth. This has become one of the central markers of value for autobiographies of childhood—a reason to buy and read this text, despite its harrowing content. An autobiography of childhood's sociological value is signaled both by its promise of didacticism and by its exposure of social injustices. For example, Fraser's traumatic autobiography of childhood, *Shadow Child*, is said to "expose the faceless bureaucracy," while Kate Shayler's *The Long Way Home* unveils "the great silence" surrounding institutionalized children in postwar Australia. Traumatic autobiographies of childhood are valued for being timely and for weighing in on issues that are circulating within public discourse. According to the book jacket, the Stolen Generations autobiography *It Is No Secret* recounts the experience of an Aboriginal child stolen from her family: "Tiny and vulnerable, she had to try and make sense of her strange new world and the loss of everything she had known and loved"; and "the loss of her sense of belonging brought Donna close to suicide. Only when she traced her birth family could her healing begin." This blurb makes quite specific references to the loss of cultural identity. The magnitude of the damage done to Indigenous people of the Stolen Generations is asserted with the reference to the author having been "close to suicide." The blurb projects these references via the innocent child who is "tiny and vulnerable," which connects the blurb to the autobiography's cover image discussed earlier.

Thus, authors and publishers select cover photographs because of their accessibility to consumers.[10] They are chosen with an eye on those few seconds when a browser chooses to become a consumer. Within these cover images the child addresses an implied adult viewer who may recognize and sympathize with an innocent child whose experiences are alien to his or her own. Or the consumer may empathize with these images and perhaps want to retrieve a little of his or her own child self in the dated fashions and childish hairstyles. Individual photographs on the covers of autobiographies are metonyms for childhoods of particular eras, especially given that the time frames of contemporary autobiographies of childhood are within living memory for many adult readers. When private photographs are made public, as Holland suggests, "a vision of a nostalgic national and regional past is constructed which parallels the continuous family history dreamt of by many an album" ("History, Memory" 13).

On the cover of *The Shark Net* Robert Drewe's childhood self poses on a beach (fig. 7). The sandy-colored cover blends into the boy's blond hair and the beach upon which he lies. This photograph is reminiscent of pictures that would likely be found in family albums across Australia. Thomas Keneally's *Homebush Boy* (fig. 8) depicts a boy dressed in uniform, saluting happily and obediently to the camera. This picture characterizes the pageantry of childhood in 1950s Australia and represents a rite of passage of Keneally's boyhood. It also serves as a reminder of the restrictions of childhood, such as being required to dress up and pose for (loving) parent photographers. In a similar way the cover photograph of Gilda O'Neill's *My East End* (fig. 14) becomes a nostalgic portrait of quintessentially British working-class childhoods. These three children, though wearing coats and carrying packages that appear too heavy for them, are smiling as happily as the young boy on the beach. The portrait suggests happiness and strength amid adversity.

If the predominant image on these covers is the innocence of the child, what sorts of effects are used to differentiate between autobiographies in the nostalgic and traumatic modes? One of the clearest indicators of the memory mode of these different autobiographies is in the juxtaposition of the child image and the book title. For example, the titles of the nostalgic auto-biographies tend to reinforce the image presented, encouraging a reading of the child as innocent. Titles such as *My East End*, *Galloway Street*, *Homebush Boy*, and *A Saucepan in the Sky* (which refers to a star constellation visible over Sydney) fix the child, unambiguously, within time and place. These titles work alongside the cover images to promise a nostalgic representation of autobiographies of childhood as autobiographies of place, as social rather than individual histories.[11]

In comparison, the book titles of traumatic autobiographies tend to be more ambiguous, offering little reference to time or place. These titles destabilize the photographic child image and its connotations of innocence. The titles function as ominous forewarnings of the text's content, for example, *Bad Blood, Before the Knife, Once in a House on Fire, Out of Darkness,* and *Shadow Child.* Subtitles are also important; Meehan's *It Is No Secret,* a Stolen Generations autobiography, is subtitled "the story of a stolen child" (fig. 10), and Shayler's *The Long Way Home,* an autobiography of child abuse and institutionalization, is subtitled "the story of a Homes Kid" (fig. 12). These subtitles lie beneath the photographs of smiling children to provide an effective contrast to the "truth" projected by the photograph. The mythic childhood happiness and innocence that are represented in the photographs will fade to unveil the traumatic events of the narrative. The effects of these constructions are multiple. These portraits reveal the illusory potential of photographs to create mythologies of innocence and happiness. In their reproduction, they draw would-be readers in by their cover images, only to demand a re-reading of the child image through the title and/or subtitle.

The "constructedness" of photographs is characteristically exposed on the covers of traumatic autobiographies through an examination of the "controlled pose": Childhood spontaneity and adult control collide. Diski's *Skating to Antarctica* (fig. 3) and Shayler's *The Long Way Home* (fig.12) both depict the sorts of posing common in Western family photograph albums, where photographs of children are produced for a predominantly adult gaze. Shayler's could be considered a typical full-face, neat-haired pose; Diski's, though clearly a posed photograph, is different altogether. Diski's photograph appears to be of a mother and daughter, but the sharp light and colors of the overexposed photograph obscure their faces and clothes. As a result it is impossible to distinguish their facial expressions or for the viewer to form an emotional bond with the child of the photograph. The viewer's gaze is disrupted, which is continued in *Skating to Antarctica*: The narrator finds it nearly impossible to represent her childhood self, who now seems like a different person and is as obscured in the narrative as she is in the photograph.

Similarly, the cover photograph of Ivor Knight's *Out of Darkness* (fig. 4) is poorly lit and out of focus. The child appears unsure about being photographed. He is unsmiling, possibly posing, and the top part of his head has been cropped. Whether this is from the original photograph or a result of the cover image reproduction is unclear. The photograph is tinged with green, and the title *Out of Darkness* asks the viewer to consider that this ghostlike child figure may be appearing from within a nightmare. In *Out of Darkness*, the nightmare is sexual abuse.

Thus, the cover images of traumatic autobiographies require a dynamic interpretation from viewers. For example, the representations of Indigenous children, children from lower socio-economic groups, and children who appear somehow disconnected or unknowable confront the viewer, revising common mythologies of what a child looks like. Higonnet refers to such images as "knowing children"—children who are visually endowed with psychological and physical individuality. Such representations require the viewer to reevaluate innocence along with childhood (12). Of the examples I have chosen for this study, the two autobiographies of childhood that do not use photographs of the child self for their book cover are Ashworth's *Once in a House on Fire* (fig. 1) and Fraser's *Shadow Child* (fig. 2). As mentioned earlier, these cover images are artist's images of childhood. Both of these autobiographies relate traumatic childhoods, so this difference is significant. The absence of a photograph of the child self may reflect a desire to provide anonymity for the child, or it may suggest that childhood photographs are unavailable to the autobiographer—a result of childhood displacement. This is how Antwone Quenton Fisher's autobiography of childhood *Finding Fish: A Memoir* (fig. 15) is offered to the reader. The reader is informed (on the back cover of the autobiography) that the blurred photograph of the young boy on the front cover is the only one the author has from his childhood. This may also explain the grainy images selected for the covers of Diski's and Knight's autobiographies. Survivors of traumatic childhoods may not have the conventional array of artifacts that other adults so often have from their childhoods. In these instances the rare photograph of the childhood becomes a means for reclaiming past identities—of using one photograph to tell a much larger story.

The cover image of Fraser's autobiography confronts the viewer with the image of a child cast in shadow. This shadowy child image prefigures the graphic events that will be recounted within this autobiography. Unlike the aforementioned childhood photographs, the child's face, and, by extension, her identity, are masked by the shadow. Therefore, the child is not constructed as knowable or available. The consumer will only learn about this child by reading the narrative within. The cover image is particularly challenging to Australians of European descent in the context of white Australia's attempts to erase Indigenous identities. The childish handwriting of the title appears to be done in white chalk on a largely black background, suggesting a black-board. This reinforces the didacticism of this autobiography. The contrast between the dark background and the chalked, childish writing of the title suggests to the viewer that however ominous this construction may appear, this is the story of an innocent child who has had her innocence stolen.

The cover image of Ashworth's *Once in a House on Fire* is of a child with a Band-Aided knee and only one rollerskate.[12] It is an evocative image of childhood playfulness amid poverty and misfortune. Though the image implies a traumatic tale, the picture is not so confrontational or graphic as to alienate the autobiography's potential readership. Irrespective of what may appear within their pages, traumatic autobiographies of childhood are consistently positioned as palatable texts. Indeed, their commercial success arguably relies on the "respectability" associated with an understated cover image. Their public display of trauma lies within. Language holds agency that visual culture does not. Cover images have clear limits, particularly when it comes to representing the child.

Consuming Childhood: Beyond the Cover

When people take personal photographs, it is not necessarily a conscious, reflective activity, nor a public one. However, the social uses of photographs continue to expand—particularly through the popularity of photo-sharing sites on the Internet (such as Flickr and Slide) and social networking sites such as Facebook and MySpace. The public display of private photographs has become a potent cultural gesture, which facilitates the intersection of private and public histories. The assembly and dissemination of visual imagery is one of the ways in which cultures produce and reproduce identities, and a nonfictional mechanism for storytelling. Marianne Hirsch proposes that because a photograph gives "the illusion of being a simple transcription of the real, a trace touched directly by the event it records, it has the effect of naturalizing cultural practices and of disguising their stereotyped and coded characteristics" (7). For this reason it is important to decode these photographic texts, and to consider them as a potent element of the autobiographical text in constructing and circulating representations of childhood.

The authority of the photograph is emphasized when the apparently "realistic" and "objective" photograph, autobiography, and figure of the child intersect. The child figure functions as a cultural symbol of the past and can offer a valuable key to understanding adult identities in the present. Cover images play a significant role in setting limits upon the meanings of autobiographies. Economically these images are being used to signify a product for sale by appealing to, for instance, sympathies, desires, and/or needs. Autobiographies gain currency from other visual images of childhood, circulating at the particular cultural moment of their release. Artistically and sociologically these images are being used to represent a childhood life and self. These autobiographical representations of the child, particularly the photograph cover image, demonstrate the socio-cultural investments in the child. They reveal the ways in which the autobiography-as-object has become a site for contesting the cultural production of childhood, particularly notions of childhood innocence. The images appeal to recognizable myths of childhood, family, and period and may rewrite them. The autobiographical photograph tells stories and thus limits meanings because of its potent representations of childhood innocence.

In representing traumatic childhoods, these cover images fall short of "undoing" ideals of childhood innocence.[13] The traumatized child is represented according to recognizable cultural templates of childhood innocence—for telling stories about childhood innocence. Though the child is not represented as happy and carefree, the child is in need of adult intervention—protection and guidance (via the adult's act of purchasing and reading the autobiography).

CHAPTER 3

AUTHORING CHILDHOOD

THE ROAD TO RECOVERY AND REDEMPTION

Personal histories—in all their varieties—serve as individualized testimonies to getting a "successful" life together (however success is defined) and/or to the failure of self-remaking in terms of the dream.
>   —Sidonie Smith and Julia Watson, eds.,
>   *Getting a Life: Everyday Uses of Autobiography*

I'm on deck the dawn we sail into New York. I'm sure I'm in a film, that it will end and lights will come up in the Lyric Cinema. . . . I stand on the deck with the Wireless Officer looking at the lights of America twinkling. He says, My God, that was a lovely night, Frank. Isn't this a great country altogether.
>   —Frank McCourt, *Angela's Ashes*

In chapter 2 I began to explore the ways in which autobiographies of childhood construct a relationship between the autobiographical child and adult reader. Following on from this, in this chapter I explore the impact of the adult autobiographical author in the production and reception of autobiographies of childhood. The adult autobiographer constructs the child self, bringing the child back to life a generation on. To write an autobiography of childhood is to inhabit and/or challenge the identities that are available for articulating childhood experiences at a particular cultural moment. What relationship is constructed between the adult autobiographical author and the child self he or she represents? What links are made between childhood and adulthood both inside and outside the text (for example, within the text's representations and in promotional material and author interviews about the autobiography)? And what tropes or templates emerge for representing this relationship, for example, the resilient child and the recovered adult?

The second question for investigation in this chapter is: How does the presence of the adult autobiographical author affect the ways in which we interpret the text? Autobiographies are unstable, dialogic, and shifting: They cannot be unified through appeals to a human author. Yet despite the prevalence of this view in theory, the adult author remains ideologically and commercially important to the promotion and reception of autobiographies of childhoods. Autobiographies of childhood are commonly promoted on the grounds that the author is a worthy subject. Autobiographies of childhood commonly make use of a child narrator—giving the impression of a rediscovered child who is able to narrate his or her own experience. Even though most readers recognize this as a textual contrivance, it has come to signify a perceptible synthesis between the author's child and adult selves. The apparently self-actualized, successful adult is qualified to speak on the behalf of both selves.

I explore these issues in light of theories of authorship and look at two case studies: Andrea Ashworth's *Once in a House on Fire* and Frank McCourt's *Angela's Ashes*. Why are these particular authors able to tell their stories at this time? Or, to paraphrase Sidonie Smith and Julia Watson, what does it mean to be an autobiographer of childhood at this particular cultural moment (*Reading Autobiography* 165–166)? For example, what are the implications of autobiographical authors such as Ashworth identifying themselves as survivors of child abuse? These narratives are commonly authenticated through the particular performances demanded from authors of traumatic autobiographies of childhood: resilience, recovery, and self-reflexivity.

To understand the significance of authorship in autobiographies of childhoods it is necessary to first briefly review the status of the author within contemporary literature and its industries. As I have suggested elsewhere, at a time when two or perhaps even three generations of literary theorists have been raised on the notion that the biography of the author is almost irrelevant to the text, in the contemporary world of book publication and marketing the author has, if anything, become even more crucial to a book's success ("Blurbing Biographical" 806).

Authorship and Contemporary Autobiography

In major cities around the world each year, you will find authors promoting their books: at writers' festivals, at book launches, at in-store appearances. Eager bibliophiles flock to "meet the author" sessions, keen to get copies of their books signed by the celebrity author and ready to hear the author's words of wisdom on writing, and on life in general. Authors—particularly autobiographers—have come to fill myriad cultural roles: public intellectual, moral compass, therapist, and teacher. But perhaps most significantly, authors are highly visible people, commonly willing to offer commentary on their own work. In this post-Oprah literary culture, readers commonly look at authors to answer questions about the meanings of their own books.[1]

Interest in authorial criticism can be read as indicative of popular culture's resistance to poststructuralist theories of the "death of the author." Roland Barthes's discussion of this "death" and W. K. Wimsatt's argument of "the intentional fallacy" both reflect a critical agenda of removing romantic notions of the human writer of a book—that is, of the "author" as an independent or unique creative genius. Creative work is "detached from the author at birth," declares Wimsatt, and becomes part of public discourse. In Wimsatt's words, the "design or intention of the author is neither available nor desirable" to critics or readers of written works (3). Also, as Thomas R. Smith notes, the widespread acceptance of "the unconscious" has challenged the notion that writers are in complete control of the work they produce (1).

Yet, despite the predominance of such views in the critical community, booksellers, book reviewers, and interviewers, to name a few examples, insist on venerating the individual writer as the author of the book. The author figure and the biography of the single author are given precedence in the promotion and reception of contemporary literature.[2] Autobiography has compounded this practice further, for as a genre it solicits and promotes even deeper connections between an author's personal life and the written work produced.[3] Leigh Gilmore discusses autobiography's "privileged rela-tion to the real" and the author's name as a "magical signifier of identity," which "focuses attention on the solid corporeality to which it refers" (*Auto-biographics* 65–66).

There is much evidence to suggest that it is the author-protagonist link that has made autobiographies so marketable at the turn of the millennium. Consider the examples of Kathryn Harrison and Maria Flook. The subjects of Harrison's *The Kiss* (1997) and Flook's *My Sister Life* (1998) had been largely covered in their earlier works of fiction, but only when these subjects appeared in nonfictional form did the writers experience media attention, highly image-conscious marketing, and controversial success. Traci Freeman explains the recent phenomena of the celebrity autobiographer:

> [There are] celebrities who have achieved fame precisely because of the success of their autobiographies.... The speed and penetrability of modern media can create celebrity writers extraordinarily quickly. After the American author Kathryn Harrison's account of incestuous relations with her father was published (*The Kiss*, 1997), she joined the talk-show circuit and was featured in national magazines. And Frank McCourt's

recent bestselling account of his impoverished Irish childhood (*Angela's Ashes*, 1996) resulted in international celebrity and a Hollywood film of his book, begging the question of how far the sequel—'*Tis* (1999)—now owed its sales to the fame of its author. In such cases the implicitly circular relationship between autobiography and celebrity is revealed, even as it is exaggerated. (189)

According to Philippe Lejeune's "autobiographical pact," the auto-biography offers the textual assertion that the author, narrator, and protagonist are the same; they have the same "vital statistics" (21). One example of the way this pact functions in contemporary autobiography is the inclusion of biographical information on the back cover or within the first few pages of a text. For instance, the third page of Ashworth's *Once in a House on Fire* contains this information: "Andrea Ashworth was born in Manchester in 1969. She is a Junior Research Fellow at Jesus College, Oxford. *Once in a House on Fire* is her first book." Though such biographical information is common to all works of literature, it can function as a plot "spoiler" in autobiography. By encouraging readers to make connections between the author's name, biographical information, and the textual plot, the autobiography enters into an agreement with readers that they will be reading about an actual person whose existence is legally verifiable (Lejeune 11). The autobiographical pact functions as a guide for reading the narrative. As suggested in chapter 2, this pact, coupled with the personal childhood photographs that are commonly found upon or within autobiographies of childhood, encourages readers to accept its truth claims.

When this contract is supposedly violated—consider the Binjamin Wilkomirski or Rigoberta Menchú controversies—the author may not only be branded a liar but, perhaps more seriously, be accused of false advertising. And yet, at least to some degree, such false advertising has also proved profitable, as "controversial" authors of experimental or renegade texts may sell scores of books. Julian Loose discusses the recent "revolutions" in nonfictional writing—the increasing number of life-writing or "creative nonfiction" texts that defy easy classification. Loose uses Dave Eggers's *A Heartbreaking Work of Staggering Genius* and Edward Platt's *Leadville* as examples of nonfictional works that disturb the conventions of life writing. We can add a plethora of others to this list—J. M. Coetzee, James Frey, David Sedaris, Lauren Slater, Tobias Wolff, Jeannette Winterson—all authors who disrupt readers' expectations of what can be written in fiction and nonfiction texts.

But, as Loose argues, "if anything is hampering experiment in non-fiction, it is, (as ever) a keen awareness of the marketplace." The available, accessible author is still very important in the marketing of contemporary literature. Why is the human writer/author so important to cultural industries? For Michel Foucault, appeals to authorship offer interpretive containment: "The author is the ideological figure by which one marks the manner in which we fear the proliferation of meaning" ("What Is an Author?" 159). Barthes suggests, "Historically, the reign of the Author has also been that of the Critic." Barthes goes on to explain that the critic has much to gain from elucidating a work in terms of its author: "To give a text an Author is to impose a limit on the text, to furnish it with a final signified, to close the writing. Once the Author has been found, the text is 'explained'—victory to the critic" (147). Those who now resurrect authors have found similarly specific and empowering functions for them: to sell books, to manipulate the economic power of the celebrity product, and to strengthen the social importance of the arts community and its cultural capital.

The cultural contexts that produce autobiography value celebrity. These contexts have seen a recent boom in reality-television-produced celebrities (or celebrities manufactured from so-called everyday people). These celebrities are marketed as accessible and "knowable," which has become one of the catchphrases associated with the latest generation of autobiographers. "Real people" are articulating their stories every day on television talk shows or current affairs programs, in newspapers and magazines, and on personal Web pages and Web diaries. "We are habitual authenticators of our own lives," Smith and Watson write. "Every day we are confessing and constructing personal narratives in every possible format: on the body, on the air, in music, in print, on video, at meetings" (*Getting a Life* 2). Since consumers of contemporary culture are predisposed to interpreting situations in autobiographical terms, marketing books by using a verifiable, authentic figure who has already entered into a contract with the reader and confided in him or her seems profitable.

Yet further to this, the author has an important and optimistic ideological function for contemporary cultural production. In response to the threat posed by postmodernists, the author becomes symbolic of the existence of individual, autonomous creativity. Lorna Sage rightly suggests that the author appears prominently on the surface of contemporary literary culture: readings, book signings, writers' festivals, and interviews, all of which position writers prominently in the public eye and in public discourse ("Living" 267).[4] Paul John Eakin notes that

> publishers today frequently ask authors to hit the road to promote their
> books, and so, willing or not, they do the book tour with its formulaic

press interviews, television guest appearances, and bookstore signings. Given the technology for media exposure, the photo- and telegenic author inevitably proves to be an asset to sales, and commentators . . . have remarked on the increasing importance of the author's looks to a book's success. (*How Our Lives* 142)

Author profiles are commonly preferred over book reviews or extracts for promoting books. Eakin muses, "We may well wonder whether the current popularity of memoirs . . .—the desire to write them and the appetite to consume them—is somehow connected to this impulse to trade on the author's flesh" (142). All of these strategies ultimately profit the industry rather than the art. Authors are constructed as the centerpiece of a widely ranging literary system over which they may exert little actual control. Just as theorists proclaimed the death of the author to ensure the life of the reader, cultural industries have resurrected the author, perhaps to ensure their own survival.

Thus, human authors are useful to consumer culture. But obviously some authors are easier to "sell" than others, and every author needs a selling point. What are some of the selling points for autobiographers? How are authors of childhood autobiographies positioned inside and outside of the text as having authority to write?

The Celebrity Childhood: McCourt's *Angela's Ashes*

McCourt's Pulitzer Prize–winning autobiography *Angela's Ashes*, which spent over a year on the *New York Times* bestseller list, was the first of a trilogy of autobiographies written by McCourt and was adapted for the screen by Alan Parker.[5] McCourt's autobiography made him a literary celebrity. As Bill Kirtz describes:

He's mixed with the likes of Sharon Stone and Francis Ford Coppola at a $500,000 gala at the New York Public Library. He's pocketing thousands for praising teaching for *Reader's Digest* ("I love them. They pay big money"), and recalling Kodakless moments with his daughter for *Rolling Stone*. He's telling Pierce (James Bond) Brosnan he's too good-looking to play McCourt's elbow-bending Dad in *Angela's* film version. (10)

Angela's Ashes is widely thought to have been one of the foundational texts of the so-called memoir boom of the late 1990s and early 2000s, and it drew praise from two other notable autobiographers of the period: Mary Karr and

Kathryn Harrison.[6] McCourt writes about his "miserable Irish childhood": "the poverty; the shiftless loquacious alcoholic father; the pious defeated mother moaning by the fire; pompous priests; bullying schoolmasters; the English and the terrible things they did to us for eight hundred long years" (11).[7] Yet despite the book's content, *Angela's Ashes* was overwhelmingly received as an uplifting and affirming tale of triumph over adversity.[8]

In an interview, McCourt talks about finding the voice to write *Angela's Ashes*:

> "I'm in a playground on Classon Avenue in Brooklyn with my brother, Malachy.
>
> "I knew then I had it—what I'd been looking for for years, the present tense of the small child. A small child has no hindsight, no foresight. He's just completely in the moment. I wanted to write without judging, to tell a story the way a camera would," he said. (Kirtz 9)

However, most readers will recognize that McCourt's voice is a construction to authenticate his memory and thus his tale. In *Angela's Ashes*, what precedes the finding of this voice is eighteen pages of an older, wiser voice that retrospectively asserts the significance of his childhood:

> My father and mother should have stayed in New York where they met and married and where I was born. Instead, they returned to Ireland when I was four, my brother Malachy, three, the twins, Oliver and Eugene, barely one, and my sister, Margaret, dead and gone.
>
> When I look back on my childhood I wonder how I survived at all. It was, of course, a miserable childhood: the happy childhood is hardly worth your while. Worse than the ordinary miserable childhood is the miserable Irish childhood, and worse yet is the miserable Irish Catholic childhood. (11)

Though McCourt's autobiography is (in)famous for its use of the naïve, present-tense child narrator, it is this retrospective voice that initially structures the tale and, having done so, is ever-present thereafter—sanctioning memories, inserting humorous anecdotes, and fashioning naïveté where necessary. McCourt has not miraculously discovered this voice within. The voice is firmly tied to McCourt-the-successful-writer, the McCourt who charismatically offers his wisdom on creative writing craft at well-paid public speaking engagements. It is impossible, and indeed unproductive, for McCourt (or his publishers) to separate the two. The adult and child each imbue each other with authority: The naïve child through his innocence reminds us that the adult McCourt was once him; and the adult McCourt brings the child back to life, apparently empowering him to tell his story through the adult medium. Where the child narrator is a literary construct, the adult author is a cultural construct. Both of these constructs, as I have suggested, have particular cultural investments underlying them.

In her review of *Angela's Ashes*, notably in the journal *Perspectives in Psychiatric Care*, Suzanne Lego comments on the relationship that the text establishes between the narrator and the reader: "I think the real reason he is so familiar to me is that I traveled through his childhood with him. It is much like the feeling of intimacy that comes from a long-term therapeutic relationship with a patient who, over the course of time, reveals many intimate childhood secrets" (42). Lego connects autobiography's penchant for "rages to riches" stories with psychological studies of "resilience." She asserts that health professionals have long been interested in the question of why some children endure horrible childhoods and end up scarred for life, while others grow up relatively unscathed (42). We might ask this question more broadly about autobiographers who write about their childhoods. Why is it that autobiographers of childhood, who have endured terrible childhoods, are not bitter but forgiving? When consuming autobiographies of childhood, why is it that the most successful, most popular texts are those that contain humorous anecdotes (often alongside representations of trauma)?

It is crucial to remember that these narratives of resilience and forgiveness are the narratives that we receive. It is these narratives that are published en masse. We readers might be forgiven for believing that these narratives of resilience and forgiveness are more broadly representative of the ways in which people remember and write about their traumatic childhoods, rather than considering these autobiographies as idealized templates that prescribe the ways in which traumatic childhood can be recalled and written about. Publishers might argue that while readers are intrigued by traumatic representations (or what Janice Haaken describes as the "romanticization of victimhood" ["Sexual Abuse" 106]), readers would prefer to read stories with happy endings, where characters triumph against adversity. The rags-to-riches template is a popular and familiar one throughout cultural representations.[9] But this is a chicken-and-egg scenario. Readers are conditioned to respond positively to these texts, and this is how the text positions us to respond. Responding otherwise is to read against the grain of the autobiography and its author construct.

Extratextually, McCourt is celebrated not only for producing an enjoyable story but for his own accomplishments. It is these accomplishments that

propel the text. For example, first we know that McCourt has survived childhood poverty and ill health (three of his siblings were not so fortunate). He
immigrated to the land of his dreams (the USA), which he describes as like
"entering heaven," worked menial jobs, served his country in the army, and
eventually entered the noble profession of teaching—all of which are covered
in McCourt's subsequent autobiographies.[10] In an interview, McCourt
explains how his childhood left him bereft of confidence and expectations:

> "I never expected to go to college. I was ready to settle for some low-level
> job, clerk in a bank or insurance company, anything. I would have made
> a great elevator operator or something like that," he says. "You get out
> (of poverty) but you don't get out; it's with you for the rest of your life
> unless you're very conscious and you go on and study what it was and
> look at the damage that was done and you remedy it. But I wasn't like
> that." (BookPage)

McCourt's narrative, though not concerned with sexual abuse, draws on the
tradition of the "survivor narrative"—life narratives that recount trauma,
attempting to go beyond therapeutic ends toward making political statements
about social injustice (Martín Alcoff and Gray-Rosendale 213).[11] McCourt
stakes out territory for telling stories about childhood poverty and intergenerational trauma—particularly how he is affected by his mother Angela's
trauma. His narrative presents a way through intergenerational trauma. And
yet, however transgressive and empowering the text may be, survivor narratives
such as McCourt's—circulating in mainstream domains—inevitably invest in
dominant paradigms for representing survival (resilience, a work ethic, gratitude). Similar tropes emerge in Ashworth's rags-to-riches autobiography.

Working-Class Girl Made Good: Ashworth's *Once in a House on Fire*

Ashworth describes growing up in working-class Manchester in the 1970s
and 1980s. The story follows Andrea, her two sisters, and their mother as
they battle domestic violence, mental illness, and poverty. *Once in a House
on Fire* ends with Ashworth winning a place at Oxford, where she earned her
B.A., M.A., and D.Phil. before becoming a Junior Research Fellow. As well as
her autobiography and academic writing, Ashworth has written for various
newspapers and periodicals. She is also a spokesperson for several British
child protection charities (Ashworth, Interview with BBC1).

    In writing her autobiography Ashworth follows other recent British
women academics and intellectuals such as Leila Berg, Annette Kuhn, and

Lorna Sage who, as Blake Morrison suggests, "scrambled clear of origins up a ladder of books" ("Importance"). Various literary critics, gender theorists, sociologists, philosophers, anthropologists, and cultural studies theorists have written autobiographies of childhood in recent years. These autobiographies commonly work to explain or justify the particular vocation of the writer. For example, in identifying themselves as working class, academics are better able to explain their ideologies, politics, and conflicts. Within this context Ashworth can be considered a reflexive intellectual, meditating on the place of her personal history within social history and the politics of class and gender in working-class Britain.

But Ashworth's autobiography is also a popular, bestselling autobiography. It has generated a massive response from book clubs and Web forums (an issue I return to in chapter 7). Ashworth's availability for interviews, coupled with her autobiographical disclosures, constructs her as accessible and know-able. She is a working-class girl who ended up at Oxford. In other words, she meets the demands of contemporary autobiography as suggested by publisher Bert Hingley: "[There has been a] definite swing away from the tradition of selecting famous subjects for autobiographies, towards finding 'ordinary people who have lived extraordinary lives'" (qtd. in Shiells 26). Unlike the "great figures" of biography, lofty academics, or mysterious writers of fiction, Ashworth, like McCourt, is constructed as an "everyday person" with notable achievements.

Gender, of course, is also a highly relevant issue in the commodification of autobiographical authors. In an age when celebrity authors and public appearances by authors are at an all-time high, examining the marketing of female authors allows for a further contextualization of the impact of gender on marketing and the commercial construction of authorship.[12] Consider Kathryn Hughes's description of a television interview with Ashworth:

> Andrea Ashworth . . . was quizzed on "This Morning" by an enraptured Richard Madeley about her love life. . . . Thirtyish, gorgeous—[she] can count on selling out any venue where [she] choose[s] to appear. Most first-time novelists, meanwhile, are lucky if their mothers turn up to hear them read at a provincial branch of Waterstone's. ("I Have Seen")

Ashworth's attractiveness is identified as marketable, and it is her status as a female autobiographer who has already disclosed information about her personal life that allows questions about her love life to be considered fair territory. While Michèle Roberts and Jane Tompkins have both explored how the autobiographical form has been utilized by women to assert the value of traditionally private or personal concerns in the public domain (Roberts 8; Tompkins 1105), marketers and "blurbers" of female autobiographies have made this trend profitable by constructing women authors according to enduring myths of femininity: women as the honest and truthful gender,[13] or women as more self-aware, emotionally attentive, generous, or saintly. Given the central concerns of this chapter, however, I will only gesture toward the potential significance of such practices.

Once in a House on Fire is "recommended reading" on various health and welfare Web sites in the United Kingdom and United States.[14] Since writing *Once in a House on Fire* Ashworth has been interviewed widely; she even appeared on Rosie O'Donnell's U.S. talk show in 1999. The presence of the autobiographical author and her availability to shed light on her own work are invariably important in how her autobiography acquires meaning. Even though readers may not directly see or read these interviews with Ashworth, book promoters and book reviewers are inevitably familiar with the author behind the work. As a consequence, this author information commonly influences the packaging and promotion of the text, for example, the review blurb, which ultimately affects the ways readers receive the text.

Thus, authors commonly have a public image that is constructed outside of the book, via interviews or articles, and upon the book, through peritextual matter such as the photograph and biographical information provided on the inside cover. As Gilmore argues, autobiography's appearance as "real" is dependent on metonymy, whereby the symbols of the self, such as the author's name and photograph, come to represent and authenticate the life narrated within the autobiography (*Autobiographics* 67). An author's biographical details have become recognizable and accessible literary evidence—symbols of the text's authenticity.

In interviews, Ashworth is asked to comment on the processes of writing her autobiography in much the same way as most writers are in interviews. Ashworth is asked questions about her personal life, which is also normal practice in interviews of writer/celebrities. However, as Ashworth is an auto-biographer of a traumatic childhood, the stakes are much different than if she were an author of fiction. In interviews Ashworth is not only called upon to explain her books and her life, as fictional writers are, but also to explain, even justify, how her life and her writing are inexorably entwined. This extratextual information forms part of the autobiographical pact, generating and limiting meanings for the autobiographical work, including creating a particular role for the autobiographer of a traumatic childhood.

For example, in interviews Ashworth speaks of her "need" to write—an idea akin to therapeutic writing models such as scriptotherapy. According to this model, the writer engages in a form of writing cure—accessing and healing traumatic memories through writing about them.[15] Ashworth suggests that writing was "therapeutic in the messiest, most painful way" (Interview with Louise Jameson); and "I wanted to get my memories out because I wanted to pin them down, so that all those ghosts wouldn't go streaking across novels" (Interview with Douglas Eby). So, although writing was therapeutic, Ashworth suggests that she wrote her autobiography out of necessity rather than choice:

> I had to capture that spooky stuff, give it a good home on paper, in order to keep it from overshadowing my life. . . . Looking back was the only way for me to move truly, freely, forward. . . . When readers began to respond with such generous warmth to *Once in a House on Fire*, I discovered a new freedom from all the old fears of my childhood. It was a fantastic relief to feel heard, understood, to finally share the story. I feel lucky, and very grateful. (Interview with BBCi)

This is a trope that is commonly used to authorize traumatic writing. These writers position themselves, and are positioned in their promotion, as people who have written against trauma. This act of writing, or breaking silences via autobiography, is celebrated because it has potency beyond the individual. Ashworth's position as a survivor of trauma makes her a powerful cultural figure and gives her a license to speak, as Haaken proposes: "The survivor as a figure of wisdom and moral authority emerged in the wake of World War II and now stands as a signifier of a moral standard, someone who must be listened to" ("Sexual Abuse, Recovered Memory" 116).

Ashworth is constructed, in her interviews and by the book jacket, as an author in control of her material, as a responsible writer who has taken charge of authoring this tale. As I suggested in an earlier chapter, critics are often skeptical of adult autobiographers of childhood, challenging them on how they can possibly remember their childhoods from so long ago. For instance, Paul Gray muses, "For those of us who have trouble remembering what was said to them at breakfast, such long-ago quotations sound like footfalls in the house of fiction" (106). The publicity for Ashworth's text preempts this criticism. For example, the blurbs on the cover of *Once in a House on Fire* emphasize that this autobiography is a controlled work of literature, crafted and remade for popular consumption. Ashworth is credited with utilizing creative new literary forms. "Ashworth has a rare capacity to describe," Susanna Rustin writes, while Melissa Behn suggests that "Ashworth has the poet's power to make language, and therefore experience seem new," and the *Kirkus Review* describes the book as "stylistically fresh." Giving little reference to other formative factors, against notions of the autonomous literary object, these blurbs suggest that the writer is the author, the producer of the work, the autonomous literary subject.

However, alongside these review blurbs that praise the author's creative originality, other blurbs suggest the opposite. Autobiographers are also held responsible for recording authentic experience, rather than for creating it, for effectively being social biographers as well as autobiographers. Such representations parallel Leon Edel's description of a biographer's task: "A writer of lives is allowed the imagination of form but not of fact" (13). When Margaret Driscoll describes *Once in a House on Fire* as rich in "vivid detail of everyday life," Julia Thorogood praises Ashworth's work as "observant and precise," or Marina Benjamin writes that "the past comes across as recollected rather than reprocessed, assimilated not analysed," they are all downplaying notions of originality to praise the author for merely responding accurately to the stimulants, prompts, and traditions of the social and literary worlds she inhabits. They imply that the author is (and should be) recalling events objectively, again suggesting the biographer's tasks as outlined by Edel: "Lives are composed in most instances as if they were mosaics. Mosaics, before they are composed, are not fiction; they are an accumulation of little pieces of reality, shaped into an image" (16). Sometimes these pieces are elements of the author's community. Thus, when the *Lancashire Evening Post* blurb describes *Once in a House on Fire* as distinguished by "never-say-die Northern humour," it suggests that Ashworth's representation of reality is unconsciously endowed with archetypal or communal meanings and attitudes.[16] Ashworth is consequently promoted almost equally as a creator and observer of her autobiography.

One explanation for this representation is that Ashworth is being constructed as the caretaker of a story that does not belong to her alone. *Once in a House on Fire* is the autobiography of her child self; Ashworth writes on behalf of a previous self. This is a recognizable strategy within autobiography: As Rosamund Dalziell suggests, "For many autobiographers who represent the child self as having been deeply shamed, the autobiographical act seems to provide the opportunity for the mature self to become visible in a deliberate way in order to confront shame and re-evaluate self-worth" (7). Despite the opening up of the autobiographical form, there is very limited space in mainstream consumer publishing for the publication of autobiographies written by children during childhood.[17] As Patricia Holland suggests, children are seen more than they are heard:

> Children remain the objects of imagery, almost never its makers. Their voices are missing, defined as incapable of meaningful expression. They should be seen but not heard. Like all groups without power they suffer the indignity of being unable to present themselves as they would want to be seen—or indeed, of even considering how they might want to be seen. They are not in a position to manufacture a public image for themselves and have no control over the image others make of them. In consequence, as they become adults, individuals have only impoverished ways of expressing their own remembered childhoods. (*What Is a Child?* 19)

Once in a House on Fire, then, is in part an apology for the absence of the child's story. In an interview that focuses on the processes of crafting her autobiography, Ashworth apologizes for trying to create, but not being able to reproduce, the child's perspective. She positions herself as the writer and custodian of this story, rather than its owner:

> What I was trying to do in the book is to show how one child finds a way to survive . . . and to see that world from a perspective that allows her to continue to live it. . . . I was trying to describe the house on fire, the sense of claustrophobia, of drama, of intense, everyday fear, of horrible things happening to the mother and the children. I wanted to zoom in, and to allow the reader to see this world through the eyes of the child, to see how she finds ways to survive what's going on around her, to interpret what's happening to her, and to re-make the world, if you like, to re-picture it in a way that allows her to live in it while all sorts of horrific things are happening to her. ("Writing from Life")

Thus, unlike McCourt, Ashworth takes the stance of benevolent custodian of her childhood story. But, more than this, she becomes an advocate for her child self and a role model for others with similar experiences. Ashworth says, "Although I've written a book that's essentially about my life, I hope I haven't written a book that's just about me" ("Writing from Life"). This gesture is taken up by "blurbers" and becomes one of the selling points for *Once in a House on Fire*.

Inside the cover of *Once in a House on Fire*, Peter Stanford writes of Ashworth, "I am in full admiration of her courage and endurance," while Hilary Mantel describes the book as "strong and admirable." By describing

Ashworth as a "role-model without parallel," Margaret Forster suggests how the worth of the human author becomes an important tool for selling the book—and hardship and suffering often endow this worth. "Andrea Ashworth escaped the fire to write a remarkable book," Linda Morrison writes, and the review from the *Scotsman* regrets that "the only pity is that she had to live it to make it." Such statements draw on therapeutic discourse to sanction Ashworth's endeavor and to encourage readers to identify with the text on a therapeutic level.

Identifying as a survivor of child abuse and domestic violence means that Ashworth the autobiographer is constructed as Ashworth-the-child-activist more often than Ashworth-the-writer. Ashworth has written a number of articles on child abuse for newspapers and is asked to speak to and on behalf of child abuse victims in interviews:

> There are too many children still trapped in dark situations. Please remember: you're not alone. It's natural to be afraid, but you mustn't feel ashamed. Take responsibility for your own well-being and happiness, not for the unhappiness and confusion and anger of everyone around you. What's happening is wrong. You don't deserve it, and you can live differently for yourself. (Interview with BBCi)

> Children can be marvellously, but also dangerously, elastic, adapting to adversity, growing to regard it as normal. As I grew up, I began to realise that what went on in my family was not normal but quite horrific. Seeing this, I was struck dumb by a deep sense of shame. Domestic abuse was not, in the 70s and 80s, something to be discussed in public. I had never even heard of terms such as neglect or abuse, let alone imagined them being applied to my family. Moreover my mother and sisters and I suffered a sense of guilt about what was done to us, as if we deserved it. Like many victims, we were caught in a web of silence, woven from sticky strands of guilt and fear. ("When I Was")

This public image of the autobiographer as an advocate enhances the truth-value of the autobiography. For example, the review blurbs praise Ashworth for telling the truth. Within this context the author becomes an almost saintly figure. This is perhaps the least complex view of authorship: the great, wise, and almost infallible writer,[18] which is probably an effect of autobiographical and biographical traditions in which "few 'ordinary' lives are written" (Edel 14). There may have been a variety of reasons for choosing to write an autobiography, but as John Sturrock suggests, the act of writing reveals the autobiographer's desire to share his or her narrative. This sharing is a public performance on a grand scale, and signals the writer's perception that his or her life is significant and worthy (23).

Although the autobiographical form has opened significantly to allow a diversity of subjects and lives to be represented, Smith and Watson have shown the ways in which the time-honored revering of authors as saints is (re)occurring as part of the consumption of contemporary autobiography: "Personal histories—in all their varieties—serve as individualized testimonies to getting a 'successful' life together (however success is defined) and/or to the failure of self-remaking in terms of the dream" (6). Such representations serve consumer strategists well, since such autobiographies can be marketed as "must read" texts—gifts from generous, self-actualized adult authors. For example, of *Once in a House on Fire*, Forster writes:

> The material Andrea Ashworth had to work with is so explosively awful and sad she had only one option—to tell it as it was, as quietly as possible. This she does, chronologically, recalling her upbringing in short bursts, and . . . [with] admirable restraint. (book jacket)

Forster suggests here that the revelations and disclosures in *Once in a House on Fire* are subtly and artfully structured by the author to protect both author and reader from the horrors of the material—an idea commonly expressed within reviews of the text. Ashworth too, in interviews, is careful to position herself and her subject matter as appropriately sensitive: "I realised that I had to write it with a certain amount of discretion, partly because my mother, and other people about whom I was writing, I needed to protect them" ("Writing from Life"). In this instance, the autobiographer speaks for and represents not only the child but also her family and makes assumptions about the needs and desires of readerships. Thus, the authorship of an auto-biography of childhood can be seen to balance upon these perceived textual and extratextual relationships between author (subject), relational subjects, and (ethically implicated) readers.

Performing Autobiographically: From Author to Subject

Eakin asks, "Why do we so easily forget that the first person of autobiography is truly plural in its origins and subsequent formation? Because auto-biography promotes an illusion of self-determination: *I* write my story; I say who I am; I create my self. The myth of autonomy dies hard" (*How Our Lives* 43). The myth of authorial autonomy dies hard, not only because the author is important in the promotion of autobiography but because it is crucial for the construction of the childhood self/subject.

At a time when "reality" in all of its forms and illusions is very marketable, the author figure has been resurrected by publishing industries able to exploit it. Publicists use biographical details of the author—as revealed within the autobiography and drawn from the author's public persona—to create blurbs and publicity, which, in turn, create a biographical frame through which the literary text will primarily be read. The revival of the author in this case has been facilitated by the autobiographical form itself, which, like biography, documentary, or fly-on-the-wall television, professes to allow a unique glimpse into the life of someone notable that will tell readers/viewers something valuable about their own lives. In this way, autobiography, which encourages the consumption of "authorized and authenticated lives" (Smith and Watson, *Getting a Life* 3), functions to validate and revalidate particular modes of autobiographical writing.

Autobiographies demand certain types of authorial performativity to make them intelligible to readers (S. Smith, "Performativity" 110). For example, in autobiographies of childhood certain narrative identities are taken up (such as the universal subject or the traumatic childhood survivor), distinctive narratives and voices are employed (such as the naïve child or the nostalgic child), and particular themes and promotional strategies recur (such as the innocent child). A performance of authorship is demanded from autobiographers of childhood, particularly traumatic autobiographers, as a means of authenticating their narrative. For instance, the author of a traumatic childhood must write and speak in interviews as a survivor who is at once a creative adult, a unique individual, and a representative individual who is able to bring his or her child self back to life in ways that will be productive beyond the individual.

CHAPTER 4

SCRIPTS FOR REMEMBERING

CHILDHOODS AND NOSTALGIA

Nostalgia itself has a utopian dimension; only it is no longer directed toward the future. Sometimes nostalgia is not directed toward the past either, but rather sideways. The nostalgic feels stifled within the conventional confines of time and space.

—Svetlana Boym, *The Future of Nostalgia*

Where did it all go right?

—Andrew Collins, *Where Did It All Go Right?*
Growing Up Normal in the 70s

In this study I have argued that autobiographies of childhood are driven by, and need to be read in terms of, a network of textual and contextual relationships. I have also argued that autobiographies of childhood are memory practices. In their initial presentation, these texts promise to tell us an individual's experiences (and memories) of growing up within a particular cultural milieu. However, I have argued, through their representations and preoccupations, the autobiography of childhood reveals more about what it is possible to remember and forget (culturally) at the time when the text was produced and circulated.

In this chapter I investigate one of the most prevalent memory models for writing about childhood: the nostalgic mode. I explore how nostalgic autobiographies work intertextually with another dominant memory practice: the traumatic childhood (which I discuss in the following chapter). In nostalgic autobiography, the past is "idealized"; there is often a "homesickness, a pain (*algos*) or longing to return home (*nostos*) or to some lost past" (Steinwand 10). Nostalgia is also a dependence on the past. The past becomes consumable in texts that promulgate the past's value in the present. Texts that appeal to a communal past assume shared values about the past, and also the present. In nostalgic texts, the present is commonly perceived as less ideal and less desirable. Nostalgic texts often represent the past imaginatively but inauthentically (Jameson).

In chapter 1 of this study I proposed that nostalgia was the dominant mode for remembering childhood in autobiographies of childhood written prior to the 1990s. As Gillian Whitlock argues, the "success of these narratives indicates the ongoing pleasure for many readers of encountering . . . familiar, repeated, cultural patterns" (*Autographs* xix). The writers of these autobiographies are adults—time has removed them from their childhoods. For each of them, childhood is past and lost. In a multitude of ways, the autobiography of childhood proves to be an ideal vehicle for nostalgic remembering. Jonathan Steinwand proposes that "nostalgia summons the imagination to supplement memory. Because nostalgia necessarily relies on a distance—temporal or/and spatial—separating the subject from the object of its longing, the imagination is encouraged to gloss over forgetfulness in order to fashion a more aesthetically complete and satisfying recollection of what is longed for" (10).

Since the early 1990s a wave of traumatic remembering has permeated autobiography. These traumatic writings have unraveled some of the mythologies (about childhood) circulated by the aforementioned nostalgic mode. For example, while nostalgic autobiographies commonly relate childhoods lost through the passage of time, traumatic autobiographies relate childhoods that are stolen or lost through trauma—particularly abuse. Traumatic autobiography has had a radical effect on the way childhood can be depicted autobiographically.

Yet traumatic autobiography has not dulled the emergence (and reemergence) of nostalgia within autobiographical writings about childhood during the 1990s and 2000s. A plethora of nostalgic autobiographies have surfaced from different locations. For example, autobiographies such as Thomas Keneally's *Homebush Boy* and Brian Nicholls's *A Saucepan in the Sky* (both autobiographies about growing up in Sydney, Australia, in the 1950s) mourn the passing of childhood (and the past)—making statements about the inferiority of adulthood (and the present) in comparison. And there are the "they don't make them like they used to" autobiographies such as Frank McCourt's *Angela's Ashes*, which suggest that, despite the difficulties the autobiographer might have faced in the past, the past was a crucial and formative time that instilled them with skills and knowledge needed for adulthood. Certain autobiographies of childhood have written back to the traumatic mode, such as Andrew Collins's *Where Did It All Go Right?: Growing Up Normal in the 70s*. On his Web site, Collins describes the book as "an antidote to all the miserable memoirs which seemed ubiquitous at the turn of the millennium but are even more so now. Boy grows up normal in Northampton in the late 60s / 70s, goes down the field, does some drawings, discovers punk rock in 1979 and frightens his parents."

Australia and Britain have been particularly fecund sites for nostalgic writings about childhood. This is not to suggest that nostalgic writings have not emerged in locations such as the United States and Ireland.[1] However, this chapter provides an opportune occasion to isolate these two locations as sites where nostalgic autobiographies have flourished due to particular cultural conditions.

Nostalgic autobiographies of childhood have an enduring cultural function. These texts, generally speaking, romanticize childhood as idyllic. Though cultural sites of nostalgia change, childhood is one site that has remained a strong location for nostalgic remembering (Goldson 2). As Svetlana Boym suggests, in twentieth-century nostalgia, the longing for home or place is expressed via the longing for one's childhood (53). For those engaged in writing and reading autobiographies of childhood, the child often functions as a symbol of the past, a cultural mechanism for reconstructing, and to some extent mourning, the distant past.

Nostalgic remembering is a cultural remembering, which results in particular histories of childhood and certain childhoods of previous eras assuming dominance—for example, perceptions of a post–World War II "golden age" (in Australia and Britain) remain important at the millennium turn.[2] Nostalgia provides a means for resisting distressing images and preoccupations of the present. Nostalgic texts fuel the propensity to contrast these golden-age images with contemporary childhoods, as Robin Gerster does in his review of Nicholls's 1950s Australian childhood, A Saucepan in the Sky: "It was a time when . . . a kid's global vision, before television, let alone the Internet, contracted to a view of the Parramatta Road as 'the busiest and most dangerous road in the world.' As I said, a lost world" (27). This idealization of childhoods from past eras allows certain social periods and historical moments to be remembered and mythologized. Autobiography offers cultural stability—providing reminders of a better time. Boym suggests, "Nostalgia is a sentiment of loss and displacement, but is also a romance with one's own fantasy" (xiii). Nostalgic remembering within autobiographies of childhood becomes a means for nonconfrontational commemoration of historical periods and regions, for example—from the postwar British football cultures in Colin Shindler's Manchester United Ruined My Life to the urban schoolyards of 1950s Sydney in Keneally's Homebush Boy.

The autobiographies I discuss in this chapter can be seen, in some instances, as continuous from the nostalgic tendencies of pre-1990s auto-biographies. For example, Nicholls's *A Saucepan in the Sky* perpetuates romantic notions of childhood innocence. Childhood in postwar Australia, as described in this autobiography, is mostly uncomplicated, centering on fun and games. The most confronting event is the end of childhood, which commonly coincides with the lamentable end of a particular social-historical era.

However, nostalgic autobiographies of childhoods are not uniform in their use of a nostalgic "I." There are instances when an apparently nostalgic autobiography complicates its classification by revealing the complexities of nostalgia as a memory mode. Consider, for example, Robert Drewe's *The Shark Net* and John Boyle's *Galloway Street*. These examples complicate nostalgia, refashioning its use within the autobiographical mode. Both books provide a useful medium for highlighting the liminal spaces between nostalgic and traumatic childhoods, and the possibility of a productive tension between the different modes. Although the powerful presence of nostalgic memory may work to counter traumatic remembering within childhood autobiographies such as Drewe's and Boyle's, nostalgic and traumatic remembering can coexist, producing bittersweet constructions of childhood.

One of the most immediate features of the selection of texts for this chapter is that all five have white male authors. While this is certainly not a large enough sample to base generalizations on, it does indicate perhaps predictable trends concerning the tendency of male writers to occupy more traditional modes of life writing, and the contrary tendency for women writers, writers from minority cultures, and nonprofessional writers to be involved in the more therapeutic modes. Though this is not a question I am able to explore at any length in this chapter, these issues raise important questions regarding what autobiographical spaces or narrative identities are available to contemporary female and male writers of autobiographies of childhood, and the extent to which these are being challenged.

The selection of texts for this chapter also provides insights into broader shifts in nostalgic memory. For example, particular nostalgic tropes continue to be represented within autobiographies about childhood. In writing about family and social relationships, maturation, and sexuality, these texts neces-sarily share cultural space with traumatic texts, settling and unsettling the past and present, and further revealing the crucial memory work autobiographical writing is engaged in.

Nostalgic Autobiographies of Childhood in the Child Voice

The nostalgic autobiographies in this study are largely affirmative, humorous stories describing the protagonists' development from childhood to adulthood. In Boyle's *Galloway Street* and Drewe's *The Shark Net*, for example, childhood is presented as a happy precursor to the bleak realities of adulthood. Nostalgic autobiographies reflect a coming to terms with this growth. The juxtaposition of adult and child selves highlights the nostalgic mode of remembering, through the use of the retrospective, knowing adult narrator in, for instance, the autobiographies of Keneally, Drewe, and Shindler.

This child-self/adult-self juxtaposition occurs through dialogism.[3] In his exploration of dialogism, Mikhail Bakhtin discusses the ways in which narrative voices are liberated or controlled within novels. Autobiographies of childhood are heavily dialogic—containing a plurality of voices that are often juxtaposed or interactive. Some voices are more powerful, or are controlled by others. Autobiographical texts are commonly constructed as containing the singular autobiographical voice of the narrator/protagonist. However, this is always an illusion; autobiographical narratives are conventionally polyvocal (Smith and Watson, *Reading Autobiography* 174). The autobiographical subject comes to understand him or herself through a multitude of social encounters with languages and meanings. Autobiography is a process "composed of many genres and constituted by a means of dialogic mirroring encounters" (Egan, *Mirror Talk* 11). Autobiographical narrators articulate their lives in relation to these encounters.

As a consequence, autobiographical narrative voices are often fragmented. While autobiographers most commonly use a single "I" as a pronoun, "both the narrating 'I' in the temporal present and the narrated 'I's of earlier times are multiple, fragmented and heterogeneous" (Smith and Watson, *Reading Autobiography* 61). As Sidonie Smith and Julia Watson propose, different voices may appear and disappear within an autobiographical narrative. Whether romantic, self-important, self-critical, or shifting in tone, these voices are subject to different degrees of narrative control. Overt relationships may be established between these different voices, or there may be tension between them. Certain narrative voices may be utilized to generate particular reader investments. For example, a narrative voice may be put forward as representative of a broader cultural group (*Reading Autobiography* 174).

Dialogism is crucial to nostalgic autobiography. The split between the adult and child selves, and between the self and time and place, is emphasized within these autobiographies. Dialogism occurs in three notable ways across these texts: via the all-knowing, retrospective adult speaking for the child, within the juxtaposition of the adult and child voices, and in the use of the naïve child voice.

For example, both Nicholls's and Boyle's autobiographies employ the naïve child voice in a narrative that is framed using a retrospective adult voice. Nicholls's *A Saucepan in the Sky*, which explores his working-class childhood in post–World War II Sydney, begins with a prologue describing his adult self at his mother's funeral. *Galloway Street*, Boyle's tale of "growing up Irish in Scotland,"[4] similarly begins with a foreword describing the adult Boyle attending his Aunt Mary's funeral. It ends with an afterword following this same event. Both texts construct the adult self as a necessary intrusion within the autobiography, but an intrusion nonetheless.

When the naïve child voice enters the text, this commonly functions as a gesture of authenticity. At the end of his afterword Boyle's adult voice worries that he cannot access his past: "I had a powerful sense that I was saying goodbye to this place I had held in my heart all these years." A memento reassures him that it is not lost: "I reached in and touched [the framed snapshot in my over-coat pocket] the only inheritance that mattered" (223). The photograph, like that on the book cover, is offered as a tool of authentication. This memento serves as a memory prompt and is a tangible guarantee of the truth of the recollection.

The adult voice that frames Boyle's autobiography suggests that it is not only possible to remember and recapture the child self, but it is a necessary rite of passage. Boyle's narrator explains, "It was a time of crisis in my life, of confusion and doubt about the way I had chosen to earn a living, about the storm clouds lowering on the horizon of my marriage, about who I was or where I belonged after years of expatriated drift" (ix). The function of the nostalgic autobiographies of childhood, as suggested in *Galloway Street*, is to explain the adult self. The autobiography provides a bridge between adult and child:

> For years I had been tinkering obsessively with reminisces about my childhood in Scotland, as if some clue might lie there to my present confusion. It did not help, I began to understand, that these events were being recalled and enhanced by the middle-aged raconteur I had become. Now I felt the need to rediscover—truthfully, without embroidery—the boy I had been. (x)

Boyle's adult voice, then, suggests that this autobiography will become a diary of his childhood. The first-person child voice is presented as Boyle's authentic child self, complete with a consistent, accented idiom: "Whit d'ye want tae

talk aboot?" (22). Yet the reader is aware that this is not a diary, irrespective
of the adult's (impossible) desire to erase himself to allow sovereignty to the
child voice. As Boym suggests, "Only false memories can be totally recalled"
(54). And Boyle's narrator is self-consciously aware of the adult posing as
the child:

> For a long time I persisted, writing this memoir in two distinct voices.
> Why not? I reasoned. Surely each has his story to tell? The raconteur
> looking fondly back, recalling a sepia-tinted boyhood across the echoes
> of the years? And the boy who lived it—insofar as he can remember it
> truly?
>
> Who's to say where truth ends and fiction begins?
>
> We shaped our truths to make them bearable. We take out sad songs
> and make them better. We grope for meaning. Much of the time we are
> lost souls whistling in the dark.
>
> But in our hearts we know where truth lies.
>
> Let the boy tell his own story. (xi)

For the adult narrator, the child's "truth" can only be told by the child.
Though this contradicts his earlier suggestion that all truths are creatively
shaped, within the context of autobiographies of childhood, it is not a
surprising narrative device. The propensity to view the child as a familiar
and sympathetic character who is the key to understanding the interior self
is already familiar to this study. This notion, as Boyle's narrator suggests, is in
"our hearts," appealing to a common belief in and sympathy for the child.

The naïve child narrator functions as a gesture of authentication in
which the appeal of the innocent child is vital. In *A Saucepan in the Sky* and
Galloway Street the naïve child is often blindly optimistic and humorously
ignorant, making the narrative seem amusing, endearingly innocent, and
engaging. Nostalgic memories are predominantly reassuring. Their value lies
in their believability and palatability, their confirmation of particular cultural
constructions of childhood history. For example, *Galloway Street* contains a
steady progression of childhood "firsts," from Boyle's attraction to girls, to his
regret over telling his brother that there is no Santa Claus, to his seeing a dead
body for the first time. Boyle's childhood self has a "favourite sin" that he "falls
back on" when attending confession, until he discovers that his sin is not a
sin at all (84). The nostalgic narrative works to suture such heterogeneous yet
stereotypical moments. Such self-representations signify the development of
the young boy into manhood.

A Saucepan in the Sky begins conventionally with the narrator's birth: "In 1938 Australia had a population of 6,935,909 people. I was one of them" (9). This diminished self functions as a gesture of his regularity—the narrator proposes his "everydayness." He refers to the "documentation" of his early progress in the form of a government health card filled out by his mother—but only for a short while. He explains knowingly, "Who wants to fill in more forms than you have to?" (9), acknowledging his mother's probable apathy after an enthusiastic start to motherhood. The narrative is unapologetically fragmented; the narrator implies that he will piece together enough information for an autobiography from the resources that he has at his disposal. This serves as an apology for both the limits of the child voice and the limits of autobiography more generally.

Where Boyle's narrative centers on the child voice, Nicholls's takes a slightly different approach. They both employ simple language and narrative structure, as well as an inexperienced, immature interpretation of events. Nicholls, much like McCourt in *Angela's Ashes*, creates the impression that it is a child's perspective that the reader is gaining:

What happened next in the world was that one day a war started. Germany wanted lots of other countries and then the Japanese decided they wanted our place, Australia, as well as their own. Dad had to go to New Guinea to tell the Japanese to go home. . . .

The Japanese didn't want to listen, and although Dad had lots of mates helping him, it was taking a very long time to make them change their minds. Dad was pretty busy. Everyone was pretty busy. (11)

The child voice exempts the narrative from describing characters, places, and events with any critical sophistication. The nostalgic child voice provides a form of admirable ignorance, a simple and defensibly self-centered interpretation of history. Similarly, despite his family's poverty and the drunken domestic violence suffered by his mother at the hands of his father, Boyle's strongest childhood memories in *Galloway Street* include going to the football with his father and playing in the streets of Glasgow with his boyhood friends. The nostalgic, child-voiced autobiography creates space for certain disclosures and not others. What might have been a traumatic narrative is taken up in a different register.

However, again as in McCourt's autobiography, there are numerous examples in *A Saucepan in the Sky* of the child voice expressing knowledge and perspective beyond his years:

My mother was a girl from the bush and my father a boy from the city. Mum's grandfather had been a grazier, but her family lost their land a very long time ago, even before Mum was born. Her father was a steam-train driver and the family moved around a lot. He was an Englishman sent to Australia as a boy of eighteen because he did something bad. He was given a fob watch and packed off to the Colonies to fend for himself and never saw his family again. (10)

This is a good example of the text's dialogism at work. The adult voice permeates the constructed child's voice, providing family background to fill the gaps of knowledge inevitably affecting the child's story. The apparently simple, child's-eye perspective of A Saucepan in the Sky gestures toward a singular child voice but is unable to sustain this child voice throughout.

Moreover, the presence of photographs in the middle of A Saucepan in the Sky works to disrupt, rather than affirm, the illusion of the child voice. This inclusion of photographs is another form of dialogism; the photographs and their annotations create the impression of a careful selection and arrangement of family history by the adult author. The photographs create a vivid picture of his family, locating them within particular moments of social history; they seem to form a separate autobiographical text to the child's-eye narrative, authored and owned more directly by the adult voice that was present at the beginning of the autobiography.

Thus, the naïve child voice proves to be both a valuable and a problematic narrative device in reconstructing nostalgic memories of childhood. As Boyle's narrative demonstrates, the child voice can be used to enhance the politics of the text. For example, his child self befriends Protestant children; however, the narrative does not explain the complexities and dangers that underlie these relationships in 1950s Britain. On another occasion the child voice of Galloway Street explains his wanting to donate money to the "Black Babies" of Africa and repeats in parrot fashion the knowledge he has about these African children: "Miss O'Neill keeps a wee box on her desk for the Black Babies. . . . The black babies live in Africa. They're poor and they don't get enough to eat. And they haven't got proper schools to go to, like St James's" (13). In such instances the reader is positioned as all-knowing, as bringing contemporary knowledge to his or her reading of this text and being in a position of greater knowledge than the child. For instance, the reader is called to reflect upon (enforced) childhood naïveté affecting children of the 1950s and 1960s.

In Nicholls's A Saucepan in the Sky, however, the naïve child voice proves to be a useful, though limiting, narrative device. The idiom and comic interpretations of events, which pervade the text, are unmistakably childlike, but the textual organization—the presence of photographs and particular knowledge, descriptions, and perspectives—overtly reveals the interventions of an adult voice. Such a construction could reflect a "best of both worlds" dialogism, which employs the appealing childhood voice alongside the adult that the child has inevitably become. *A Saucepan in the Sky* does, however, reflect a commitment to sustaining the childhood voice. For instance, early in the autobiography the narrator describes his responses to the attention he received as a baby: "I responded with a display of gleaming gums and a cascade of bubbles from the corners of my mouth that all but soaked my little pillow. Anyway, that's what Mum said. Mum said I got 'over-excited'" (10). In this example, the lucid description of his baby self is concluded with the quick return of the child voice quoting "Mum." Such containment is important for the logic of the text.

This narrative structure works to assume that the reader will comprehend and accept this dialogism, perhaps as a consequence of the reader's knowing acceptance that the child voice is a deceptive convention. Both of the autobiographies I have discussed to this point include an adult voice within a narrative that is otherwise constructed around a child voice. I have suggested that the presence of the adult voice is a dialogic inevitability within nostalgic autobiographies of childhood. Though the child voice is important, nostalgic autobiographies reveal the limitations of its perspective. The overt intervention of the knowing adult is crucial to nostalgic writing. The idealization of the past and the insertion of nostalgia into the present can only be owned and advocated by someone who has experienced both the past and the present, and is firmly entrenched in the present—that is, the adult.

Nostalgic Autobiographies of Childhood in the Adult Voice

It is not surprising, then, that retrospective, all-knowing, adult narrators are a common device in nostalgic memory texts. These narratives are also dialogic, subject to narrative fragmentation, particularly as a result of the intervention of voices from the past. However, nostalgic autobiographies of childhood that employ an all-knowing adult narrator display a resistance to this fragmentation as they constantly assert the retrospective adult voice as the textual authority. *The Shark Net*, *Homebush Boy*, and *Manchester United Ruined My Life* each contain frequent reminders that it is the adult self that is narrating this autobiography of childhood. Most often this is signaled by the narrators' mastery of language and imagery, but adult narrators also commonly criticize the foolishness of their child self. For example, Keneally's narrator suggests, "I was a strange little bugger" (3). This complicates the idea that the nostalgic mode is concerned with idealizing childhood. In these examples writing about childhood becomes a means of retrospective interpretation, whereby the adult narrator, for the contemporary reader's reflection, appraises the experiences of childhood. In *Homebush Boy* the adult narrator is positioned to repair the childish errors he recalls:

> It is a truism which people, even memoirists, can't forebear repeating: that to survive childhood is to have memories of non-recurrent chances for filial and fraternal solidarity, for crucial words which went unuttered, for concessions that went unoffered, for gestures which went unsignalled. (114)

Homebush Boy is thus inscribed as an adult interpretation of childhood, rather than a recapturing of childhood experiences. The adult reader is invited to occupy this knowing space by recognizing the significance of the child life being narrated, as well as his or her own (perhaps similar) childhood. Nostalgia is more than a longing for a lost past; it is an overt longing for a past that may not have existed. Childhood will not be remembered as the child experienced it; it will be overtly reconstructed as the adult has re-experienced it. As Jonathan Steinwand argues, "Nostalgia cannot be dismissed as merely an imaginative improvement on the lost past. Rather the possibility should be retained that nostalgia offers a compensation for the lost proximity by supplementing a memory invigorated through absence" (10). These memory and writing practices have implications beyond the self. Jerome Bruner suggests that "in rewriting our autobiographies, we often 'rewrite culture' as much as we rewrite our lives, privileging different conventional turning points such as adolescence and retirement" (40). Nostalgic autobiographies are instrumental in privileging certain childhood experiences over others.

Another way in which the adult narrator inscribes himself into the narrative of *Homebush Boy* is through the voicing of retrospective regrets—(superior) adult perspectives critique childish mistakes. For instance, Keneally's narrator discusses his introduction to rugby: This sport was "one I would later come to love" (95), and "I would regret not having the humility to play in the Thirds. All my life I have retained a curiosity about whether I would have been good enough for the Seconds or even the Firsts" (97). This foreshadowing, which reflects a mastery of temporal space, is also utilized by Drewe's narrator in *The Shark Net* and Shindler's in *Manchester United Ruined My Life*. Drewe's and

Shindler's narratives do not contain the plethora of overt foreshadowing that occurs in Keneally's *Homebush Boy*, but *The Shark Net* and *Manchester United Ruined My Life* regularly disrupt their chronology, for instance, through connecting narrative incidents to future events. This functions to suggest retrospective narrative control, interrupting any immediacy.

The examples of nostalgic autobiographies of childhood that I have selected for this discussion are characterized by sensitive, often comic representations of the child self. Though each is an autobiography of childhood that seeks to explain the adult in terms of the child, they differ generically. Shindler's *Manchester United Ruined My Life* is an accessibly comic sporting autobiography; football (soccer) provides a filter for self-examination.[5] The title of Shindler's autobiography is itself a comic play on "miserable childhoods." Though not an autobiography of trauma, it is notable that the particular traumatic event within the narrator's life, the sudden death of his mother, did not "ruin" his life and is not the center of the narrative. Instead, it is the success of his least favorite football team, Manchester United, that becomes the bane of his young life in 1950s and 1960s England. The narrator explains, "This book is an attempt to understand why a rational man should be reduced to such a level of irrationality by sport" (3). As in Boyle's autobiography, the answer is sought within the events of his childhood.

The Shark Net and *Homebush Boy* are concerned with relating the experiences of growing up in 1950s Australia, in Perth and Sydney, respectively. Drewe's and Keneally's autobiographies are literary childhoods: The child self is juxtaposed with the adult self to authenticate and ground the adult literary self. These narratives are poetically structured, using adult language and interpretations. The adult narrator is positioned in a space that the child could never occupy—an understanding of the significance of his childhood in political, social, and cultural terms. For example, Drewe uses his childhood autobiography to consider a violent crime; Keneally uses his childhood to consider Catholicism in the 1950s. Drewe's autobiography concludes with his leaving Perth, effectively leaving his childhood behind. The narrative suggests that only retrospectively can he know the significance of this moment. Similarly, Keneally's *Homebush Boy* uses childhood experiences to draw attention to political and religious issues affecting the inhabitants of 1950s Australia.

Keneally's narrative begins, in much the same way as Nicholls's, with his birth:

Born in Sydney in the southern hemisphere's spring of 1935, after Mussolini had in another unimaginable continent invaded Ethiopia, and while my parents were down from the country town of Kempsey trying their luck in bad economic times, I had been named Michael Thomas by my mother. (1)

Yet the primary difference is the suggestion of the broader scope and relevance of Keneally's narrative, made directly by an adult narrator. The references to the southern hemisphere, Mussolini, and Ethiopia all seem self-conscious, ironic gestures of the relative (un)importance of a boyhood spent in Homebush, Sydney. The narrator's statement regarding the structure and scope of this autobiography is a further suggestion of its significance:

This is not an exhaustive tale of boyhood but of the one, reckless, sweet, divinely hectic and subtly hormonal year. That is, in my case, 1952. It seems to outweigh the other years, to be the most succulent and the most dangerous. Its consequences, lightly embarked on, have not to this day ceased to tease, govern and turn on me. (1)

On the one hand, this narrative choice reflects an acknowledgement of the impossibility of an "exhaustive boyhood." On the other hand, this can be read as a supremely nostalgic gesture—the suggestion that one year of his boyhood was the most formative, representative, or significant. The adult narrator inscribes this nostalgic gesture upon the child self: "I was a far more turbulent spirit, and felt that something massive was about to descend upon me" (61).

The narrative of *Homebush Boy* does not adhere to its promise of being the autobiography of one year; it begins with describing the narrator's birth, details of his childhood illnesses, his father's experiences of the war, and his family's move to Homebush. Further on in the book he describes various episodes of his childhood, such as incidents that happened ten years earlier. The early pages of *Homebush Boy* suggest that the broad purpose of this autobiography is to explore the childhood of this first-person narrator who was "incorrectly registered" as Thomas Michael Keneally, born in Sydney in 1935 (1). The title *Homebush Boy* functions to inscribe the place and cultural moment upon the boy—he is a "Homebush Boy," the product of a particular place and time. It also serves to inscribe the boy upon the place—he is an exemplar of a Home-bush Boy. Some of the readers of this text may also be "Homebush" boys, and thus *Homebush Boy* appeals to communal memory.

From the title and the early intimations of broader socio-historical events, the reader is invited to interpret this autobiography as a social history of 1950s

Sydney, as much as a tale about Keneally. In locating his experiences of child-hood alongside larger socio-political events, he creates the impression that this childhood has been reflected upon, contextualized, and contained within this autobiography. The child is as much a trigger for remembering a place as the place is for remembering the child. As such *Homebush Boy* presents physical and temporal sites for nostalgic remembering, such as the home, the family, the suburb, and, most importantly, the period.

Each of these locations is remembered affectionately and nostalgically, just as they exist within cultural memory of 1950s Australia. Keneally's and Nicholls's texts in particular commemorate the same authority figures and institutions that the traumatic childhoods dismantle—parents, teachers, priests/brothers, and nuns.

Such nostalgic remembering is inherently political as it functions to perpetuate particular experiences of family life within cultural memory. As Michael Lambek and Paul Antze suggest, "Memory is widely called upon today to legitimate identity" (xv). The representation of cohesive Australian communities in autobiography functions to confirm notions of egalitari-anism, interrelationships, and family values. Nostalgic autobiographies of childhood commemorate certain social and familial relationships that are explicitly and implicitly interpreted through contemporary Australian fami-lies.[6] The growing awareness of Australia's traumatic history, along with its complex (multicultural) present, triggers a desire to reactivate the past that can be managed by autobiography. The Australian cultural scene has traditionally been conducive to narratives of resilience and survival, which can be found in both nostalgic and traumatic autobiographical modes but are also strongly evident in the plethora of autobiographical sporting, rural, and travel narratives that still dominate the nonfiction sections of Australian bookstores. These texts function as intertexts of nostalgic autobiographies of childhood; their commonality is that they do not take a conflict view of history. Nostalgic remembering combats growing uncertainty of the past by linking autobiography to specific social constructions of the golden age—Nicholls's Sydney without crime, Drewe's beachside childhood, and Keneally's school filled with sporting heroes. Thus, as argued in chapter 1, nostalgic memory reveals more about the present—its concerns and preoc-cupations—than it does about the past. This association of nostalgia with the present, highlighted by Boym in the epigraph for this chapter, suggests that nostalgia is not necessarily about the past or the future but can also be directed sideways (xiv). This complicates conventional uses of nostalgia, which associate it with the past. When nostalgia becomes most strongly associated with the present, it reveals it to be the site of interaction between past and future. Indeed, the preoccupations of the present incubate the representations of the past.

Keneally's narrator idealizes his parents. When discussing his childhood deliberations over whether he will become a priest, the narrator writes of his mother's protective support:

> She knew that the Orders meant that she wouldn't see me for years, the child she had nursed and urged back to breathe and coaxed to some scholarly eminence, and she broke into tears. I was of course of an age where everything is easily sacrificed—family, love and even life. (131)

Keneally's narrator explains his parents' sacrifices: "My father went without drink. My mother, who was by everyone's account a beautiful woman, had to line her holed shoes with newspaper . . . in the hope that my brother and I would become academic stars" (22). The narrator's description of his father returning from war appeals to communal childhood memories: "I had a sense of proudly surrendering care of the hearth back to him. Yet I felt odd with him, like many of the children of that era who greeted returning fathers" (6). Similarly, Nicholls's narrator in *A Saucepan in the Sky* remembers loving parents as well as an extended family full of comical characters, including a range of larrikin "uncles" who teach the young Brian to be a larrikin himself. The narrator describes this relationship: "I knew uncles for a long, long time. Uncles are good. They can teach you a lot of things. It's not good for a boy to be too good. That's what my uncles taught me. Your mother and father wouldn't teach you that" (22). The inclusion of these details suggests the importance of family in accounting for the narrator's experiences of childhood. Families are contextualized as a site for nostalgic remembering. The autobiography of childhood becomes a means for commemorating families as nostalgic figures and iconic Australians.

As a result of these fondly remembered family lives, the nostalgic narrators each foreground their own developing sexualities as a key concern in the narrative. Sanitized, romantic descriptions prevail. In *Homebush Boy* Keneally's narrator remembers the first time he witnessed a "real kiss." He narrates his first adolescent attraction to Bernadette Curran, who he describes as his "*belle dame sans merci*" (7), while Boyle's narrator in *Galloway Street* writes of his first kiss, "When I tasted her mouth I was that dizzy I thought I was fainting. I wanted to kiss her again but they started a new game" (10). Drewe's narrative recounts the first time he saw people having sex, and later his first kiss and first romance while holidaying on Rottnest Island.

The boyhood memories of Drewe, Keneally, and Nicholls are presented as rites of passage for conventional male development in the 1950s, perpetuating the social ideal that all children have the freedom to explore their sexuality. These developing sexualities are often explored in terms of guilt or discomfort. For example, both *Manchester United Ruined My Life* and *The Shark Net* explore the consequences of unplanned pregnancies in late adolescence from a male point of view. However, sexuality is significantly implicated in narratives of nostalgia as a memorable and formative "first," becoming a trope of nostalgic autobiographies of childhood. Virginity is "lost" rather than stolen, while sexuality is experienced as pleasure rather than abuse, as it so often is in traumatic autobiography.

Keneally's narrative does acknowledge the occurrence of child sexual abuse perpetrated by priests in the 1950s. However, Keneally's narrator explicitly exonerates the priests he encountered during his boyhood: "The old bigot rumour was that the priests got indecent thrills listening to people's sexual admissions. But I couldn't imagine anything garish being confessed by the staid parishioners of St Martha's" (100). The all-knowing adult voice in *Homebush Boy* encourages the reader to attribute this particular interpretation to the adult narrator. The narrator provides a humorous reminder of a golden age of naïveté. In another incident, the narrator's mother reads reports in the newspaper of Christian Brothers "interfering" with young boys, and she asks her son if anything like this has ever happened to him. The narrator mockingly reflects that the only way he has been interfered with is by the brothers criticizing his choice of reading (51). Though this conversation works as an acknowledgment that child abuse was occurring in the Church at this time, it is presented in the narrative as marginal within the cultural memory of this period.

Nostalgic autobiographies of childhood contain affirmations of the golden age and rarely take a conflict view of history. In *Manchester United Ruined My Life* Shindler's narrator attributes his childhood development to a lost era, when football was, in Shindler's opinion, much superior to the game today: "Personally, I regret this new bile. . . . The hatred in football has grown exponentially" (131). Such a statement reveals one of the ways in which nostalgia is useful in times of crisis (returning to Steinwand's argument). Moments from the past are juxtaposed with the apparent crises of the present.

Aside from this particular critique, Shindler's autobiography is, generally speaking, mockingly uninterested in politics: "The only thing that mattered to me in the universe was the ninety minutes of football. . . . Elsewhere during the week, Enoch Powell was warning of rivers of blood flowing through the streets of England if immigration controls were not tightened" (234). This is another example of the adult autobiographical voice challenging the limits of his previously childish view. However, this framing also provides a pretext for the narrative's avoiding the broader contexts and politics of the period it recounts.

Despite its downbeat title, *Manchester United Ruined My Life* is not a denunciation of Manchester United; far from it. Shindler's autobiography does not focus on adverse events. His childhood is filled with sport and play, a good education, a happy family, lots of friends, "Blytonesque" family vacations, and adventures abroad (90). Shindler's narrator describes his childhood as "a John Major–like world of Fifties security and respectability" (61). The narrator refers to his poverty as "genteel" and describes himself as "middle-class" (9). He writes, "I never felt unduly poor, not like the kids from the council estate on the other side of Park View who came to school with holes in their clothes, but all my life I felt I had lived in a time of austerity" (79). Apart from his mother's death, his tragedies, such as his Uncle Laurence moving to London and his father's business failing, are constructed as minor within the narrative.

The nostalgic autobiographies of Nicholls and Keneally depict a predominantly white, masculine Australia where a sense of Britishness prevailed. Nicholls's narrative represents "a lost world"; as Gerster suggests, "This is a Sydney that has largely vanished. There's neither a non-Anglo-Celt nor a discarded needle ('the grog' being the resident social demon) in sight" (27). *Homebush Boy* is predominantly concerned with boyhood friendships, poetry, and sport. Keneally's autobiography is implicated in particular dominant cultural memories of 1950s Australia. The narrator is obsessed with rugby and refers to a number of Australian sporting greats that attended his high school.

Keneally's narrator describes 1950s Australia as an age of "hugest innocence," explaining that immigrants suffered "casual malice" at the hands of white Australians: "Italians had begun to arrive in numbers, and Balts of every stripe—Lithuanian, Estonian, Latvian—and Poles and Greeks, but they had not yet changed the Australian equation. . . . Britishness prevailed, and even the Irish-Australian working class were part of that Britishness" (25). As David Cannadine suggests, writers born during and after World War II are privileged children of the colonial era, and thus may be unable to write in any other way (194).

As discussed earlier, Keneally's narrator offers political contexts to mock his childhood naïveté:

This was the year in which Singapore had fallen to the Japanese and the occasional Japanese reconnaissance plane went over Sydney, the year in which the entire Australian world scheme—development as a working man's utopia under the umbrella of Imperial power—had been disrupted by the humiliation of British and Australian arms. Yet it was our urinary crimes which seemed to cry to the heavens. (85)

The dialogism of the narrative results in the adult narrator grappling with his child self for narrative ascendancy. The quotation above reveals his self-consciousness about the limitations of nostalgic memory. It serves as an apology for the ignorance of youth and a rewriting of his childhood history to frame experiences that would not necessarily have been within the child's consciousness. The narrator writes of his childhood "hunger for grandeur, which Homebush and the Western Line could not slake" (29). These triggers of adolescent embarrassment are the inspiration for nostalgic remembering within autobiography.

Nostalgic Unease: Toward Traumatic Memory

Drewe's narrator in *The Shark Net* complicates this discussion of nostalgic remembering and lacks some of the conventions of other nostalgic auto-biographies discussed in this chapter. For instance, though Drewe's childhood dominates the text, subplots describing a murderer and a murder hearing regularly interrupt this narrative. *The Shark Net* begins with the adult narrator acting as a journalist at a murder trial. He assumes the role of describing events for the reader, including the courtroom, the trial, and the murderer. The narrator soon becomes implicated in these events; he is more than an observer. He is experiencing unease, he is restless, and his focus on the trial is waning. He feels detached from events, because he knows the murderer and one of the murder victims: "With a sickening shock I'd remember that the subject of the police photographs on the court clerk's table, Exhibit 14—the shattered head, the blackened mess of blood and matter—was a friend of mine" (8).

The narrator feels ashamed that he cannot stop looking at the photograph and the murderer:

Suddenly I felt him staring at me. I'd been avoiding his eyes, hoping he wouldn't recognise me, but a moment later he winked, I winked back, then I felt a hot wave of embarrassment that quickly turned into anger at myself. I hoped that no one, not the magistrate or the other reporters, and especially not the victim's family had seen me. (11)

His overwhelming sense of guilt is due partly to this incident, but also to something else that is not yet revealed. This first section of *The Shark Net*, along with the title, establishes the text generically as a murder mystery. The presence of a conflicted character who is experiencing personal shame creates a more general sense of fear and foreboding. The final sentence of this section asks, "What happened?" seeking answers to both the murder and the confusion that is affecting the adult narrator.

It may prove surprising to some readers that *The Shark Net* proceeds to seek the answers to these questions within the narrator's childhood. Here the autobiography of childhood becomes a mechanism to explore not only the adult narrator's personal conflicts but also the serial killings that shadowed his seemingly idyllic 1950s Perth boyhood.

Why do I describe this autobiography as nostalgic? When Drewe's narrator remembers his childhood, he does so nostalgically; his memories are influenced by, and actively shape, the cultural memory of 1950s Australia. The physical sites that trigger nostalgic memories in *The Shark Net* include beaches, the school, the home, and the backyard. Drewe writes of quintessentially Australian childhoods, inviting the reader to recognize these images as familiar to the dominant culture of childhood at this moment:

> Those grazed ankles and blackened toenails, the blood-blistered heels, the festering reef-cuts, criss-crossing their soles, showed a boy's familiarity with reef, surf and cliff-face. Their feet were painted so boldly with Mercurochrome and flavine antiseptic they looked like they were wearing red and yellow socks. (35)

Drewe's vivid description of "the Sand People" of Western Australia creates a sense that this was a time and place that was racially white and wholly innocent: "Sun and wind had rearranged the appearance of the Sand People, too—sand, freckled, scabbed and bleached them. With their darker skins, red eyes, raw noses and permanent deep cracks in their bottom lips, they looked nothing like Melbourne people" (34). The narrator constructs these Western Australian children as innocent and prosperous; he covets these traits:

> I envied the superior foods they claimed to live on. Salad was for smearing on their burnt bodies—what they ate was fish and chips, chocolate-coated ice-creams, spearmint milkshakes. Passiona drink and hamburgers, the aroma of whose frying grey mince patties and onions attracted both Sand People and outsiders after dark. (41)

Carmel Bird suggests that these images invite the reader's recognition:

> The structure of the work itself is seductive, with scenes selected from
> personal domestic life playing against the larger dramas of crime and
> accidental death. In spite of all this I sometimes laughed aloud, often
> with a laugh of recognition at a locution or a turn of events that brought
> back live memories of the time. (7)

Drewe's childhood life parallels the development of Perth. For example,
when Drewe's narrator writes of his schoolboy dances and his first trip
to Rottnest Island, he also describes the fast-developing Perth, with its
expanding suburbs and the opening of the Narrows Bridge. By the end of
his childhood he has emulated the lifestyle he envied and perceives it as
paradisaical.

As Joy Hooten argues, Australian autobiographies commonly acknowledge
that the "security and identity offered" by nostalgic memories of place are
"illusory" (*Stories* 67). *The Shark Net* debunks various symbols of middle-
class prosperity—the secrets within the family, the unstable houses built too
close to sand dunes, and the gaudy material wealth provided to his family
by Dunlop Rubber. In her review of *The Shark Net* Rebecca J. Davies argues
that Drewe's family is "acutely observed as a microcosm of 1950s Australian
suburbia. His father is not above ripping pages of naked breasts from the
National Geographic magazine, nor burning the weekly tabloid after viewing
the so-called filth for himself" (1282).

Though, as Mieke Bal argues, nostalgia can lend itself to political
manipulation and is commonly thought to be regressive in establishing
an ideal relationship between the past, present, and future, "nostalgia can
also be empowering and productive if critically tempered and historically
informed" (xi). In *The Shark Net* nostalgic remembering is widened and
used to reflect on the junction between the favorable and unfavorable events
of Drewe's childhood. The narrative pinpoints the moment when both the
narrator and the city he lived in experienced their loss of innocence, their
coming of age. The central theme of Drewe's autobiography is an inquiry
into what happens when physical location becomes insecure—how could
something as terrible as serial killings happen somewhere as idyllic as
Perth? In using an autobiography to explore this concern, Drewe's narrative reveals the utility of nostalgic remembering. On one hand, Drewe's
autobiography is filled with notions of the 1950s as a golden age similar to
those in Keneally's and Shindler's texts. On the other hand, these memories

are explicitly referenced to juxtapose the innocent times of the past with the traumatic times that followed. This employment of nostalgic memory is what Boym describes as "reflective nostalgia," which "thrives in longing" but dwells on the ambivalences and contradictions of this longing, as opposed to "restorative nostalgia," which "attempts a transhistorical reconstruction of the lost home" (xviii).

Do these traumatic interventions—for instance, the descriptions of the "Saturday Night Boy," Eric Cooke, and his serial killings—work to suggest, as Hooten argues, that innocence was an illusion all along? *The Shark Net* implies that the narrator was not aware of this undercurrent during his childhood, and therefore, like Keneally's autobiography, *Homebush Boy* functions to reexamine his childhood memories via adult knowledge.

And yet the overarching impression created within *The Shark Net* is that it idealizes the time prior to the serial killings: The autobiography appeals nostalgically to these times to emphasize the magnitude of the change that came after. In an interview with Drewe, Ramona Koval asks him if *The Shark Net* challenges the idea that Perth was ever a place of innocence. Drewe responds by arguing that Perth was exactly that,

> a place of innocence. No one locked the doors of their houses. You'd go into a shop and leave your keys in the car, for instance. People always slept with the windows and doors open. When the serial killer was on his various rampages, even after he'd killed a couple of people, he never had to break into a house. (9)

Thus, *The Shark Net* warrants a close reading with regard to its use of nostalgic memory. This autobiography in particular reveals the difficulties faced by autobiographers occupying nostalgic spaces. Because of this, *The Shark Net* provides a useful transition point for examining the relationship between nostalgic and traumatic memory modes in autobiographies of childhoods.

Nostalgic autobiographies of childhoods work with certain ideologies, mythologies, and histories that surround childhood. Nostalgic autobiography permits a focus on commemorative events of childhood and lively or humorous reflections on cultural life and community; traumatic autobiography centers on personal sadness and loss. Traumatic autobiographies of childhood are concerned with the child's alienation from a personal community, as a consequence of his or her childhood being "stolen."

In these instances, do nostalgic and traumatic childhood narratives work in opposition to each other? Has traumatic remembering been enhanced by nostalgic remembering? For instance, in what ways can traumatic autobiographies of childhoods be read as a challenge to the nostalgic autobiographies they coexist with? The tension between nostalgic and traumatic remembering is productive rather than damaging. These texts cannot function as they do without each other; each works in reaction to the other and, read comparatively, they assert a plurality of identities for childhood. Steinwand argues that nostalgia is more than merely an "imaginative forgetfulness perfecting memory"; nostalgia should not be simply dismissed as distortion "because every reflection on where we are going and where we have been depends on some distortion" (10). Traumatic and nostalgic memories are different cultural modes of remembering, rather than simply "false" and/or "accurate" memories. Other factors are also significant in revealing the social function of autobiographical texts of childhood, such as the moments and locations within which these memories occur and, most importantly, the other memory practices in circulation at the same moment.

CHAPTER 5

SCRIPTS FOR REMEMBERING

TRAUMATIC CHILDHOODS

One of the most compelling reasons trauma has become important to life writing is its sheer scale and pervasiveness. Life writing about trauma moves personal experience onto the historical stage, it provides a way to reconceive the relation between private and public, and it produces a counter-discourse to the historical muting or erasure of the kinds of violence that have been regarded as violating dominant cultural norms and narratives.
—Leigh Gilmore, "Trauma and Life Writing"

The happy childhood is hardly worth your while.
—Frank McCourt, *Angela's Ashes*

In the 1990s and 2000s, autobiography and trauma have gone hand in hand—with the publication of a plethora of child abuse survivor narratives. But what do autobiographers do with childhood trauma? What are the limits of traumatic representations in autobiographies of childhood, and what layers can autobiographers add to broader cultural understandings of childhood trauma? The previous chapters have revealed a diversity of traumatic representations within autobiographies of childhood—from Mary Karr's restrained representation of her childhood rape to Rosalie Fraser's graphic depiction of sexual abuse at the hands of her foster mother. This chapter takes a close look at more examples of traumatic autobiographies of childhood to suggest some of the different templates for writing survivor narratives, and to examine how these texts have found their cultural moment.

The U.S. literary scene has witnessed an outpouring of traumatic autobiographies of childhood during the late 1990s and 2000s. The majority of these autobiographies have related the experience of child abuse within the family—whether biological families (such as Rick Bragg's *All Over but the Shoutin'*, Julie Gregory's *Sickened*, Dave Pelzer's autobiographies, Barbara

Robinette Moss's *Change Me into Zeus's Daughter*), by family friends or stepparents (Mary Karr's *The Liars' Club*, Jennifer Lauck's *Blackbird*), or by foster families (Antwone Fisher's *Finding Fish: A Memoir*). The U.K. witnessed similar trends—with the family asserted as the key site of child abuse. For example, Constance Briscoe's *Ugly*, published in 2006, recounts Briscoe's experiences at the hands of her physically abusive mother. Jenny Tomlin's *Behind Closed Doors* (also published in 2006) recounts Tomlin's experiences of abuse by her father and neglect by her mother growing up in London. Sarah Davies's *Running from the Devil* (also 2006) tells the story of an abusive father and a mother who was unable to offer any escape.

These autobiographies, to name just a few examples, form part of broader cultural initiatives that circulate meanings for child sexual abuse. As Ian Hacking suggests, child abuse "is a story that is developing every day" ("The Making and Moulding of Child Abuse" 255). Popular cultural forms such as film (for instance, Gregg Araki's *Mysterious Skin*) have been instrumental in breaking silences and creating cultural templates for stories to be told. As *Mysterious Skin* exemplifies, these narratives can be extremely provocative, and the lines of acceptable representations are constantly shifting in line with changing cultural mores.

As Leigh Gilmore suggests (in the quote I use for the epigraph to this chapter), trauma has been central in contemporary self-representation. The term "trauma" is "from the Greek meaning 'wound,' [and] refers to the self-altering, even self-shattering experience of violence, injury and harm" (Gilmore, *Limits* 3). For Sigmund Freud, trauma has a double meaning; trauma may be a new wound or the opening up of an old wound (100).[1] There are different schools of thought (within theoretical and therapeutic disciplines) regarding the advantages and disadvantages of speaking out about trauma, for instance, within autobiography. Gilmore discusses the paradox that trauma is largely considered "unspeakable" or "unrepresent-able"—that language is inadequate to articulate trauma—yet, at the same time, writing and speaking are authorized as the primary modes for healing trauma (*Limits* 6). These are a means via which the previously disempowered person (in this instance, the child) can "write back" (as an adult) after the fact, to offer a revised version of events.[2]

Traumatic autobiographies have long been recognized as therapeutic "silence-breakers" for individuals who have suffered pain or distress.[3] More recently, however, traumatic remembering has been repositioned "from the individual psyche to the social sphere, where it rightfully belongs" (Martín Alcoff and Gray-Rosendale 200). Given this repositioning, much of the dialogue that surrounds contemporary traumatic autobiographies interprets these narratives as socio-political performances. Memories, as Michael Lambek and Paul Antze suggest, are at once "a source of authority and a means of attack" (vii). Autobiographical writings are used to legitimate experiences and to mediate the confrontational transmission of personal narratives into public life and socio-cultural history.

In interpreting their childhood experiences, however, autobiographers of childhood are influenced by their contemporary social and political contexts (for instance, prevalent ideologies of childhood). These contexts have significant impact on what stories can be told at particular moments (a point I discussed in chapter 1). In a Foucauldian sense, speaking out about trauma is a mode of confession—and those writing about trauma within autobiography are bound to make particular types of confessions. Particular confessions are culturally valued (over others) at particular cultural moments. And confession is one of the ways in which the body is managed, made to conform to public and cultural values (Foucault, *History of Sexuality*).

The idea that trauma stories "must be told," or indeed "must be witnessed," is one of the catalysts for their publication. Yet the adult autobiographer's right or ability to narrate his or her childhood experiences retrospectively has triggered much debate, from questions about how adults can remember events from their childhoods to debates over authority—such as who has the right to narrate these stories and what kinds of disclosures are considered "appropriate" at particular historical junctures.[4] As Lambek and Antze argue, "The right to establish authoritative versions never rests with the individual telling the story alone. It shifts from communal institutions and collective memory to the domain of experts and beyond—to market forces and the power of the state" (xvii).

For example, the "false memory syndrome" movement, which arose during the 1990s, warns against the fabrication or exaggeration of child abuse narratives—offering protection to parents who have been falsely accused of abuse by their children (who are now adults). There are obviously serious consequences for parents who are falsely accused of child abuse—particularly emotional hardship, and financial hardship if litigation ensues. False memory syndrome focuses on the fragility of repressed and recovered memories (Loftus and Ketcham; Ofshe and Watters). Recovered memories might in fact be culturally suggested memories, deriving from therapy, or affected by the individual's consumption of memories other than his or her own. Critics of false memory syndrome argue that there is no evidence of its existence as a widespread phenomenon. It is generally acknowledged (among therapeutic professionals and scholars working with trauma and memory) that those experiencing trauma commonly experience difficulties in remembering—and that notions of "truth" and historical accuracy are relative to those experiencing the events rather than objective measures (Freyd; Whitfield). These memory controversies function as a reminder: that debates about truth and lies are fundamentally irresolvable. As Marita Sturken contends, memory controversies and the representations they evoke need to be explored within larger cultural frameworks and beyond true/false binaries. Traumatic memories must be understood

> along a continuum of cultural memory, spanning from actual experience to remembered experience, with the understanding that these locations are impossible to measure. To say that recovered memories are part of cultural memory means, among other things, that the question of their origins and their relationship to experience must necessarily be thought of as a complex mix of narrative, displacement, shared testimony, popular culture, rumor, fantasy, and collective desire. All recovered memories are part of cultural memory; even those that are not derived from specific instances of abuse are still elements of the memory landscape that we inhabit. To remember something *is* an experience. (Sturken, "Remembering of Forgetting" 106)

Though life narratives of child sexual abuse are commonly found on television talk shows and in current affairs media, as well as within autobiography, there are obvious limits on these representations. Autobiography is a genre that values "good subjects"—where displays of resilience and recovery are evident throughout the autobiographical project. In the introduction to this study I suggested that distrust, even condemnation, of popular autobiography became a regular feature in literary media in the late 1990s.[5] In recent times, autobiographical interventions into child abuse have been met with a great deal of skepticism. Accusations of sensationalism and distrust over the veracity of autobiographies of childhood abuse have pervaded the media. As Paul John Eakin argues:

> Life writers are criticized not only for not telling the truth . . . but also for telling too much truth. . . . The public airing of private hurt . . . was not universally welcomed; many of these narratives not only featured abuse as a primary content but also were perceived by some reviewers to *be* abusive in their candour. (*How Our Lives* 3)

For example, U.S. author Kathryn Harrison's controversial autobiography *The Kiss* was the catalyst for a literary backlash against traumatic autobiography, or what Laura Frost terms "memoirs of extremity."[6] It was a common assumption that popular autobiography, like television talk shows, was becoming too sensationalized in its depictions of people in distress. Sensationalized depictions of abuse are commonly thought to be counterproductive to survivor discourse, because they focus on individual pathology rather than social inequalities and issues of power.[7]

Yet this is not the only ground upon which traumatic autobiography has been criticized; these autobiographies are critiqued on the grounds of "good taste." Malcolm Jones, writing for *Newsweek,* offers this description of traumatic autobiography: "Style doesn't count . . . the grit of life—is what we crave"; "the success of memoir has little to do with good taste" (59). Similarly in Britain, Ann Treneman derisively observes,

> you don't have to have had a rotten childhood to get a book published these days, but it helps. Actually it needs to be a little worse than rotten. Nor is difficult, lonely or sad really good enough. Publishers are looking for urban, poor, abusive, or—even better—all three. Death is good, drugs a plus. It helps if you can write, but it's not essential. . . . "There are so many of these 'They fuck you up, your mum and dad' type books," said one publicist. "It really is this thing now."

For some critics, then, traumatic autobiography has the potential to be self-indulgent, self-pitying, lacking in self-discipline, and generally in "bad taste."

As Sonia C. Apgar suggests, the wider acceptance of traumatic narratives is dependent on their fitting within social constructions and norms of the time (48). Traumatic autobiographies of childhood are most commonly offered to the public as testimony of their narrators' endurance of trauma. For many autobiographers who represent their shamed childhood selves, the autobiographical act becomes a means for "the mature self to become visible in a deliberate way in order to confront shame and re-evaluate self-worth" (Dalziell 7). Authors of traumatic autobiographies of childhood commonly emphasize that it is only through the adult voice, and the particular contemporary cultural environment they find themselves in, that they are able to recite their narratives. This also seems to be an axiom of therapeutic discourse, for, as Apgar suggests, "writing provides the survivor with a psychological distance that allows her [or him] the possibility of analyzing her [or his] past" (48). Thus, autobiography has become a mechanism for mediating between the past and the present, between the child and the adult self, and between trauma and healing.

Traumatic childhoods are often contrasted with the idyllic constructions of postwar childhoods (discussed in the previous chapter). For example, the so-called authority figures of nostalgic autobiographies of childhoods—priests, parents, and stepparents—are dismantled within these traumatic autobiographies of childhood. In doing so, these autobiographies offer their narratives as counter-discourse to nostalgic memories. They circulate childhood experiences, which, when framed within dominant Western ideologies of childhood, seem notable, unusual, and unacceptable. Moreover, these autobiographies are often overtly politicized, containing diatribes against the institutional causes of child abuse in the mid- to late twentieth century.

These points are best illuminated through examples of autobiographies of childhood that represent trauma and take up some of the cultural debates associated with representing child abuse: the reliability of memory—trauma and "forgetting," socio-economic and gender issues associated with trauma and its perpetration, and trauma and the rights of the child.[8] Apgar writes, "With the increased awareness of sexual abuse in the past decade has come a growing number of texts on the subject, including psychological treatises and sociological studies, popular press and self-help books, autobiographies and anthologies of first-person narratives in which survivors tell their own stories" (47). In the new millennium autobiographical narratives of childhood trauma can be found in a range of nonfictional literatures, from poetry and plays to self-help books. Amazon.com lists hundreds of traumatic autobiographies under the categories of "recovery," "family and relationships," "abuse," "incest," "psychic trauma," "child abuse," and "adult child-abuse victims." Traumatic narratives are also a constant presence on television talk shows and current affairs bulletins. Indeed, mainstream cultural domains—particularly film, television, and documentary—have recently played an increasingly important role in representing and defining child abuse.

Although each of the autobiographies I discuss in this chapter offers a representation of child sexual abuse perpetrated by an adult, the representations of abuse and the methods of its disclosure differ significantly between these texts. In some instances abuse is a central concern of the autobiography. Centering the abuse functions to situate it as central to the childhood experience and challenges its previous marginality. In other instances abuse is represented with a shadowy complexity that underlies its "unspeakability." On other occasions abuse and neglect are constructed on the periphery or as frames for the narrative. In these examples abuse can only be spoken of in light of deeper ideological concerns such as mental health, class, history, or gender.

Another significant movement within autobiographies of childhood is the prevalence of abuse narratives written by men. Given that sexual abuse remains one of the most underreported crimes—and that men are less likely to report sexual assault than women—these become important texts (Andrews, Gould, and Corry).[9] I have chosen three texts written by men in this chapter as a means of looking at the particular ways in which male survivors of child sexual abuse use the autobiographical form to frame their experiences.

Exposing and Disclosing: Antwone Fisher's *Finding Fish: A Memoir* and Duncan Fairhurst's *Our Little Secret: A Father's Abuse, a Son's Life Destroyed*

"On 16th August 2004," Duncan Fairhurst writes in his autobiography, "I walked into Grantham police station and reported my father as a child abuser and paedophile" (263). Fairhurst was sexually abused by his father for thirteen years—for most of his childhood. It took Fairhurst more than twenty years to report this abuse. Eventually, his father, Clifford Fairhurst, was prosecuted and jailed for eleven years.

Duncan Fairhurst waived his anonymity and became a vocal advocate for child protection in the United Kingdom. Outside of the text (in interviews), Fairhurst has commented publicly about his disappointment with British child protection institutions: "One of the friends who supported me during the case revealed that he had also been abused, but he said he wouldn't be reporting it because he wouldn't put his family through the same treatment I got from the police child protection. So the guilty go free" (qtd. in Gould). Janice Haaken proposes that many abuse survivors are "able to convert pain into a social cause" ("Sexual Abuse"116). Like many other social justice campaigners before him, Fairhurst's response to the failures of the justice system was to write a bestselling autobiography, which details his experiences of childhood sexual abuse. Autobiography becomes a counter-discourse—a powerful means for circulating a narrative when other discourses prove inadequate or fail. *Our Little Secret: A Father's Abuse, a Son's Life Destroyed* was first published in the United Kingdom in early 2007.

As previously suggested, Fairhurst's narrative of abuse joins a corpus of child abuse narratives in circulation during the 2000s. When writing about childhood sexual abuse, autobiographers are bound by, and draw upon, available cultural templates for describing abuse, for example, the abused body. For instance, Haaken argues that trauma stories are believable and communicable if there is a social dimension for remembering this type of story (*Pillar of Salt* 111). She gives the example of how the feminist movement (particularly in the 1970s and 1980s) enabled family child abuse stories written by women to find witnesses. Similarly "stories of clerical abuse of children galvanized rebellion against authority within the Catholic Church in the 1980s" (*Pillar of Salt* 122). These contexts have also resulted in the increased disclosure of child sexual abuse by male survivors. Although most studies contend that (as with child abuse generally), male child sexual abuse remains grossly underreported, there is an increasing number of conducive discourses emerging for the disclosure of childhood sexual abuse. Fairhurst's narrative provides a window into the ways in which the traumatic mode of childhood autobiography enables (and also regulates) the disclosure of abuse.

One of the missions of Fairhurst's narrative is to disclose (in intimate detail) the abuse that he suffered at the hands of his father. Many autobiographies of childhood take a different road. For example, many autobiographers choose to disclose, but not graphically represent, child abuse, preferring the literary equivalent of fading to black at crucial moments. Fairhurst's narrative represents (and perhaps employs) the body as a means of authenticating his narrative. Writing about the body within autobiography is a realistic strategy at a time when autobiographical writers have found themselves under increased scrutiny regarding the veracity of their tales and the ethics of representation. However, those writing graphically about abuse are also commonly accused of sensationalism and/or attempting to "up the ante"—transgressing the boundaries of acceptable representation.

Fairhurst's *Our Little Secret* is, at least in part, born out of a desire to raise community awareness of child sexual abuse. This is suggested in his comments quoted earlier. Autobiography is a receptive genre for these stories, and book sales figures suggest that readers consume traumatic life narratives in large quantities. Whether this is a symptom of "wound culture" (to use Mark Seltzer's term) or can be attributed to increased community empathy and/or interest in childhood is a debate for another time. Traumatic autobiographies attempt to establish particular exchanges between the autobiographer and reader that inevitably prescribe and limit a reader's consumption of these texts. As Gilmore argues, autobiographers who write about trauma place themselves in "testimonial contexts. . . . These contexts are reproducible; [and the] repetition of the forms that characterize them establish expectations in audiences" (*Limits* 3). A question that has forever pervaded the construction of autobiographical writing about child abuse is: How can child abuse be written, and how can the (traditionally unspeakable) traumatized, abused body be represented within autobiographies? At any given time, as Sidonie Smith and Julia Watson contend, "cultural discourses determine which aspects of bodies become meaningful—what parts of the body are 'there' for people to see. They determine when the body becomes visible, how it becomes visible, and what that visibility means" (*Reading Autobiography* 38). At a time when the body is highly visible across all levels of culture—from television makeover programs to academic discussions of the disembodied self, the post-human and cyber-selves—the body remains (as it has been traditionally) a site where political and ideological struggles can be fought (Terry and Urla). Autobiography becomes a discursive site for the exploration of the relationships between autobiography, memory, and the body. Smith and Watson argue that "the body is a site of auto-biographical knowledge, as well as a textual surface upon which a person's life is inscribed. The body is a site of autobiographical knowledge because memory itself is embodied. And life narrative is a site of embodied knowl-edge because autobiographical narrators are embodied subjects" (*Reading Autobiography* 37). The body is a site upon which childhood memories can be ascribed and confirmed, which is to say that the abused body can provide a means by which an abuse narrative becomes authorized. Representing an abused body provides "evidence" to confirm the experience of abuse as "real." The survivor comes to own his experience through his graphic disclosure; within the autobiographical narrative transaction, the reader has very little else to do other than witness this disclosure and accept its truth.

Our Little Secret is what literary critics would describe as a "popular" autobiography rather than a "literary" one. Like many of the autobiographies already discussed in this study, this autobiography was not written to impress critics or win awards for its literary merits. Fairhurst is not a professional writer. *Our Little Secret* is written in plain-English style and does not contain complex prose or description. The intended audience is everyday readers, so this approach is perhaps inevitable. But there is more at stake here. Fairhurst's narrative is constructed as a transparent depiction of the abuse he suffered at the hands of his father. And in the field of contemporary life writing, this requires the adherence to particular conventions. Fairhurst's narrative appears constructed as an open, straight-to-the-point depiction of events, and his representation of bodies (his own and his father's) is a crucial component in this approach.

Fairhurst was regularly abused by his father over a period of thirteen years. In his autobiography, Fairhurst describes his father's incessant surveillance of his bathing, and his eventual molestation of Duncan while bathing:

We always shared a cubicle to get dressed [at the public baths]. Dad would make extra sure my genitals were dry. It didn't matter if I had water on my back, under my arms or if my hair was wringing wet, he always dried my penis . . . quite thoroughly, even when I was capable of doing it myself. (18)

Fairhurst's father abused him by forcing Duncan to masturbate him, and by masturbating Duncan. According to the autobiography, he performed oral sex on Duncan, and forced Duncan to perform oral sex on him on numerous occasions, many of which are described within the autobiography: "Up and down his mouth went while I lay there motionless. It seemed to go on forever and I did not ejaculate. I was too young. Soon it began to hurt" (20). Duncan was anally raped by his father on more than one occasion:

I felt a movement between my buttocks and then a push as my whole body shuddered forwards. And then, for a few seconds, nothing. . . . I had never been in so much agony in my life. The sensations were sudden and confusing. I could feel a mixture of burning, ripping, stretching all at the same time. His penis was in my anus. (53)

Within *Our Little Secret*, Fairhurst regularly describes erections and ejaculations (both his father's and his). He describes both his emotional and physical reactions to the abuse he suffers. Paragraphs are devoted to describing pain and soreness and his attempts to cleanse himself that often result in self-mutilation. Very little is withheld from the reader.

Fairhurst's representation of his traumatized body challenges the notion that trauma is unspeakable or unpresentable, responding instead to therapeutic discourses such as narrative therapy that propose that "reauthoring" life experience can lead to self-awareness and/or healing.[10] Therapeutic evidence becomes "literature" to be examined and critiqued. Again, that Fairhurst is able to do this via a frank discussion of his abused body suggests the extent to which the body has become a site for autobiographical exploration, perhaps promising complete disclosure (and even complete exposure) on the part of the autobiographer.

Fairhurst's self-critical tone and his admissions of love for his father—but perhaps most significantly the extent to which his narrative is written upon and through his own bodily experiences—seem self-conscious attempts to circumvent criticism of his narrative. Gilmore discusses the difficulties faced by autobiographers who disclosure trauma: "The portals are too narrow and the demands too restrictive. Moreover, the judgments they invite may be too similar to forms in which trauma was experienced. . . . The risk of being accused of lying (of malingering, or inflating, or whining) threatens the writer into continued silence" (*Limits* 3). Within contemporary autobiographies, the body is a "truth-text," to appropriate Gilmore's term; "truth claims about identity are made through the body" (*Limits* 124).

In Fairhurst's *Our Little Secret* the body becomes a site for consciousness raising—a space upon which abuse claims can be made and the authenticity of his life narrative can be asserted. Arguably, literature can go where film and television cannot, in terms of graphic representations of child sexual abuse. Language has an agency that visual mediums do not, and popular auto-biography has a license that other literatures lack, because of its connections to therapeutic discourses.

Although I have talked about autobiographical representations of abused bodies in this discussion, I have said very little about the more particular autobiographical representations of abused *masculine* bodies. This is topic for a longer discussion, as gender is a crucial variable in these representations. Within autobiographical writing, the body can be employed in significant ways. Fairhurst employs his abused body to explore "cultural norms determining the proper uses of bodies" (Smith and Watson, *Reading Autobiography* 42). In this instance, the body permits the most intimate of all disclosures, and thus can be constructed as a symbol of autobiographical truth.

Another autobiography of childhood that seeks to address childhood abuse through detailed disclosure of childhood shame is Antwone Fisher's *Finding Fish: A Memoir*.[11] *Finding Fish* recalls Fisher's early life living with an emotionally and physically abusive and neglectful foster mother, Mizz Pickett, and being sexually abused by a babysitter, Willenda. He eventually leaves the Picketts and lives on the streets for a period before enlisting in the navy. The autobiography culminates with Fisher reuniting with his family (including his mother) and coming to terms with the traumas of the past. In *Finding Fish*, Fisher, like Fairhurst, suggests the redemptive power of writing—of disclosing trauma as a means of shifting the shame from the victim to the perpetrator. Representing the abuse he suffers allows Fisher to meditate on deeper questions about race, identity, and inequality in 1950s America.

Like Ivor Knight's *Out of Darkness* (which I discuss in the next section), *Finding Fish* is centrally critical of welfare systems that allow abuse to go unnoticed. Fisher intersperses welfare documents—the reports made by social workers during the time he was a ward of the state—within his auto-biographical narrative. His text becomes a dialogic encounter as he attempts to piece together the fragments of his life and to assert the truthfulness of the story he constructs. Fisher writes back to these documents describing his childhood, refuting certain claims and elaborating on others, attending new layers of "truth" to the official versions.

Fisher is beaten and emotionally abused by his foster mother. Her abuse includes regular whippings, forcing him to bathe in bleach, tying him up, racially vilifying him, depriving him of food, and threatening to cut his penis off. Fisher also describes how from age three, he is sexually molested by his twenty-something-year-old neighbor Willenda. She forces him to perform cunnilingus on her. Fisher writes:

> And it wasn't really the fear of her punishing me that kept me from telling anyone all those years. It was the unspeakable shame I felt about what went on with her in the basement, and my unspeakable shame that maybe it was my fault. (44)

Fisher contextualizes his own traumas within a deepening awareness of communal trauma:

> A few months later, I awoke to the morning after Robert Kennedy was killed. The Pickett house was filled with sadness. Everyone kept mentioning Martin Luther King and Robert Kennedy in the same sentence, charging the air with an unbearable weight that pressed down on my shoulders and around my heart. It was obvious that I was responsible for Robert Kennedy's death, too.
>
> Until that day, I only understood my own sadness. But all at once, I became aware that there was more sadness out there than I could even begin to imagine, enough to fill every ocean full of tears. With too many tears of my own to hide, I ran outside, out to the backyard, behind the garage. Then I leaned my head in my hands and cried for a long time. (98)

Fisher's narrative is filled with inspirational nuggets of knowledge that he has acquired and wants to share with the reader. Like many other trauma narratives, it is overtly didactic, owing much to therapeutic and motivational discourses to find its language. For example, Fisher recounts being praised by a teacher:

Her honest, careful words are the equivalent of lightning bolts and thunderclaps. Outside I shyly accept her praise, but inside I'm flying with the birth of revelation. It's the first time I've ever realized that there is something I can do to make things different for myself. Not just me, but anyone. That no matter how often someone says you can't do something, by simply working harder and trying, you can prove them wrong and actually change your circumstance. This lesson is a piece of gold I'll keep tucked away in my back pocket for the rest of my life. (127)

The reader is well aware that it is this Fisher who is triumphant—we know that despite his despair (described recurrently in the autobiography), Fisher survives. Fisher uses an extract from a letter he wrote to his foster sister (Teresa) to open up a monologue on the relationship between his child and adult selves:

In many ways I have forgiven those persons, for my benefit. . . .
    I was a child with no responsibility for being on earth or in her home. With no way to protect myself, she had the power to crush out my spirit, and she did. . . . She had the power to beat me to dust, and she did. . . .
    Now this calf has grown to be a bull with horns, able to protect himself from others. . . .
    Now, here I am this day, with my accomplishments, reflecting on my years with the Picketts. No credit due. Yes, the gusty winds of my melancholy youth have shifted, and brought to me a fine sunny day. (324)

Fisher frames his childhood experiences of abuse within recognizable paradigms of masculine adult success: a career in the armed forces, a solid work ethic, a decent job, a wife and young family. Through the act of writing, Fisher is able to further assert his ascendancy over his abusers. As suggested in chapter 3, the act of writing—of being published and circulating your story among a readership of thousands—is another conventional marker of success. It symbolizes intelligence, creativity, hard work, and resilience—setting him apart from his humble origins.

The narratives of Fisher and Fairhurst share a focus—to expose their abuse through constructing transparent and accessible narratives that task memory and memory texts (in Fisher's case, child welfare documents; in Fairhurst's case, embodied memory) to support their claims. As suggested earlier, this approach to writing trauma is often lambasted by critics who see this (apparently verbatim) mode of constructing childhood experiences as lacking in authenticity. It is not surprising, then, that other autobiographers of childhood have taken a different approach to representing trauma and memory.

"I Just Wanted to Forget": Ivor Knight's *Out of Darkness* and Jenny Diski's *Skating to Antarctica*

Ivor Knight's *Out of Darkness* (1998) forms part of a significant band of autobiographies of childhood to emerge—particularly in Australia and Ireland during the 1990s and 2000s—attempting to expose child abuse in religious welfare institutions.[12] The emergence of these autobiographies follows the exposure of high-profile child abuse cases involving the Catholic Church—the Magdalene laundries in Ireland, the Stolen Generations in Australia, and the long history of pedophilia in the Australian Catholic church (for which Pope Benedict XVI apologized in his 2008 visit to Australia).

Knight was the second youngest of ten children. His mother died when he was two, and shortly after (at age five), Knight was declared a ward of the state. He lived in various Christian Brothers institutions during his childhood, during which he suffered years of emotional, physical, and sexual abuse. The main focus of *Out of Darkness* is to expose childhood traumas perpetrated by welfare institutions: "My unhappiness dates from the time when we three boys were forcibly separated. Perhaps the authorities regarded us as budding criminals" (13). The narrative does not overtly defend its truth or authenticity; *Out of Darkness* is presented as an autobiography constructed from imprecise memories. The narrative opens with the adult, retrospective narrator struggling with the autobiographical convention of summarizing his family history. He confesses, "I don't recall too much of my earliest days" (10). The narrator reveals how his childhood memories conflict with versions he hears later in life: "I do not recall those days being unhappy ones. Much later in life I heard about how my father knocked my mother around, but other members of the family shielded me from all that" (13). Thus, the narrative becomes a site of dialogism; the fragmented narrative contains inconsistent memories and conflicting versions of events. The narrator struggles unsuccessfully to uncover the "truth" behind his confusions, because this is what the autobiographical form demands. He constantly apologizes for what he does not remember: "Those first four years at Castledare compress into my mind as weeks—very much as a blur in time. Specific memories are fragmentary" (25). The narrator recognizes that this memory loss was induced by the traumatic events of his childhood and the shame that these incidents caused him:

Now I just wanted to forget all that early episode of my life. None of it
meant anything anymore. None of them could reach me or touch me now.
Although, I was still not able to discuss it with people; shame would overcome me, embarrassment, and the feeling that no-one would believe it all.
Possibly, I thought, a lot of it was my fault. (177)

According to the narrator, forgetting was easier than remembering, and it was
only from the temporal distance of adulthood that he was able to recognize
and interpret (rather than remember) some of the events of his childhood:

> I spent many years after leaving the orphanage deliberately trying to forget
> all about it. Those earlier years were the easiest to forget, due not only to
> the time frame and my age, but my inability to recognise that many things
> I regarded as "normal" were anything but that. I was not to discover this
> until much later. (25)

As in the nostalgic autobiographies discussed in the previous chapter,
the act of writing an autobiography is presented as a means of comprehension, of understanding the adult self within the context of childhood, and
of the autobiographer offering the community of readers the opportunity
to understand her or him better.[13] As discussed in earlier chapters and by
numerous autobiographical scholars, writing about trauma is commonly
thought of as a healing strategy; this is regularly invoked as a justification
for writing autobiographically about childhoods. For example, Knight dedi-
cates his autobiography to helping his family achieve a better understanding
of each other.

One of the key issues here is that the earlier admissions of memory loss
do not obstruct the writing of an autobiography of childhood; the narrator
reassures the reader that it is quite the opposite. Despite his admissions of
memory loss, the narrator of *Out of Darkness* stresses the "truth" in what
he does record. Amid the popular criticisms outlined earlier relating to
memory recall in traumatic childhoods in particular, this is a significant
assertion. On the one hand, this narrative could be viewed as a defender of
traumatic memory, accepting the limitations of both human memory and
the autobiographical form.[14] On the other hand, Knight's truth claims could
be considered a narrative strategy, part of the constructed authenticity of
this autobiography. For instance, in *Out of Darkness* the narrator is precise
about the first instance of sexual abuse he suffered, but mostly imprecise
about what followed. He remembers that it happened "every three weeks

or so" at the hands of a brother "(I think the same one)" (23). The narrator suggests that though the first incident remains "vivid,"

> most of the later nights are confused. Yet I know what occurred. I cannot recall the name of the particular brother, because later in life, when full realisation came to me as to what it was all about, I made a deliberate and conscious effort to repress it; to deny that it had ever happened. Many years were spent attempting to forget; not to re-live the experiences. In some ways I felt that I must have been responsible for what had happened. Certainly I was no saint and deserved many of the hidings I was later to get. (24)

In refusing narrative conventions, such as chronological details and the filling of memory gaps, the narrator makes important assertions on behalf of this particular autobiographical form. Details are not important—they do not "prove" the accuracy of his memory. *Out of Darkness* is concerned with breaking the silence imposed upon the child and revealing the falsities of the "official records" that represent the only documentation of his childhood. For example, the narrator explains how his childhood experiences were entirely marginalized in his official records. After running away and being apprehended, he writes, "no one from the department ever interviewed me. They were not interested in hearing any reasons from me for running away" (110). Knight is nicknamed "Nitty" by the brothers. In denying him his name, they inscribe an identity, a personal history, upon Knight that does not belong to him. It is a particularly empowering moment for the narrator when he is able to shed the nickname given to him and regain his sense of self through his real name: "Henceforth I was simply ME, not 'Nitty Knight,' a State Ward, who had to report his whereabouts to an uncaring authority" (177).

Out of Darkness maps the difficult movement toward creating a narrative of Knight's life, particularly the tension that exists between personal memory and cultural memory. The narrator describes an incident when he was working on a farm and disclosed some of the events of his childhood to his employers and workmates:

> Some of the Trigwell family questioned me about life in the various orphanages. I replied with some candour about things generally, but not too specifically about my own bad experiences. I found they lost interest very quickly. Later, on the way to the toilet I overheard one say to another that I "was a lying little shit." Obviously, they were convinced that I was

fabricating or exaggerating, or both. The incident made me more wary of discussing such matters with anyone. Who would believe me? (139)

The narrator cannot tell his story openly at this time because his memories are not part of cultural memory. In comparison, the autobiography of childhood mode of the 1990s and 2000s creates grounds for the recovery of these memories as truth. The authority of this autobiography lies within the plain-speaking autobiographical voice that stresses its limitations. The broader revelations of institutional abuse outlined earlier that circulate at the same moment as Knight's narrative work to authenticate *Out of Darkness*. The permeation of traumatic memory into cultural memory fills the gaps in his narrative.

In constructing an autobiography of childhood as a reaction to official histories, and despite acknowledgments of the fragility of his childhood memories, *Out of Darkness* foregrounds autobiographical "truth" as a leveler, with the capacity to redress the injustices of the past. It is the autobiographical form, a dialogic encounter, that brings this narrative and the child who endured it "out of [the] darkness." For example, the adult narrator seeks to liberate his child self from feelings of guilt:

> Why didn't I simply refuse to go to the brother's room? Why did I partici-
> pate in what he did? Couldn't I have yelled and screamed and kicked and
> refused to be compliant? To whom would I have addressed my complaint,
> had I dared to complain? When one does not know any better, even the
> grossest behaviour becomes normal. Quite simply, I did not know any
> better, and so came to accept things, even though I was unable to reconcile
> the behaviour of the brothers with their teachings. I always had more ques-
> tions than answers. (24)

This admission of confusion again reinforces his childhood disempowerment. It is only as an adult, in a cultural environment that supports his claim, that the narrator can address this shame.

One of the key consequences of presenting an autobiography of childhood with distorted memories is that it demands an active reader. *Out of Darkness* employs a simple, conventional narrative structure: Chapters represent different blocks of one- to six-year periods of his life. These chapters are based around the different locations of his childhood, from the institutions he lived in to his eventual laboring jobs. The narrative is chronological. It also often foreshadows the implications of events, such as the consequences of his childhood optimism: "Little simpleton, I did not know what Clontarf was really going to bring me" (53). Although *Out of Darkness* does not make use of a naïve child narrator, the adult narrator stresses his childhood naïveté throughout the autobiography. For example, he describes the first time he was molested by a brother: "That bed looked very warm and inviting. Gratefully, I climbed into it. What would any five-year-old boy do?" (21). The narrative presents graphic depictions of abuse; often these incidents are framed within the child's consciousness, and consequently the retrospective narrator does not name or explain them to the reader. For instance, the narrator explains his childhood reaction to abuse: "I was frightened, not knowing what was happening, nor what to do" (22). In such constructions the narrator, like the child, appears vulnerable. The reader is placed in a position of knowledge and responsibility, to witness and recognize these events as a consequence of abuse.

Thus, Knight's *Out of Darkness* works to convince the reader of its truthfulness through its acknowledgment of memory loss. In doing so, the text shapes its authority through connections to cultural memory, such as its timeliness alongside other "stolen" childhoods.

Jenny Diski's *Skating to Antarctica* (1997), though a very differently styled autobiography, also makes use of an adult retrospective narrator who writes about childhood despite acknowledging memory loss. In *Skating to Antarctica* novelist Diski merges the story of her 1950s–1960s childhood with a travelogue of a 1990s trip to Antarctica. She refashions particular incidents previously used in her fictional writing into the autobiographical form. Traveling to Antarctica represents Diski's desire for peace, quiet, and emptiness, which she believes she will find in the "whiteness" of Antarctica. What the experience does provoke, however, is memories of her youth and childhood—of the whiteness of the psychiatric institutions she found herself in as a child.

As suggested earlier, Diski's narrative is inconsistently concerned with narrating her childhood and adolescent experiences, interweaving these events with that of traveling to Antarctica as an adult in search of an "other" space. For the narrator whiteness is symbolic of escape, like the psychiatric wards that provided an escape from her traumatic childhood and adolescence.

Diski's narrator implies that she is able to forget about her childhood for some years until her daughter begins researching her family. Her daughter's research coincides with the narrator's trip to Antarctica, and the physical journey, which represents a highly unconventional travel narrative, becomes the catalyst for an autobiographical journey and, eventually, the writing of this childhood autobiography. Francis Spufford suggests that there are three selves in *Skating to Antarctica*:

> There's the present Diski, with her all white flat and her practised grasp on
> survival; there's young Diski with her Nembutal, a lemming prancing on
> a clifftop; remoter again, and much more disturbing to the present status
> quo, there's little Jennifer, who was too small in relation to the parental
> thunderstorm. (12)

The "self" that is missing from this equation is the literary narrator, who
appears in the mold of literary autobiographers such as Robert Drewe and
Lorna Sage discussed in earlier chapters. This narrative is dissimilar to the
uncomplicated, conversational style of narrative used in Fairhurt's, Fisher's,
and Knight's autobiographies. Amid the numerous admissions of memory
loss in *Skating to Antarctica* (which I discuss later), there is a sense that this
narrator represents a writer who is well aware of the artistry of, and debates
surrounding, autobiography. The narrator refers to herself as "Jenny Diski,"
author of previous novels, who is preoccupied with questions of consciousness and memory.

Such gestures imply that this will not be a conventional traumatic autobiography of childhood. When compared with the other autobiographies
discussed in this chapter, which disclose their politics and ideologies readily,
Skating to Antarctica is ambiguous and even contradictory. There is very little
reassurance of its "truth"; it is not chronological, and the narrator presents the
story of her childhood, from birth to mid-adolescence, in two pages. There is
a parallel (travel) narrative occurring alongside the narration of the childhood, which disrupts any easy generic classification of this text. The narrator
addresses the reader and wills him/her to be confused by the structure of her
narrative: "You are, perhaps, by now a little chronologically confused. It's
hardly surprising, my childhood and adolescence were busy times. Sometimes
I get confused myself about the order of events during those days. Why
shouldn't you?" (101) Here the narrator is making specific appeals to readers
of autobiography and their presumed expectations, as readers of literary
fiction would be likely to be familiar with such complexities. Thus, the
narrator urges her readers to consider this text an autobiographical anomaly,
but an autobiography nonetheless; this appearance is crucial to the issues
explored in *Skating to Antarctica*.

The narrator approaches her childhood memories with a great deal of
postmodern skepticism (perhaps appropriate for a writer of literary fiction).
She painstakingly establishes herself as an unreliable narrator: "Sometimes
I think I don't think at all, if thinking means some conscious process of the
mind working out the nature and solution of a problem. I'm a little ashamed

of this. I wish I thought properly, like proper people seem to think" (4). The narrator muses over the possibilities of self-representation through memory. Such musings seem self-consciously reminiscent of debates on cultural memory that occur in theoretical debates. In addition, Diski's narrator admits to not respecting the truth because her parents never did: "Truth, I learned, was up for grabs, entirely dependent on who was doing the telling" (100). The overall suggestion is that the reader should approach this narrative with the same skepticism with which it approaches itself. And yet such an apology, seemingly necessary within the literary context in which it is produced, also works to convey an authority upon this text. The narrator has acknowledged and continues to openly insist upon the limitations of the autobiography of childhood form.

In *Skating to Antarctica* the adult narrator refers to her child self in the third person, similar to John Boyle's adult narrator in the framing of *Galloway Street* discussed in the previous chapter. Boyle's narrator does this to suggest the accessibility of his child self: "He stands on the sidelines of my life, in the shadows, watchful, reproachful. He knows all my anecdotes; he beats me to the punchlines; he is not impressed" (xi). But Diski's narrator suggests the difficulties, even impossibilities, of accessing the childhood self. In the chapter titled "Whatever Happened to Jennifer?" the narrator refers to her child self as Jennifer, as if she were a fictional character in a book she was reading or writing:

> I remember Jennifer with about the same clarity that I remember the young Jane Eyre, Mary from *The Secret Garden*, Peter Pan and Alice. Rather less clarity, in fact, since the last four are readily available on my bookshelves. . . . Jennifer, I've merely remembered from time to time over an increasing distance of years, and with each remembering, each re-remembering, the living, flesh-and-blood fact of her slips incrementally from my grasp. (85)[15]

The narrator takes this proposition even further by suggesting that her child self is no less fictional than a fictional character: "The thing about Jennifer is that there is no corroborating evidence for her existence these past thirty years, as there has been for the child characters in books I once read and continue to read" (85). The narrator suggests that she might have "made her [the child self] up" (86). In proposing this, the narrator invites the reader's suspicion about any representation of childhood that *Skating to Antarctica* (or any other autobiography, for that matter) might offer:

> I am not fettered by history, by an absolute sense of telling-the-truth
> or making-things-up. I'm free to play around with who Jennifer was,
> might have been, never could have been. Sometimes it seems that I can
> get closer to her, or an essence of her precisely because of the distance
> between us. (86)

In an intriguing twist, the narrator then allows herself to remember and write
about her childhood by qualifying the validity of anything she may write. For
example, after introducing Jennifer in the third person the narrator proceeds
to slip into a first-person narrative to recount her experiences.

These stylistic choices prompt a number of questions: What is this autobiography for? Why is it not written as fiction? Was it penned merely as
a critique of the autobiography of childhood form? There is no strong
evidence to suggest that the latter is the case. A more likely explanation is
that this narrative seeks to broaden the parameters of the form and to use
it to incorporate and explore some of the debates about autobiography and
memory. In offering new possibilities and presenting new challenges to the
autobiography of childhood, *Skating to Antarctica* may be seeking to avoid the
kinds of criticisms that have plagued others who have chosen to write about
their childhoods.

Diski's narrator, like Knight's, considers how "forgetting" is often a survival
strategy, which is a very important feature of traumatic autobiography. Diski's
narrator asks, "Shouldn't I be grateful to my unconscious for the protection
it provided? Surely, it is neurotic to seek pain, where ordinary unhappiness
is available?" (22). Yet *Skating to Antarctica* extends the notion of productive
forgetting to suggest how the value of remembering has become a modern
cliché of popular psychology:

> That fully analysed person, the one whose unconscious is laid bare, who is
> in command of their psyche: what dreams do they have, what games can
> they play, and who can they talk to on equal terms, in a world where the
> vast majority of us are rubbing along leading an altogether murkier sort
> of inner life? . . . I gave up searching for anguish and settled for naïve tran-
> quillity. What I didn't know didn't seem to hurt me. (22)

The need to write and know one's past represents the antithesis of the narrator's aforementioned desire for whiteness or nothingness. Thus, her "naïve
tranquillity" does not last (or does it?) as the narrator begins to construct
her childhood. Throughout this construction the text "skates" paradoxically
around the narrator's need to remember and her ability to forget phases of

her childhood. For example, when the narrator visits her parents' former neighbors she is affronted when one of them, Mrs. Rosen, presumes that she would not remember that her childhood was not "a very happy childhood" (96). This section of *Skating to Antarctica* quotes dialogue that apparently occurred between the narrator and Mrs. Rosen. The insertion of this dialogue provides another fascinating dimension to the debates about memory and knowledge that pervade the text:

> I was thrown by Mrs Rosen's genuine surprise that I recollected my childhood as being less than classically happy. At first I wondered if the idea of false memory syndrome had seeped deeper in to the general consciousness than I had supposed. Why would I have blanked out what she seemed to remember? Because I couldn't stand to remember it, would be the post-Freudian supposition. But more likely the source of her surprise was the pre-Freudian notion that children are not really conscious entities. A comforting thought this for parents who can manage it. (96–97)

The narrator uses this instance to assert her ability to remember her childhood and to affirm the consciousness of the child, such as the capacity of the child to recognize and evaluate her circumstances. Such statements reveal something more about the politics of this narrative, including its interest in advocating the child's consciousness of trauma and the rights of the child. "Remembering" plays an important part in such advocacy:

> The sound of my parents fighting in our two-roomed flat on the third floor echoed through the corridors of Paramount Court, my father leaving several times, my mother being stretchered away to hospital, the furniture and fittings being confiscated by debt collectors when we were on the fifth floor: these were all public events, but somehow, it was assumed, I wouldn't retain a memory of those things. Adults experience, children don't. (97)

It is from this exchange with Mrs. Rosen, amid tense explorations of memory, that the narrator's childhood abuse is revealed: "After a quiet moment Mrs. Rosen asked hesitantly, lowering her voice, 'Tell me, did he ever abuse you, your father?'" (113). This incites the narrator to return to the process of externalizing and contextualizing her personal history. The narrator expresses skepticism regarding this conservative, middle-aged woman's ability to engage with the issue of child abuse:

This [suggestion of abuse] was jolting, coming in this room of respectable, elderly people, for whom discretion and decency were keys to contentment. Extraordinary that the delicately thoughtful Mrs Rosen could have voiced this thought, amid the china ornaments and professionally posed photographs in her immaculate living room. In the hush that awaited my answer, I realized fully how the word "abuse" has become such a pervasive modern euphemism, suggestive yet unclear, a declaration of something shocking without saying anything shocking. . . . It felt like a trick question, one that needed careful definition, this company would not want too frank an answer. (113)

It is the presumption that Mrs. Rosen would not want to know what happened that convinces the narrator, who has already acknowledged her ambivalence about truth, to lie to her. Her presumption proves correct; what remains unsaid to Mrs. Rosen is communicated to the reader.

In writing about the abuse she suffered, the narrator asserts the fundamental difficulties of autobiographical representations of childhood: the inability to capture and represent an event as it was (or for the reader to witness it as it was). For example, the narrator denies the reader the opportunity to immediately comprehend and judge the victims and perpetrators of these events:

What flashed into my mind as I considered what to say next, were those nights, many of them, when my naked mother . . . would enter my room . . . shake me awake telling me I had to go and sleep with my father because she wasn't going to sleep in the same bed as him. . . .

I adored being held in his arms and feeling his big hands stroking me. Stroking me where? Everywhere, I think. I took in his physical affection like draughts of delicious drinks. I don't ever recall feeling anything but safe and loved in this private midnight comforting. . . .

There was a game both my parents used to play when I was small on the occasions when they were in accord. Usually after an evening bath, I would dry myself in the living room and then run naked between them as each, on opposite sides of the room reached out for my vagina and tried to tickle it. When they caught me, their fingers at my vulva, I would squeal and shriek and wriggle with the equivocal agony tickling engenders, and the game would go on until I was exhausted and they were weak with laughter. (115)

Diski's narrator does not label her parents' actions as abuse, nor does she discuss it at length within the text. This increases the impact of the depiction because, as in Knight's autobiography, it may unsettle the reader's expectations and make particular demands on them to recognize and interpret events the narrator is unable or unwilling to. This representation of abuse serves to demonstrate the difference between a child's and an adult's perceptions or consciousness of abuse. The narrator suggests that as a young child she was unable to distinguish between affection and manipulation or affection and abuse.

This marginalization of the abuse narrative in Diski's narrative works to emphasize her experiences of abuse in ways very different from the more graphic descriptions of Fairhurst and Knight. One explanation is that this less explicit mode of narration is a consequence of Diski having been silenced on this issue throughout her childhood. She is looking for ways of speaking, of explaining the events of her childhood; existing templates prove to be inadequate.[16] Diski is concerned with the complexities, even impossibilities, of writing about abuse in the form of a deeply personal, experiential narrative. Yet, as I have previously argued in relation to Diski, this mode of writing can also be considered a product of the socio-literary positioning of the particular autobiographer. For example, what and how an autobiographer can write are affected by the writer's authorial position, whether as a literary autobiographer or a first-time author using the autobiographical mode. As Linda Martín Alcoff and Laura Gray-Rosendale argue, "In many speaking situations some participants are accorded the authoritative status of interpreters and others are constructed as 'naïve transmitters of raw experience'" (202). Similarly, in autobiographies of childhoods some writers are perceived to be writing from a critical distance, whereas others are thought to be writing from crude honesty. The lines are often drawn depending on whether an autobiography is seen to be "literary" (like Diski's, Drewe's, or Sage's, which are credited with having critical distance) or "popular" (like Fisher's or Fairhurst's, which are thought to be imbued with crude honesty).

Autobiographies of childhood have the potential to broaden the socially constructed limits of traumatic narratives by, for example, provocatively complicating notions of victim and perpetrator, healing and forgiveness. However, while the act of speaking out against abuse can reform power relationships, it can also (through repetition) work to enforce accepted patterns of speech and disclosure—maintaining existing boundaries of acceptability and sanctioning particular norms for the survivor narrative—such as

Fisher the protective father, Fairhurst the child advocate, and Knight writing
for familial catharsis (Martín Alcoff and Gray-Rosendale 198).

This chapter has found a plurality of traumatic narratives that work in
different ways and reveal diverse investments in childhood trauma and its
narration. These texts circulate meanings for childhood abuse, and they
have found their cultural moment (paradoxically) through repetition and
novelty—through repeating established tropes of survivor narrative templates
and by attempting to extend the boundaries of acceptable representation,
from Fairhurst's graphic representation of his abused body to Diski's refusal to
brand her parents as abusers. I agree wholeheartedly with Haaken, who argues
that the circulation of diverse trauma narratives can only deepen our collective understanding of the complexities of being a "survivor." Haaken writes,
"We need to claim as much cultural space as we can for meaningful debate,
for exploring the ambiguities and uncertainties that emerge as . . . [survivors]
struggle to find their own voices, past and present" (117). Rather than focus on
the veracity of autobiographical writing, and make accusations about sensationalism, literary critics should focus more closely upon abuse narratives as
cultural texts that link therapy and literature in important ways. Literature,
like therapy, has become a powerful mediator of child abuse.

CHAPTER 6

ETHICS

WRITING ABOUT CHILD ABUSE,
WRITING ABOUT ABUSIVE PARENTS

What are the author's responsibilities to those whose lives are used as "material"?

—G. Thomas Couser, *Vulnerable Subjects*

I always win the [bleeped]-up-childhood contest . . . no matter who's in the room.

—Augusten Burroughs, quoted in
Hank Stuever, "Growing Up Truly Absurd"

In the prologue to her autobiography of childhood *Ugly: The True Story of a Loveless Childhood*, Constance Briscoe describes a visit she made to Social Services when she was eleven years old. She asks the woman at the reception desk if she can book herself into a children's home. The woman replies: "You cannot refer yourself to a children's home, luvvie. You need to get your parents' consent first. Why don't you go home and think about it? . . . I can't book you in just because you feel like leaving home. Do you want us to contact your mother?" Constance replies, "No thanks . . . I'll handle it myself" (1). Afraid that she will receive another beating from her mother, Constance goes home and drinks a glass of diluted bleach. She writes: "I chose Domestos because Domestos kills all known germs and my mother had for so long told me that I was a germ. I felt very sick, happy and sad. I was happy because tonight, if the bleach worked, I would die" (2). Briscoe survived to write her autobiography. She went on to become a barrister and one of the first black women to sit as a judge in the United Kingdom (Meeke).

Briscoe's autobiography describes the physical and emotional abuse she endured from her mother during her childhood. Writing about child abuse presents a way for abuse sufferers to address the abuse, disclose intimate details from the past, and declare oneself a survivor. However, in declaring oneself a survivor of abuse, someone else must be declared as the perpetrator; in autobiographies of childhood, as in life, this is most often the parent or guardian. Autobiographies of childhood are necessarily relational; they become "auto/biographies" conveying the life narratives of both the author and his or her parent/s. They are also what G. Thomas Couser refers to as "intimate life writing—that done within families or couples." Couser writes, "The closer the relationship between writer and subject . . . the higher the ethical stakes" (*Vulnerable Subjects* xii). Who is the auto/biographer responsible to in constructing his or her life narrative, or, as Couser asks, "What are the author's responsibilities to those whose lives are used as 'material'?" (34). And do the stakes shift if the author is writing about child abuse? In comparing and contrasting three auto/biographical depictions of abusive parents—Constance Briscoe's *Ugly* (2006), Augusten Burroughs's *Running with Scissors* (2002), and Dave Pelzer's *A Child Called "It"* (1995)—I explore the ethical dilemmas that underlie these different auto/biographical projects—whether the author demonstrates an awareness of these ethics or not. In these auto/biographies we can see the tension between the weight of traumatic life writing, or the need to write, and the ethical responsibilities that relational auto/biography, and more particularly children writing about parents, summons.

Humor and Trauma: Augusten Burroughs's *Running with Scissors*

Running with Scissors, published in 2002, is a highly comic autobiography of childhood. Told in a series of hilarious vignettes, it recounts Burroughs's experiences living with the highly unusual Finch family—led by his mother's psychiatrist, Dr. Finch—in Massachusetts during the 1970s. Burroughs was sent to live with the Finch family shortly after his parents split and his mother began her association with Dr. Finch. *Running with Scissors* is filled with witty, often outrageous anecdotes, as the reader follows the young Augusten Burroughs through (what Burroughs depicts as) a neglected and exploited childhood. *Running with Scissors* was made into a film (released in 2007). Burroughs has penned two nonfictional accounts of his adult life: *Dry* (2003) and *Possible Side Effects* (2006). He also wrote a second autobiography of childhood, *A Wolf at the Table* (2008), which details his early childhood spent with his mentally ill, alcoholic father. Burroughs's father is largely absent from *Running with Scissors*, save an early reference and sporadic mentions in the latter part of the text.

Running with Scissors turned out to be a highly successful and highly contentious memoir. In 2005, six members of the Turcotte family sued Burroughs's publisher for defamation—believing that the Finch family is based on their lives. The Turcottes claim that Burroughs fabricated and/or exaggerated behaviors and events, portraying the family as "an unhygienic, foul, and mentally unstable cult engaged in bizarre and, at times, criminal activity" (Mehegan). According to the Turcottes the book overtly aligns the fictional Finch family with the Turcottes—for example, providing directions to the family home—and apparently Burroughs dropped the Turcotte name in an interview with *People* magazine in September 2002 (a point Burroughs rebutted). As a result, the Turcottes have been subject to embarrassment and ridicule. They spoke back to Burroughs's claims in an interview with *Vanity Fair* in 2007 (Bissinger; Mehegan). The Turcottes are upset that Burroughs did not tell them he was writing about them. They are disappointed in what they see as lies and exaggeration within the text, and generally that he has done nothing to protect their identities within the text.

Literary critics observed the Burroughs case carefully for what it might reveal about the legal and ethical boundaries affecting autobiographies of childhood (Mehegan). It reopened a range of questions around the ethics of representing family and friends in "your" autobiography. For example, what *Running with Scissors* revealed to publishers was that it is not enough simply to change characters' names when the location and events remain so identifiable. Perhaps not surprisingly, in the post–James Frey era, Burroughs and his publishers settled out of court with the Turcottes. Burroughs agreed to refer to *Running with Scissors* as a "book" rather than a "memoir" in the author's note (it is still referred to a "memoir" on the cover) and to alter the acknowledgments section to recognize that his version of events may be very different to that of the Turcottes (Ngowi).

One way to interpret *Running with Scissors* is that it is an exploitative, exaggerated attempt to gain laughs (and a successful writing career) at the expense of deeply flawed people such as Dr. Finch and deeply disempowered abuse sufferers such as Burroughs's mother, her girlfriends—Fern and Dorothy—and the Finch offspring.[1] As the lawsuit demonstrates, there are large ethical stakes here, and at the center of these debates are questions of truth in representation and the ethics and responsibilities of representing others. During an interview with *Vanity Fair* in 2006, Burroughs stood by his story, asserting that it was his story and that he had a right to tell it:

> This is my story. . . . It's not my mother's story and it's not the family's story, and they may remember things differently and they may choose to not remember certain things, but I will never forget what happened to me, ever, and I have the scars from it and I wanted to rip those scars off of me. (Bissinger)

At this point, it is worth considering what Burroughs is trying to accomplish through his representation of his mother and the Finches. Can we make an argument in favor of Burroughs's right to represent his life in the way that he has?

The title *Running with Scissors* emphasizes the extent to which Augusten (and the Finch children) lived a life removed from regular conventions of adult/child relationships. The children are allowed to "run with scissors"—to engage in potentially risky behaviors without parental admonition. *Running with Scissors* is preoccupied with what it means to be a child and to be a parent and what might lie beneath middle-American family façades.

To summarize: In *Running with Scissors*, parents are largely failures. The two parents whom Burroughs chiefly depicts in his autobiography are his mother and his designated father figure: Dr. Finch. We know (from the epilogue) that Burroughs's mother is still alive at the time he is writing but that he and his mother are estranged. In interviews, Burroughs is very frank about his feelings toward his mother: He has no desire to apologize for her or protect her. He says: "I love her but I don't like her. Some things are unforgivable" (Interview with Jane Sullivan). The reader is informed early in *Running with Scissors* that Burroughs's mother and father have a volatile and abusive relationship—with both possibly affected by mental illness:

> As time went on, my parents' relationship became worse, not better. My father grew more hostile and remote, taking a particular liking to metallic objects with serrated edges. And my mother began to go crazy.
>
> Not crazy in a *let's paint the kitchen bright red!* sort of way. But in a *gas oven, toothpaste sandwich, I am God* sort of way. Gone were the days when she would stand on the deck lighting lemon-scented candles without having to eat the wax. (28)

Burroughs describes one screaming match that escalated "until my father was chasing my mother through the house with a Danish fondue pot held high above his head" (22). This vivid, comic image constructed by the adult autobiographer belies what the young Augusten may have been experiencing at the time, and thus functions to sharpen the reader's interpretation of this event as traumatic.

In representing his parents this way, Burroughs uses humor as a means to defuse his own trauma. More specifically, he uses humor as a mode of self-defense against, even aggression toward, trauma perpetrators. As Sigmund Freud contends, humor is commonly used by those who have been repressed as a point of counter-aggression and/or confrontation (*Jokes*). Burroughs also uses humor as his primary mechanism for self-defense—as a means of stepping away from the trauma toward alternative experiences of the events of the past. For example, he uses humorous language to disparage his mother; it is unlikely that he was able to use humor to do so in the past. His representation of his mother and the Finches as absurd people rather than simply "bad" people makes his representation all the more complex and potent. Burroughs's story becomes all the more accessible precisely because he does not adopt the status of victim. He positions himself as a survivor and as an intelligent observer and commentator. His mother, Deirdre, according to Burroughs, is a shrink-dependent, matchstick-eating failed poet, who comes out as a lesbian shortly after divorcing his father. Burroughs describes his reaction to his mother's abandoning him to Dr. Finch: "As far as I was concerned, my mother was a bitch, period. She was a rare psychotic-confessional-poet strain of salmonella" (32); and later "I fantasized about slicing my mother's fingers off with the electric knife that was hanging by its cord from the curtain rod" (55). Such statements seem to be fueled by anger—but since the anger is a child's (and seems wholly founded) and is strongly couched in humor, Burroughs never allows his autobiography to become self-pitying or overtly hateful.

Despite his affection for Finch's daughters Hope and Natalie, particularly the latter, Augusten feels trapped and alienated in living with Dr. Finch: "There was enough confusion and distraction here to keep my mind off the fact that my parents didn't seem to want me" (66). Dr. Finch is represented as highly eccentric—a man who lives in squalor, who has a room in his house devoted to masturbation (the "Masturbatorium"), who believes that God is appearing in his feces, and who is ultimately accused of raping Burroughs's mother. He is constructed as an extremely unconventional role model. For example, Dr. Finch fakes a suicide attempt for the young Augusten—a ploy to allow Augusten to miss as much school as he wanted.

At the core of *Running with Scissors* is a consistent and overwhelming representation of adults failing their children. According to Burroughs, both Dr. Finch and his mother failed to discourage Augusten's adolescent sexual relationship with a thirty-something patient (and "adopted" son) of Dr. Finch, Neil Bookman. When Augusten "broke down" at age thirteen and confessed his relationship with Bookman to his mother, Burroughs recounts,

> she couldn't have been happier. "I am very, very fond of that young man," she told me, gazing off into a space beyond my left shoulder. "He's always been very supportive of me and my writing."
>
> "So you're not pissed?" I said, wondering if the fact that I was involved with a man twice my age would be yet another thing she had to worry about.
>
> "Look, Augusten," she began. "I don't want you to suffer from the same sort of oppression that I suffered from as a girl. Because I know"—she lit a More—"how difficult it is to reclaim one's self. I'll tell you, sometimes I wish I had been raised by a mother like me. You're very lucky that I've done so much work, emotionally. And it makes me so happy to be able to support you." (133)

From Dr. Finch, the adolescent Augusten learns that "living arrangements needed to remain fluid" (83). Dr. Finch "believed a person should choose his or her own parents" (83). Dr. Finch's daughter Natalie has a legal guardian— "Terrance Maxwell, who was forty-two and rich" (83). Natalie ends up a victim of domestic violence and returns home at age sixteen.

Continuing the theme of the pedophilic "pimping" of adolescents into adult relationships, Deirdre has a relationship with Dr. Finch's suicidal eighteen-year-old patient Dorothy. According to Burroughs, Dorothy was endowed with a large trust fund "because when she was younger he [her father] showed her his penis on a rowboat" (203). Burroughs's almost glib depiction of this incidence of molestation reveals the extent to which pedophilia had become an ingrained part of this world. Such statements allow the adult author Burroughs to be provocative—the humor reveals the absurdity, but also the danger, of the life that these children found themselves in. Later on in the memoir, Deirdre and Dorothy very briefly take on a "husband," Cesar Mendoza, who attempts to anally rape Augusten. Mendoza has sex with Deirdre, Dorothy, and Natalie (210). Again, Burroughs employs humor (they each contract a yeast infection) to distract from (and perhaps thus to draw attention to) the seriousness of his attempted rape.

Augusten feels that he is in love with Bookman. This is very different to the adult Burroughs, who in interviews describes himself as "freaked out" and "damaged" by his experiences with Bookman. It is notable, as Jane Sullivan asserts in her interview with Burroughs, that Burroughs is more overtly damning of his mother and the Finches in interviews than he is in books:

> When Burroughs talks about his childhood, he condemns the damage in an outright way he doesn't use in his writing. The psychiatrist: "Just pure evil, destructive, a complete cult that destroyed so many lives. I don't think he was intentionally malicious but he was completely insane."
>
> His mother: "Blame, blame, blame. Victim, victim, victim. She's literally said I've had such a hard life, you don't know how much I've suffered. I just think, Unless you were in Auschwitz, shut up, you privileged Southern woman."

However intertextual and complementary, the interview is an entirely different discourse to autobiography—imbued with different rules and reader expectations. In this interview, this is Burroughs the adult speaking—working to justify himself and his autobiography to the literary community. In *Running with Scissors*, Burroughs constructs the child Augusten via humor rather than anger. As I have argued in earlier chapters (and will continue to show in the chapter that follows), anger and regret are not valuable commodities in autobiographical writing about childhood. Humor and resilience amid trauma are. Ultimately, though *Running with Scissors* is not a narrative of forgiveness like many of the others I have discussed in this study, the humor employed within it provides Burroughs with a means for addressing his trauma, which, in turn, asserts his resilience. Humor provides Burroughs with literary kudos and a firm place within the writing-from-recovery paradigm.

Further, the humor in *Running with Scissors* makes this a highly provocative text. Burroughs is very likely well aware of the glut of traumatic texts that preceded his autobiography. This awareness is demonstrated in the quote from Burroughs that forms the first epigraph of this chapter. As a writer of an autobiography of childhood, Burroughs has to up the ante, to achieve something more than the stock coming-of-age-despite-trauma narrative. So, in *Running with Scissors*, events that might have been depicted as traumatic in the hands of another author are depicted with humor by Burroughs. But the trauma remains evident and potent. For example, as previously suggested,

Burroughs represents an incident in which he is almost raped by his mother's boyfriend:

> At just after midnight, I was awakened from a dream that a hard penis was pressing against my ass. It turned out there *was* a hard penis pressing against my ass.
>
> "What the fuck are you doing?" I said, shoving him off.
>
> He was completely naked, even his teeth were out of his mouth. "I only want to try," he gummed. "I love you, new son."
>
> "Get away from me," I said.
>
> I locked him out of the living room and went back to sleep on the sofa. My powers of denial were strong even then, and I was able to convince myself that it *didn't really matter because it didn't really happen*. When I heard him climbing the stairs to go find Deirdre and Dorothy, I figured he'd finally leave me alone. (210)

Amid the absurdity of the scene is a young boy who is almost raped, and who exhibits resilience beyond his years to cope. Burroughs emphasizes his survival instincts throughout the book—as a child he is intelligent and resourceful, growing up before he should:

> Like a sheep or a dog that can predict an earthquake, I had always been able to sense when my mother was about to go crazy. Her speech quickened, she stopped sleeping and she developed a craving for peculiar foods, like candle wax. (230)

Through all of this, Augusten is coming to terms with his own sexuality and making a future for himself. It is only when he emancipates himself from both his mother and the Finches that he is able to become an autonomous adult:

> So it came to this: Was I a turd-reading Finch? Or was I my crazy mother's son?
>
> In the end, I decided that I was neither. (299)

Burroughs-the-author has an agenda: to align his child self with his adult self in an unapologetic battle against his mother and the Finches. Ethics flies out the window. Burroughs gives his mother and the Finches no right of response. And *Running with Scissors* most probably appeals to readers on this level: precisely because it is a one-sided version of the truth that is digestible because it is so humorous; precisely because it is a renegade, unethical text with unconventional heroes and wacky villains. Burroughs, like Frank McCourt, presents himself as a heroic survivor of a miserable childhood:

> [I had] a sense that I must propel myself forward at all times. I didn't allow myself to feel scared or depressed or sorry for myself. . . .
>
> Humour was my life raft. I focused on the eccentric or the hilarious. I found it, even where there wasn't necessarily anything funny. It was a way to fool myself into believing everything was OK, when everything absolutely wasn't OK for many years.
>
> The other emotion I felt was hope. I always felt and believed that even if things were appalling today and yesterday and the day before, they might not be appalling tomorrow. (Interview with Jane Sullivan)

It is this construction of an authorial hero rescuing the child who could not rescue himself during childhood that draws the reader in. In suggesting that the child needs an adult advocate (the adult author), the author provides what the parents or guardians did not—protection for the child. We come to know the child and the adult author more than we can ever know the parent or guardian, and as a consequence the reader might be unlikely to care to hear the latter's version of events. The autobiographer's rights become paramount—primarily because he has chosen to share his story with us.

In this way, autobiographies of childhood tap into cultural contexts that are receptive of trauma stories. Janice Haaken proposes that there has never been a better time to circulate childhood trauma narratives; cultural environments have never been more receptive:

> Survivors who tell their stories do have more cultural support than they have had in the past, and there is a growing challenge to parental authority from the professional community. Standards and expectations of good parenting have risen, and the right of parents to control their children is no longer considered absolute.
>
> Such advances in the recognition of children's rights mobilize tremendous ambivalence in many parents, particularly in a society where parents, and most particularly mothers, are blamed for the problems and suffering of their children. (*Pillar of Salt* 33)

Haaken highlights the potential cost to parents of the privileged centering of the child's narrative truth. This is nowhere more evident than in Burroughs's text—which highlights the ethical contest that occurs when people remember differently, and when memories become public. The ascendancy of these texts relies heavily on their relationship to rights-of-the child debates—in a universal belief in, and commitment to, hearing the traumatized child. This commitment is also evident in the circulation of Dave Pelzer's autobiography *A Child Called "It."*

The Rights of the Child: Dave Pelzer's *A Child Called "It"* and Constance Briscoe's *Ugly*

In *A Child Called "It"* Dave Pelzer writes of the physical and emotional abuse he endured at the hands of his alcoholic (and possibly mentally ill—though this is not addressed) mother when he was between the ages of four and twelve. His mother stops calling him by his name (calling him "boy" or "it") and banishes him from family life, forcing him to live in the basement. He is tortured, humiliated, poisoned, starved, and denied contact with his siblings. His father does not act to save Dave from the abuse. Dave was rescued by schoolteachers at age twelve and taken into foster care. *A Child Called "It"* was an international bestseller and featured on *The Oprah Winfrey Show*. Pelzer has written two sequels to *A Child Called "It"*: *The Lost Boy* and *A Man Named Dave*. He has also penned a self-help book titled *Help Yourself*. Pelzer is well known as a motivational speaker—a high-profile spokesperson against child abuse.

Like Burroughs, Pelzer has been challenged over the veracity of his memoirs. Pelzer's younger brother Stephen and his grandmother have each suggested that Pelzer exaggerated events depicted in his memoir—and misrepresented his own behavior.[2] Pelzer has also been criticized on the grounds that he is a "professional victim"—milking his experiences opportunistically for fame and money:

> Pelzer is relentless in peddling his books. He speaks more than 270 days a year, and after many of his talks he sells copies of his books to the crowd assembled there. To watch him work is to be put in mind of those itinerant preachers of the early part of last century. They traveled the dusty back roads of America, put up their revival tents in an open field and then laid on hands and healed, or swindled, their believers. In Pelzer's case, how much he is healing or how much he is swindling is unclear and

depends in large part on whether or not you believe the horrific story he has so profitably told and retold and continues, day after day, to tell. (Jordan)

There is even a suggestion that he buys his own books to keep them on the bestseller lists (Jordan).

Like Burroughs, then, Pelzer is a controversial autobiographer—accused of exploiting his experiences—and labeled as unethical. However, Pelzer's approach to his abuse narrative is entirely different to that of Burroughs. Though Pelzer's aim, like Burroughs,' is to expose abusive parents, Pelzer represents the abuse he suffered in graphic detail, employing a somber tone and using highly emotive but entirely accessible language (compared with Burroughs's humorous, often flippant representations). The abuse that Pelzer suffered at the hands of his mother includes being repeatedly beaten (including having his face smashed, and his tears smeared, against a mirror while being ordered to repeat "I'm a bad boy! I'm a bad boy" over and over), a broken arm, burns, poisoning, an attempted drowning, a stabbing, and being deprived of food and clothing. *A Child Called "It"* reads like a long list of abusive incidents and behaviors. Just when the reader thinks he or she has reached the limit, Pelzer adds a layer.

A not so sophisticated between-the-lines reading of the events in *A Child Called "It"* suggests that Pelzer's mother is suffering from a mental illness, not coping with raising children alone while her husband is away working. According to Pelzer:

About this time, Mom's behavior began to change radically. At times Father was away at work, she would spend the entire day lying on the couch, dressed only in her bathrobe, watching television. Mom got up only to go to the bathroom, get another drink or heat leftover food. When she yelled at us, her voice changed from the nurturing mother to the wicked witch. . . . After a while, I could determine what kind of day I was going to have by the way she dressed. I would breathe a sigh of relief whenever I saw Mom come out of her room in a nice dress with her face made up. On these days she always came out with a smile. (30)

By positioning his narrative as a child's-eye view of events, Pelzer is able to bypass assessing or commenting on his mother's illness. As a consequence, Pelzer's mother is simply demonized within the narrative as a Jekyll-and-Hyde character who oscillates between being very loving and being extremely abusive. Meanwhile, the innocent child is left to suffer through horrific abuse, and through the shame that followed, and to fantasize about a better life.

Pelzer seeks to shift his childhood shame from his childhood self and onto the perpetrator of his abuse—his mother. Pelzer represents his mother's actions as inexplicable. For example, after one instance (of many) in which his mother deprives him of food, Pelzer recalls:

> I stood before her dumbstruck. I didn't know what to do or say. All I could think of was "Why?" I couldn't understand why she treated me the way she did. I was so close that I could smell every morsel. I knew she wanted me to cave in, but I stood fast and held back the tears. (106)

Apart from the teachers who eventually rescue him, the young Dave is positioned as entirely alone. As his mother is abusing him, he imagines that God has abandoned him:

> I lost circulation in much of my body, as I sat on my hands in the "prisoner of war" position. I began to give up on God. I felt that He must have hated me. *What other reason could there be for a life like mine?* All my efforts for mere survival seemed futile. My attempts to stay one step ahead of Mother were useless. A black shadow was always over me. (111)

In the scheme of Pelzer's narrative, it is only Pelzer (no one else, not even a higher power) who can save him. Such statements are important in establishing Pelzer (both inside and outside of the text) as the survivor and hero of this story. In *A Child Called "It,"* Pelzer overtly positions himself as a survivor—as a child who is able to strategize to save himself from the abuse:

> Standing alone in that damp, dark garage, I knew, for the first time, that I could survive. I decided that I would use any tactic I could think of to defeat Mother or to delay her from her grisly obsession. I knew if I wanted to live, I would have to think ahead. I could no longer cry like a helpless baby. In order to survive, I could never give in to her. That day I vowed to myself that I would never, ever again give that bitch the satisfaction of hearing me beg her to stop beating me. . . .
>
> Even the sun seemed to avoid me, as it hid in a thick cloud cover that drifted overhead. I slumped my shoulders, retreating into the solitude of my dreams. (43)

The narrative functions as an extended justification of Pelzer's right to speak—his ethical right to expose this abuse, for his own sake and for the sake of other abuse sufferers. For Pelzer, no one else's ethical rights can surmount this.

In the afterword to *A Child Called "It,"* titled "Dave Pelzer: Survivor," Pelzer assumes an adult voice—the voice of a survivor—to add the final layer to his narrative. Pelzer contextualizes his story:

> As a child living in a dark world, I feared for my life and thought I was alone. As an adult I know now that I was not alone. There were thousands of other abused children. (161)

Yet Pelzer, who paradoxically asserts that this is "my story and mine alone" (165), again declares his agenda—the rights of the child to protection over the rights of an adult to "discipline" his or her child:

> Sources of information vary, but I estimated that one in five children are physically, emotionally or sexually abused in the United States. Unfortunately, there are those among the uninformed public who believe that most abuse is nothing more than parents exerting their "right" to discipline their children and letting it get out of hand. (161)

Again, such statements work as a defense of the autobiography of childhood—the right of the adult to tell the story of childhood without admonition. Pelzer's narrative celebrates openness and disclosure, defending the child's right to tell—to speak out and to speak back—over the parent's right to privacy. Perhaps anticipating challenges to his story, Pelzer's text is polyvocal—constructing a child's voice (the apparent eyewitness), the adult Pelzer in the afterword, and finally the narrative of Stephen E. Ziegler, Pelzer's teacher, following the afterword. The three voices we hear each work to affirm the veracity of Pelzer's story, as if, in the current climate of doubting life writing, one voice is not enough.

Pelzer's autobiography is overtly didactic:

> What you have just read is a story of an ordinary family that was devastated by their hidden secret. The story has two objectives: the first is to inform the reader how a loving, caring parent can change to a cold, abusive monster venting frustrations on a helpless child; the second is

the eventual survival and triumph of the human spirit over seemingly insurmountable odds. (164)

Again, it is not simply enough for Pelzer to position himself within the survivor narrative paradigm—he feels it necessary to overtly guide the reader toward the text's greater purpose. Pelzer likens his defending the rights-of-the-child mandate to his previous military service:

> For over 13 years I served my country in the military. I now serve my country giving seminars and workshops to others in need, helping them to break their chains. . . .
>
> Today there are millions around the world in desperate need of help. It is my mission to assist those in need of a helping hand. I believe it is important for people to know that no matter what lies in their past, they can overcome the dark side and press on to a brighter world. It is perhaps a paradox that without the abuse of my past, I might not be what I am today. Because of the darkness in my childhood, I have a deep appreciation for life. I was fortunate enough to turn tragedy into triumph. (165)

Pelzer gains his authority to speak (like McCourt and Ashworth, as discussed in chapter 3) from his adult successes. He positions his adult self as a survivor who has succeeded despite, and in spite of, his childhood. But more importantly, he constructs himself as the antithesis of his mother—a worthy citizen of America whose autobiography and motivational speeches provide a "service" to fellow abuse survivors.

However, if *I* wanted to know more about Pelzer's mother, it is probable that many readers would also be dissatisfied with Pelzer's treatment of her and of his childhood self more generally. Readers of autobiographies of childhood such as Pelzer's are placed in a difficult bind: To challenge Pelzer's claims or even his methods of storytelling is to lack empathy and to risk inflicting further shame upon the traumatized subject. For this reason, traumatic autobiographies of childhood—particularly those that testify to child abuse—often appear to be critically untouchable. But this should never be the case. The spirit of testimony is writing back to resist enforced silences and to assert previously marginalized narratives. In turn, testimony should invite informed debate upon itself.

In *Ugly*, Briscoe finds herself in very similar ethical terrain to Pelzer's. Briscoe, like Pelzer, recounts how her biological mother subjected her to constant abuse throughout her childhood: from name-calling to punching and kicking, spitting at her, and depriving her of food. Briscoe writes:

> By the time I was seven, my beatings were as regular as ever. The [bed-wetting] alarm failed to wake me, yet my mother always heard it. She would dash into my room when she heard it ring and drag me out of bed. Sometimes when she came into my room, she would remove the wet bedclothes and give me a mighty slap on the bare backside, then leave me naked and shivering. My humiliation was complete. Not only was I unable to prevent myself wetting the bed, the mere presence of my mother and/or a bedtime beating made me so nervous that I sometimes emptied my bladder in front of her. (11–12)

According to the autobiography, in Briscoe's late adolescence, her mother tried to disrupt her efforts to go to university. And Deirdre Fernand states, "In 1999 [Briscoe's mother] tried to sabotage Briscoe's career, writing to the Bar Council to allege that her daughter had hired a hitman to kill her. The council dismissed the claim as unsubstantiated" (Fernand). Briscoe's mother is now reportedly suing Briscoe for defamation because of the contents of *Ugly* (Saunders).

This is clearly not a happy story, and the writing of it has deepened the conflict. Pelzer, Burroughs, and Briscoe each face a multitude of ethical dilemmas when writing about a parent. John D. Barbour discusses these dilemmas:

> One of the most significant ethical dimensions of life writing is the writer's evaluation of his or her parents. . . . A central theme in many autobiographies is judging one's parents, as the author sorts out what parental virtues he affirms and which things he denies, at least as normative for his own life (73).[3]

In other words, an adult autobiographer who retrospectively writes about his or her parent necessarily contextualizes his or her parent's life within his or her own adult life—within his or her own values and morals. The parent's life experiences are thus decontextualized and reinterpreted years on by a child (now adult) who might (at best) remember only particular aspects of his or her experiences with the parent, and whose perceptions have since become infused by an assortment of inescapable cultural memories. Barbour goes on to argue:

There are several reasons why we should be careful about judging others. . . . To the degree that a writer focuses on her relationship to a parent, she must explore the parent's life, explaining how the parent came to have specific values and a certain moral character. . . . Intergenerational autobiography is a matter of both judging and "not judging." Moral judgment is not negated but made more complex by causal interpretations of behaviour, by forgiveness, and by scruples about the appearance or reality of self-righteousness. (73–74)

There is a much-spoken-of unspoken rule within contemporary autobiography that writers must not appear too bitter in their depiction of their childhood or too condemnatory of their parents. Bitterness appears as uncontrolled emotion. And as I have argued elsewhere, "forgiveness" is a highly valued commodity in autobiography (Douglas, "Blurbing Biographical," 819).[4]

So what are we to do with autobiographers that do not forgive their abusive parents and write their autobiography from this position? In her autobiography *Ugly*, Briscoe goes against all of the standards set down by Barbour regarding the ethical responsibilities of representing parents. Briscoe is judgmental and unforgiving of her abusive mother and never seeks to explore or explain the reasons behind her mother's abuse. For instance, though the autobiography makes references to the domestic violence suffered by her mother, there is little detail or discussion about it. Briscoe's mother is clearly abused and oppressed by the various male partners she has. Bella Brodzki argues that autobiographies by daughters "often present themselves first and foremost as having been 'sinned' against—by their mothers and . . . by the patriarchal structures that have made her mother an unknowing collaborator with male authority" (159). Briscoe does not delve into this feminist terrain. Of her mother, Briscoe writes: "I never knew why my mother wanted children. Not once did I think that she liked me or my sisters and brothers. Why she had so many of us is a mystery" (24). In an interview Briscoe is asked if she "made an effort" to try to understand her mother's actions. Briscoe replies:

I have never thought about her motivation. I took the view that she didn't like me and I caused her problems by wetting the bed and so on. Why did it happen? Because I was a problem child. Do I understand her? Now that I have my own children, I do not understand it for one moment. I hope that my mother will, one day before she goes to her grave, realise that I was not a bad kid. It would please me if she knew me as her daughter. (Meeke)

Briscoe's mother becomes a vulnerable subject (to again use Couser's term). Like the Turcottes and Pelzer's mother, Briscoe's mother also has little right of reply to Briscoe's charges against her. However, Briscoe's position, like Pelzer's, is that she is writing about a traumatic event and her writing reflects particular needs—to speak out against the previously unspeakable. Traumatic autobiographies are offered to the public as testimony of their narrators' endurance of trauma. They are a means via which the previously disempowered person (in this instance, the child) can "write back" (as an adult) after the fact, to offer a revised version of events. Briscoe's auto-biography is angry and triumphant. She writes from a position of power: She is part of a conventionally happy family; she is a mother and a wife. She has a very successful career. To paraphrase Sidonie Smith and Julia Watson, Briscoe has "got a life" (*Getting a Life*). But this "self" is an autobiographical construct, a performance. Part of Briscoe's project is to set herself up against her mother and to set her adult self up against her child self—to offer a comparison between the different selves and the different mothers—and to thus authenticate her experience and herself.

Briscoe's autobiography is not burdened by sympathy because she has none for her mother, whom she represents as not having one redeeming quality. Briscoe's autobiography is not an act of forgiveness; Briscoe says: "My mother's behaviour was a combination of temperament and circum-stances. But now that I am a mother, I think even more that her treatment was completely incomprehensible and unacceptable. I do not forgive her" (Fernand). In writing this autobiography, Briscoe's responsibilities are to Briscoe and her immediate family only.

Trauma, Anger, and Ethics

Richard Terdiman rightly contends that memory is especially fraught with emotional content when it comes to intergenerational relations. Terdiman writes, "The stories a culture tells about parents and children frame, as if in microcosm, the culture's conception of the inevitably problematic inheritance, of the present's perplexing relation to the past" (214). Autobiographies of childhood such as those written by Briscoe, Burroughs, and Pelzer interrogate this problematic inheritance while highlighting the ethical complexities it poses. These are writers who have experienced trauma and are looking at ways to authenticate themselves and their stories. In writing their relational autobiographies, various scripts are available in relation to where or how they will position their abusive parent within the texts. The ethics too are up for negotiation. These representations reflect shifts in the cultural representation of mothers and fathers (stepmothers and stepfathers). In light of contemporary acknowledgments of the rights of the child, it is possible to say more about a parent than it once was. As more autobiographies about abusive parents are published, particular narratives will be enabled and written into the cultural memory of child abuse and parenthood.

Ethically, what do we do with the conflict between Burroughs's, Pelzer's, and Briscoe's right to tell his or her story, to expound the trauma, and the parents' right to be represented in a more complex manner? Do these authors have a responsibility to their parents to try to understand them as part of the autobiographical project? Or is the author exempted because of the trauma he or she suffered? While the narratives of Burroughs, Pelzer, and Briscoe are not simply vitriolic attacks on abusive parents, at times they are not too far from this mark. Where *Running with Scissors* uses humor to defuse traumatic representation, *A Child Called "It"* and *Ugly* are embedded within politically vehement rights-of-the-child debates. Each justifies its approach (ethically) within this paradigm. The writers use the autobiographical form to exercise agency denied to them as a child, to purge trauma and to direct anger toward the perpetrators of their abuse, and to transfer their childhood shame onto the perpetrator parent. Briscoe's and Pelzer's autobiographies are angry in tone, against the grain of contemporary autobiographies of childhood. The anger represents attacks against child abuse and its perpetrator and functions as an internal justification for the tone of these texts. That neither author chooses to forgive his or her mother is obviously significant. This again functions to silence the perpetrator and to position the child, and thus the author, as "right" and as having the primary right to speak.

The appeal of the autobiographies in this chapter—autobiographies that firmly juxtapose the (potentially mentally ill) perpetrator parents with the successful adult autobiographers—suggests the continuing influence of conservative rhetoric demanding clear-cut heroes and villains within autobiographical writing. Ethical responsibilities to relational subjects become unbound by trauma. The traumatic form asserts that the autobiographical author's needs supersede those of the parent. Other autobiographers, such as Rosalie Fraser and Jenny Diski, are able to address this tension through a complex representation of abuse, parenting, and social inequality. These varied representations and the tensions inherent within them mirror broader cultural debates about what is remembered, forgotten, and represented in parent/child relationships.

For Couser, "Readers are likely to be more receptive to writers who face up to the ethical challenges inherent in their projects" (201). This is perhaps the primary grounds upon which we might criticize the narratives of Burroughs, Pelzer, and Briscoe as unethical. Each of these texts ultimately lacks an overt consideration (and thus, seemingly, an awareness) of the ethical responsibilities the authors have to their parents and guardians who appear as relational subjects in their texts. These texts offer very little (if any) discussion of the potential ramifications of circulating their stories. The author's right to tell the story is paramount. Trauma, testimony, and witnessing provide an enduring defense for authors in these instances—providing the survivor the right to speak, which supersedes that of the accused perpetrator. To deny this is to deny the trauma and to potentially retraumatize the survivor.

And yet survivor testimony that fails to consider (and, indeed, criticism of this testimony that fails to account for) the complexities of trauma narration surely does very little to enhance our understanding of traumatic experience or to further the cause of traumatic life writing. This is not to suggest that traumatic autobiographies of childhood must offer balanced treatments of parents, guardians, and other relational subjects—rather that these trauma texts should demonstrate some overt consciousness of ethics, and of the autobiography as relational. As previously discussed, there are many ways in which autobiographies of childhood accomplish this—for instance, through assertions that this narrative is subjective and that the memories it contains are fragmented. Such acknowledgments greatly extend autobiography's ongoing critical conversations on subjectivity and the ethics of life writing.

CHAPTER 7

THE ETHICS OF READING

WITNESSING TRAUMATIC CHILDHOODS

*A reader's involvement with the painful details of another's story entails both
the pleasures of the imagination and the defenses of personal boundaries—and
these reactions shape the exercise of identification across the borders of the
unfamiliar. Accounts of extreme experience set in motion an ambivalent desire
to look, to grapple with real suffering, and at the same time to look away—to
put the book down. . . . The forging of community is both an arduous and
utopian project . . . but any reader can take a first step toward collective self-
consciousness by negotiating pathways of responsiveness and responsibility
between what is both strange and familiar, distant and all too close.*
                —Nancy K. Miller and Jason Tougaw, "Introduction: Extremities"

*I am a similar age to Andrea and related fondly to her sharp memories and
observations of growing up in the 70s and 80s. I felt ashamed of my some-
what-luxurious-in-comparison upbringing, and ached for Andrea every step
of her humble journey through childhood and adolescence.*
                —R.H., *Amazon.com*

Readership provides a further context for interpreting autobiographies of
childhood. At other points in this book I have discussed the reader investments required of traumatic and nostalgic memories of childhood and
the ways that readers are anticipated and addressed by autobiographies of
childhood. Readers shape autobiographies of childhood as much as any
of the other contexts I have discussed in this book. These texts depend on
readers to sanction the narratives they offer. Readers play a crucial role
in interpreting and inscribing meanings upon these childhoods. These
readers may be "professional readers"—researchers engaged in scholarship, reviewers, or media critics—or "recreational readers" responding to
these texts in reading groups or in online discussion forums. Within these

different categorizations there is a heterogeneous readership for autobiographies of childhood.

Where in the previous chapter I discuss the ethical responsibilities that
authors have to their child subjects, in this chapter I explore the ethical
responsibilities that readers have, or consider themselves to have, to child
subjects of autobiographies. Following on from the discussion in chapter 5 on
traumatic narratives I ask: Why have so many readers responded to traumatic
narratives of childhood, for example, those depicting child abuse or bereavement? There is a range of potential methodologies for exploring the ways in
which readers take up traumatic autobiographies of childhood. As this study
is necessarily limited to one chapter, I have narrowed my methodological
approach to a particular example: review discourse (professional and recreational reviewers). I explore the reception of traumatic autobiographical texts,
predominantly by analyzing online reader responses to these autobiographies
(for example, on bookseller Web sites).

Witnessing via Autobiography

The primary way in which readers have come to approach autobiographies
of childhood is through witnessing the testimonies offered within. Autobiographies of childhood are commonly commended for offering insights
into traumatic experiences. In this instance, literature is thought to play a
reparative role after trauma, mediating between the trauma and the witness.
According to Leigh Gilmore, readers commonly look to autobiography to
gain perspective—reading individual experiences as a means of translating
community, national, or global events:

> Autobiographical representations of trauma make an invaluable contri-
> bution to the study of literature and culture. They offer indispensable
> eyewitness accounts of large-scale and everyday violence and, through
> their elaboration of specific scenes of terror and trauma, provide an anti-
> dote to universalizing narratives about evil, suffering and history. (367)

As previously discussed, trauma has been the boom product of autobiographical writing since the mid-1990s. Karyn Ball anticipated trauma's
decline in her editorial in a special issue of *Cultural Critique* on trauma,
written in 2000. She cited "the backlash against Holocaust studies" as one of
the factors affecting this declining interest in trauma (10). It turned out that
Ball's predictions were premature. It would have been impossible for her to

foresee the new wave of traumatic texts (and their witnessing) that would follow September 11, 2001. Since 2001 there has been a renewed focus on trauma, and recognition that people are witnessing terrible atrocities every day in unprecedented ways, particularly through media representations. Universities teach courses on trauma that commonly go beyond discussions of the Holocaust toward examinations of more contemporary traumatic events (for example, wars/contemporary conflict, cultural persecution and incarceration, genocides, and terrorism). In other contexts, recreational readers are consuming autobiographies that graphically detail child abuse, domestic violence, illness, and injury. Traumatic autobiographies have been valuable commercial products for the past decade, and this literary trend shows no sign of abating. Readers are commonly drawn to the life narratives of vulnerable subjects. There has been a range of explanations offered for the high level of reader interest in traumatic narratives. Where some theorists suggest that in consuming traumatic autobiographies, readers are developing empathic relationships with the subjects, others see this literary trend as a form of voyeurism or schadenfreude.

Recent scholarship has explored the position of the "witness" in literature of trauma—such as Holocaust testimony or Stolen Generations testimony in Australia. In their landmark study *Testimony: Crises of Witnessing in Literature, Psychoanalysis, and History*, Shoshana Felman and Dori Laub ask, "How is the act of writing tied up with the act of bearing witness? . . . Is the act of reading literary texts itself inherently related to the act of facing horror? . . . And by virtue of what sort of agency is one appointed to bear witness?" (2). The witness may be a person who is present at a traumatic event and gives testimony as a firsthand witness. Alternatively, a witness might be "the second person." The second person reads a testimony in textual form and, in this act of reading, sanctions and empowers the testimony. The second person may understand the text as relational—accepting his or her connection to the traumatic event depicted (Kennedy; Whitlock, "In the Second Person"). Witnessing has traditionally been constructed as a mode of intelligent, informed, and necessarily empathic reading. As a reading practice it reveals the political power of reading: Reading can raise awareness, challenge historical knowledge, shift power relationships, and redress inequalities.

Felman and Laub explain that witnessing occurs as a result of identification, transference, and secondary trauma. In other words, the second-person witness develops empathy for the first-person trauma sufferer by experiencing something akin to trauma him or herself: "The listener to trauma comes to be a participant and a co-owner of the traumatic event: through his very listening he comes to partially experience trauma in himself" (57–58). And yet, as Rosanne Kennedy argues, while this model works particularly effectively in Holocaust studies, its application might be limited in other contexts. For example, Kennedy argues that Stolen Generations testimonies "often construct complex subject positions for listeners, who do not necessarily identify with the speaking positions of the person giving testimony. And some of the constructed subject positions, such as 'perpetrator,' work against identification" (58).

There is a long-held, perhaps even axiomatic, belief in literary studies that readers will find themselves confronted by the literature they read. While this seems a reasonable assumption, as scholars it is important that we reflect upon the consequences of what we, and, in turn, the reading public, are consuming. As Nancy K. Miller and Jason Tougaw argue, literary critics are prone to putting themselves at the coalface when it comes to reading challenging material: "We look to meet if not to match the wounds of others. We demonstrate a willingness to be bruised, to have our indifference challenged. Reading for the extreme is a way to consider the politics of empathy and acknowledge the limits of our civic engagement" (18). Miller and Tougaw warn against "the dangers we incur by being overly confident that our theories can accommodate all the contingencies our reading practices may encounter" (19). The representation and reception of trauma are extremely dynamic processes. We need to be aware of the shifting contexts affecting the production, circulation, and reception of trauma texts. And we must be accommodating of the varied subject positions that readers will bring to reading these texts.

For example, recent studies of traumatic representations have examined some of the possible adverse effects of witnessing upon the second-person witness. Kirby Farrell suggests that the second person might overempathize with the traumatic testimony and suffer psychological trauma as well. There is a very fine line between affective witnessing and traumatic transference— between the recipients feeling empathy and becoming vicariously traumatized by the traumatic life narrative they consume (Kaplan 2). Other studies have explored the damaging effects of witnessing on the traumatized subject. Mark Seltzer uses psychoanalytical theory to explain the voyeuristic interest people might take in traumatic events. And for Lauren Berlant, the rampant "use" of traumatic imagery in cultural texts can mute and/or commodify the traumatic subject (48).

It is impossible to know the broad-ranging effects that the outpouring of traumatic childhood life-narrative texts has had upon those who have read them. However, it is possible to speculate by looking at some of the contexts in which these texts have been taken up, and by examining some of the recurring themes that emerge within the reception of autobiographies of childhood.

Reading Traumatic Childhoods

There is a multiplicity of factors affecting the ways in which readers might respond to traumatic texts—not all of which can be measured in a small study such as this one. E. Ann Kaplan argues that "[it is difficult to generalize] about trauma and its impact, for, as Freud pointed out long ago, how one reacts to a traumatic event depends on one's individual psychic history, on memories inevitably mixed with fantasies of prior catastrophes, and on the particular cultural and political content within which catastrophe takes place, especially how it is 'managed' by institutional forces" (1). Autobiographies of childhood, like all autobiographies, have intended and/or implied readers. Publicists and sellers of autobiographies agree that one of the keys to autobiography's success is the connection it elicits between author and reader (McPhee; Gray). What autobiographers can write about depends on what readers want to read; and what readers want to read is heavily influenced by the broader cultural milieu that surrounds their reading—from politics through to literary trends.

Autobiographies seem to suggest a simple relationship between text and reader, but the relationships they require are extremely complex. Susanna Egan suggests that autobiographies are interactive or constructed by a number of relational or mirroring encounters (*Mirror Talk* 3). Childhood narratives are driven by these encounters among fragmented selves and voices, mementos and intertexts. Egan describes autobiography as an " 'encounter of two lives' between reader and writer of life and of 'life,' repeated both outside and inside the text" (3). The appeal of autobiographies of childhood is dependent on particular reader positionings and investments. These texts solicit an active reader who will participate dynamically in the politics of the autobiography either by being represented by the autobiography or by being confronted into witnessing what occurs within it.

As suggested in earlier chapters, autobiographies of childhoods engage their readers in particular relationships through the narrative's positioning of the reader. For example, the nostalgic memories of Thomas Keneally and Brian Nicholls appeal to cultural memory and to the reader's identification and acceptance of these autobiographies as representative Australian childhoods. Lorna Sage's consciousness-raising narrative functions as a call to action: The reader is asked to recognize the gender inequalities suffered by girls during Sage's childhood era. In the autobiographies of Andrea Ashworth, Antwone Fisher, and Mary Karr, the reader is positioned as a knowing confidant. The child discloses his or her abuse to the reader but not to characters within the autobiography. The autobiographies of Constance Briscoe, Duncan Fairhurst, Rosalie Fraser, Ivor Knight, Dave Pelzer, and Donna Meehan are constructed as highly accessible texts, each aiming to reach a broad readership. Each text overtly advocates for the rights of the child—the authors are less interested in the literary aspects of writing and more concerned with the political potential of their words. For instance, of her Stolen Generations autobiography, Meehan is quoted as saying, "I just wanted it to be something my mob could read," but also as hoping that the book will go "where my feet can't go," advancing the cause of Reconciliation (Scott).

In traumatic autobiography the protagonist is rarely presented as a unique individual. The relationship between author and reader is explicitly foregrounded with an "emphasis upon the referential and denotative dimension of textual communication" (Felski 83). Readers are encouraged to consider the similarities and differences between the autobiographical life and their own.[1] The personal disclosures of an autobiographical narrator may produce a sense of intimacy between the narrator and reader (although disclosure may cause the reader to feel shamed and responsible) or, because the events of the narrative are unfamiliar, may alienate the reader. Readers respond in these ways because of the particular conventions of interpretation that are circulating at that cultural moment. Inevitably, certain disclosures and notions of truth and identity make sense at particular times for particular readers (S. Smith, "Performativity").

The readership for autobiographies of childhood is initially designated by the book-as-object—as suggested in chapter 2, book jacket cover images and blurbs define autobiographies of childhoods and often make explicit statements about what a reader will gain from reading this particular autobiography. The intended reader or readership is heterogeneous, which is obviously important for book sales. But book jackets work to encourage particular, preferred relationships between reader and text. As was also suggested in chapter 2, the autobiography can be positioned as a therapeutic provider, moral guide, or testimony, and the reader is most commonly positioned as a witness—a moral respondent to the events depicted in the text.

Professional and recreational readers play a significant role in making connections between different autobiographies and in suggesting the value and meanings of these texts. For example, book reviews are becoming ever more pervasive in terms of their occurrence, influence, and critical significance. For many contemporary literary releases, these reviews serve as the only critical material available in the early stages of release. Just as reviews are important to literary scholars, they have a significant function for the publishing industry in the marketing and selling of books. Book reviews, while still present in their literary-critical forms, are increasingly found in the popular press and on the Web in shorter, more accessible formats. For example, book reviewing is increasingly produced by "everyday" readers, especially in online book clubs and fan forums and on bookseller Web sites, personal Web pages, social networking sites such as Facebook's "i read," and "virtual bookshelves." Book club recommendations and the word-of-mouth promotion that they solicit have come to play an increasingly significant role in the popular circulation of literary texts. Online bookseller Amazon.com has a section for "customer reviews": Readers are encouraged to write short reviews, which become part of the Web site's publicity for selling books. This phenomenon indicates the importance of reader/author/bookseller interactivity in autobiography. In customer reviews, the reader's personal revelations become important forms of criticism and for marketing.

I agree with Richard Woodward, an essayist for the *Village Voice Literary Supplement*, who suggests that Amazon.com's reviews reflect a move away from professional criticism toward reviews that can be more easily manipulated for the bookseller's gain (1). But the most intriguing aspect of these developments is the centering of the recreational reader in review discourse. Recreational readers have become crucial to the reviewing and promotional processes, in determining what books people buy, in asserting meanings for books, and in suggesting how they should be read.

Scholars within autobiography studies have recognized the significance of reviews in circulating meanings for autobiography. Though there are no studies of customer reviews of autobiographies (to my knowledge), three studies use book reviews to frame their analyses: Paul John Eakin's "Breaking Rules: The Consequences of Self-Narration," Laura Frost's "After Lot's Daughters: Kathryn Harrison and the Making of Memory," and David Parker's "Counter-Transference in Reading Autobiography: The Case of Kathryn Harrison's *The Kiss*." Frost uses reviews to define the "history" of the autobiography and the environment in which it was received, particularly emphasizing the "moral valence coloring most criticism" (51). Eakin examines the ways in which truth in autobiography is publicly tested, and Parker explores autobiographical disclosure and the moral judgments that are made by reviewers.

Such studies provide a place to start when considering what investments professional and recreational readers are making in autobiographies of childhoods. For instance, why do readers value some stories of childhood and not others? The line of judgment between what makes a "good" or "bad" autobiography of childhood seems arbitrary to some professional readers, but very clear to others. The judgments made by reviewers of autobiographies of childhoods reveal a number of important features of reader and textual positionings within and around these autobiographies.

"Public Interest" and "Good Taste" : The Professional Reader

Literary critics in various media have devoted considerable space to discussions of autobiography in the mid-1990s to 2000s—ranging from affirmations to declarations of how damaging this genre has been within the literary landscape.[2] Critics agree that this period has been a fruitful time for writing about traumatic childhood, that "we wolf down terrible stories of abuse and neglect, we gobble up lives that somehow chime with our own; we nibble at the exotic, the strange and the exciting" (Armitstead). In his review of Harrison's *The Kiss* James Wolcott describes the plethora of traumatic autobiography as "agony-overload" (32). Malcolm Jones observes that "[in the 1990s] the need for authors—especially young authors with miserable childhoods—to get something off their chest has grown from a fad to a genre" ("It's Better to Tell All"). In Australia, freelance writer and editor Nicola Robinson suggests, "weekend newspaper colour supplements are bursting with excerpts from the latest autobiography, or interviews with their subjects. Real-life stories—especially salacious events, family abuse, meteoric rises to fame or heroic struggles against illness—slip easily into journalist hyperbole" (33). The focus here seems to be on what should and should not be disclosed within autobiographies of childhood—from what seems appropriate to what seems "salacious."

The majority of these critiques of autobiography are highly suspicious of the genre. For example, most commonly propose that autobiography is of value if it evades controversies of authenticity and identity; autobiography is "bad" if it is vindictive or blatantly profiteering from sensationalized depictions (Begley and Moss). Madeline Blais outlines some rules for good autobiography, which include "No sentimentality, especially when applied to childhood. Even the most fortunate childhoods are more than just lollipops and licorice." This returns us to my discussion of ethics in the previous chapter. There is a clear trend emerging here toward what is perceived to be an ethical autobiographical representation: one that offers balance and consideration of themes outside of its primary mandate, and one that does not seek to represent and profit from the misfortunes of others.

Reviewers value autobiography that is written in "good taste" and that demonstrates some restraint in terms of personal disclosure (Treneman). For example, in her review of Ashworth's *Once in a House on Fire* Mary Paumier Jones praises the autobiography for being "understated" (118). Another reviewer of Ashworth's autobiography writes of the trepidation that s/he had before reading it:

> When I first picked up Andrea Ashworth's *Once in a House on Fire* I did so doubtfully. However, a few of her brave, funny chapters about her northern working-class childhood of the Eighties are enough to bring even the strongest confessional objector round. Despite the beatings and the tears, Ashworth's writing is about as far from victim culture as you get. ("A Kiss and Sell Affair")

The *Economist*'s review of *Bad Blood* expresses a similar trepidation about the autobiography of childhood form: "[The packaging of this autobiography] might lead the reader to believe that he or she is about to be served up another fashionably grim account of childhood deprivation and misery. Yet the overall effect of *Bad Blood* is far from gloomy" (91).

Despite the glowing reviews of Ashworth's and Sage's autobiographies, these reviews expose the autobiography of childhood's increasingly infamous reputation as sensational self-indulgence. Parker provides an explanation for this reaction against traumatic disclosure. He suggests that counter-transference may be the reason why some reviewers react so harshly against traumatic disclosure. These disclosures may confront the reviewers' shame, causing them to shame the autobiographer by writing a poor review (500). Criticism's preoccupation with the resilient, forgiving autobiographer, which I outlined in chapter 3, strengthens Parker's theory. Resilient autobiographies are considered most appropriate. For example, in his review of Meehan's *It Is No Secret*, Paul Kraus writes: "Although the author's life journey has understandably been punctuated by sadness, her story also carries much that brightens the heart. . . . Despite many setbacks, Donna Meehan gradually overcame these traumas, strengthened by a radiant Christian faith and its accompanying abiding hope" (8). An Aboriginal writer whose writing reflects forgiveness and also professional success is applauded. Rosalie Fraser's forgiveness is also emphasized in Jan Mayman's review of *Shadow Child*: "Fraser was four years old when her foster mother raped her with a knitting needle during one bout of drunken madness; yet she has forgiven this monstrous woman: 'I realise how sick she was. . . . I still put flowers on her grave.'" The discursive effect of such reviews, particularly their valuing of resilience, is that they place responsibility for the eradication of racism and social inequality with individuals rather than institutions. Consider the opening lines of Mayman's review of *Shadow Child*: "At two, Rosalie Fraser was a stolen Aboriginal child destined for years of abuse. At 14, she was an alcoholic street kid. Today at 40, she is a newly acclaimed writer whose Cinderella story will touch many." Mayman asserts, "With five children of her own and over 20 years of happy marriage, Fraser is serene, poised and deeply fulfilled today." These statements invariably position the Indigenous author very much in terms of conventional Western capitalist indicators of success: a rags-to-riches "Cinderella" figure with a successful job as an "acclaimed writer." When noting the explosion of recently published childhood narratives and the reviews that accompany them, readers could assume that people overcome adversity more often than not.

As suggested in chapter 3, particular templates have emerged for articulating trauma within survivor narratives. Certain types of narratives are more likely to solicit a sympathetic or empathic response. For example, as Janice Haaken contends,

> the ability of victims to mobilize support depends on their capacity to convey an essential goodness, in spite of the traumatic effects of victimization. "Good" victims are virtuous and always tell the truth. . . . This political construction of the victim—as "all good" and never prone to distortion of events—works against complex truths and honest self-exploration on the part of adult children and their parents. ("Sexual Abuse" 122–123)

However, a belief in such black-and-white constructions of abuse is commonly evident in the assessments that professional readers make of these texts. For example, James Wolcott proposes that "some memoir-writers are legitimately trying to clarify for themselves and the reader the experience of a cruel upbringing or an unfortunate twist of fate; others are simply peddling their stories for fame" (32). Such either/or binary constructions belie the complexities of writing about child abuse—reducing these texts to narrow survivor scripts.

What makes an autobiography of childhood worth reading? Michael Rust proposes that "narcissism and a focus on personal experiences with problems such as alcoholism and child abuse are the characteristics of much of the memoirs written in the 1990s. These books tend to focus on the self at the expense of the public interest" (19). And Patrick Smith condemns autobiographies that are not concerned with "the human condition," "a dedication to public discourse in one form or another, or to some object or event outside of the self" (30).

According to these critics, the best way to avoid solipsism is to construct your autobiography as representative or as being worthy of "public interest" (Rust 19). Writing about a childhood is not enough (in itself) to secure relevance for the autobiography. Children's lives are traditionally constructed as valuable only for what they can tell us about adult lives, or about adult preoccupations with childhood. The subject of the autobiography must be deemed "worthy" to the critics of the time—or else it risks being labeled trivial or inconsequential.

Pierre Bourdieu's theory of "taste" is relevant here. There is an implicit suggestion, within these reviews, that an autobiography can be objectively "good" or "bad," rather than simply to certain readers' culturally constructed taste of what constitutes good literature or intriguing subject matter. To value only certain autobiographies or to unequivocally condemn the form— consider Kathryn Hughes's suggestion that autobiography is ruining literature ("Remembering Imagination")—reveals the complex fixation that literary culture has with autobiographies of childhood. Autobiography's popularity has made this fixation necessary, but autobiography remains something of a disobedient genre as far as many of its critics are concerned.

Not surprisingly, some recurrent themes emerge in the commendation of particular autobiographies of childhood. These autobiographies are celebrated if they are "literary" and/or if they tackle sufficiently momentous subject matter, particularly humanist "truths." As Frost suggests, and as I argued in chapter 3, "Athough academic critics accept the intrinsic fictionality of autobiography . . . non-academic audiences hold their authors to Lejeune's autobiographical pact" (55). For example, writing for the *Literary Review*, Maggie Gee credits Jenny Diski for the "astringent truthfulness of her prose" in *Skating to Antarctica* (book jacket). Colin Shindler's *Manchester United Ruined My Life* is described as "honest" and "genuine" by Anthony Quinn from the *Daily Telegraph*. (book jacket). Clive James and Margaret Drabble also refer to Lorna Sage's "honesty" in their reviews of *Bad Blood* (book jacket).

This perceived or constructed honesty is associated with another theme of reviewing: that reviewers praise autobiographies of childhood for representing consequential subjects. For example, the traumatic autobiographies in this study are praised for the ways that they redress particular myths of childhood. Kraus commends the political value of Meehan's autobiography in writing, "I hope the publishers have sent a copy to [Australian prime minister] John Howard" (8). Suzanne Moore, reviewing *Skating to Antartica* for *New Statesman*, refers to Diski's "genuinely horrific childhood" (44). Mary Beard, reviewing *Bad Blood* for *TLS*, describes it as "a brilliant reflection on the nature of family life and family memories; an experiment in exploring the myths of one's own childhood" (36). Similarly, the majority of reviewers commend Ashworth's *Once in a House on Fire* for its social relevance as an autobiography concerned with childhood abuse, class inequality, and social mobility. Tim Lott describes *Once in a House on Fire* as a "poetic of social history" (book jacket); Margaret Driscoll writes, "It is almost a sociological resource as much as a family story, so rich is it in vivid detail of everyday life on the wrong side of 1970s Manchester" (book jacket). Margaret Forster's *Daily Telegraph* review discusses Ashworth's autobiography within the context of the inequalities suffered by working-class females in Britain: "This is not so much a memoir as a war report from the front line. Andrea Ashworth is like a soldier who wins through after a hellish time in the trenches suffering a steady bombardment. And this war she courageously reports from isn't over either—girls like her, born into seemingly hopeless circumstances, still have to wage it." Peter Stanford emphasizes the social work that is done by autobiographies of childhood such as Ashworth's: "I will press a copy of Ashworth's book into the hand of any government minister I hear holding forth of the adequacy of the benefit system" (book jacket); Forster writes that Ashworth "has written a book which is a rare thing, a book that is needed. It should be issued immediately by all inner-city educational authorities to girls at their comprehensives."

These reviewers commend the autobiographers for their painful, public disclosures and for the knowledge they impart. These reviews reveal the responsibility of autobiographies of childhood to redress myths of childhood by providing so-called honest images, the implication being that they provide sociologically pertinent images of childhood. Asserting the sociological value of autobiographies of childhoods allows critics to declare the representativeness of these narratives, their connection to cultural memory, and a shared past between autobiographer and reader.

Kraus writes of Meehan's *It Is No Secret*: "This is not a book about one stolen child. Donna Meehan gives voice to the thousands of silent stolen children" (8). Bert Hingley, the publisher of *Shadow Child*, is quoted as saying, "At times it is horrific, yet it is an affirmation of life, of the victory of the human spirit over cruelty and suffering. This is a book for the world, a heart-felt cry for all suffering children. . . . It is a tragic tale with a happy ending, offering hope and inspiration for others" (qtd. in Mayman). Hingley's quote emphasizes that this is "a book for the world," asserting the universal value of Fraser's narrative using phrases such as "affirmation of life," "human spirit," "a heartfelt cry for all suffering children," and "inspiration for others." The recurrence of these particular themes and concerns in reviews of autobiographies of childhoods might be simply explained as a predictable consequence of literary journalism and commercialism. Reviewers have to define these texts simply and succinctly, according to recognizable signifiers of value. But reviews play an important ideological role in demarcating good books from bad books and in telling recreational readers how these autobiographies should be read. As I suggested earlier in this chapter, review criticism has been the primary site for debate about autobiographical writing at the turn of the millennium. One of the intriguing features of these reviews is their commendation of autobiographies that can be deemed "sociological" or "historical." In making this judgment, autobiographies of childhood are offered as privileged access to social issues. There is an implicit assumption that particular narratives are "key texts." As Cath Ellis argues, this is particularly problematic in the instance of Indigenous autobiographies. She argues that it is not enough for readers to take their act of reading an Indigenous autobiography as sufficient apology for two hundred years of white domination (76).

Thus, autobiographies of childhood provide a difficult challenge for professional reviewers who are bound by the conventions of reviewing and the expectations of literary culture. Positioning these autobiographies in terms of their sociological value seems the best ideological fit for these reviewers.

Recreational Readers: "Getting a Life"

Professional reviewers construct autobiographers and their works as worthy subjects for print and for a wide readership. And yet one of the primary appeals for recreational readers of an autobiography of childhood is that an apparently accessible and perhaps even "ordinary" person wrote the autobiography. This perceived accessibility is crucial in gaining the trust of a readership but constructs a paradox whereby the protagonist must be both "extraordinary" and "everyday" at the same time. Where professional readers emphasize the extraordinary, recreational readers more often refer to the everyday aspects of the autobiography. The perceived accessibility of the author and autobiography creates a bond between author and reader. In deciphering his or her own life experiences, the reader uses the autobiography as a guide. Autobiographies of childhood, particularly traumatic narratives, encourage readers to think relationally, to consider how this narrative represents them or relates to their own life. For example, in her study of teenaged readers of autobiography, Jane Kurtz proposes that the main attraction for adolescent readers is the coming-of-age aspects of these texts (250). Teenagers read autobiographies intertextually with music lyrics and poetry and value these texts as rebellious acts of defiance (250). In consuming autobiography, readers are able to align themselves with the life they consume, particularly to offer ideological support to the autobiographical subject and designate their own ideological or political stance.

In the absence of empirical studies of autobiographical readers, I turn to Amazon.com as a means of examining a particular context for recreational readers.[3] In Amazon's customer reviews, readers do not simply mirror the critical responses of their professional counterparts, though the articulations of professional readers clearly set some parameters for these nonprofessional critics. Recreational readers often use these forums to react against the reviews of professionals. For example, one reader of Sage's *Bad Blood* writes, "I was disappointed with this, but probably because my expectations were too high after having read the glowing reviews" (R.O.). But recreational readers predictably offer types of literary criticism similar to professional readers,' as well as offering their opinions on the autobiography and why and how they came to read this particular book.

One theme that recurs strongly in these customer reviews is readers' personal reflections. Reading autobiographies of childhood and responding on this forum commonly results in readers reflecting upon their relationship to the autobiographical text. They engage explicitly in "mirror talk." These readers reflect upon their own lives and offer critical responses framed within their own biographies. Through this interaction the truth of the text is created as much by the reader as by the author.

Reading these Amazon.com customer reviews offers only a limited perspective on how recreational readers respond to and create meanings for autobiographies of childhoods. For example, we cannot be certain that readers do not respond to fictional texts in exactly the same way (though a quick search of customer reviews of recent realist fiction does not reveal as much self-reflexivity from Amazon customers). Furthermore, it could be the forum that facilitates these autobiographical responses as much as the text under review (or an equal combination of the two). A certain type of reviewing quickly becomes the norm and may then be perpetuated ad infinitum. Further research into the customer comment phenomenon would be a significant contribution to autobiography studies. But for the present study these reviews provide some valuable insight into how recreational readers respond to these texts and engage in a reflective dialogue, negotiating the limits of these autobiographies.

Readers interpret the autobiographical lives they read using their own experiences as markers of the autobiography's representativeness. Examples of this can be seen in the customer reviews of James McBride's *The Color of Water*. For example, R.B. writes:

> Loved this book. My son is also bi-racial. I was born in 1956 and could really relate and re-read the book with my son. He never experienced most of the things in the book so it was an incredible sharing and bonding experience for us and it opened a whole new dialogue with his dad whose family originated in North Carolina. Great read for all parents and children. Truly enlightening.

And R.G. says:

> *The Color of Water* really spoke to me. In fact in many ways I felt he could have been describing my own mother for her beauty both physical and spiritual. However, I think this is a great story excellently told for anyone.

In these reviews, McBride's autobiography becomes a relational text, and its appeal lies in the ways in which it connects with the broader experiences of readers' childhoods. Similarly, of Pelzer's *A Child Called "It,"* R.W. and R.D. offer the following reviews:

> I read this book about ten years ago, after my first child had turned one and as I read it I found myself picturing my child as David. I connected with him in that way—like a real loving mother should have. I've never forgot the horror that he went through and still cannot believe that it's true. I was happy to read that he finally escaped his terrible monster of a mother, but then saddened deeply to read that his brother was his mother's next victim. This story is truly one of brutal courage and not for the faint of heart. I was truly touched by David and he lives in my heart to this day. (R.W.)

I just finished this book today, in tears. It is one of the, if not the most inspirational books I have ever read. I grabbed my baby and didn't wont [sic] to let go of him, and I want to give the author a hug for sharing his story with us. (R.D.)

The reader's engagement in the text involves his or her imagined affinity with the accessible author and with the innocent child figure. In reading the text, the reader becomes the child's protector—fantasizing about "saving" the child from trauma. The child within the autobiography becomes metonymic of children generally—and the right of the child to protection.

This tendency of readers to interpret autobiographies of childhood relationally can also result in readers disengaging with a text on the grounds that the reader cannot relate to the experiences the autobiography depicts. For example, of Sage's *Bad Blood* R.C. writes:

Even though I was born in the early 50s and could remember the basic "no mod cons" way of living in the years after the 2nd world war, I didn't find Lorna Sage's life story in any way as interesting as I thought I would. I asked for the book as a birthday present from my sister (born in the late 50s) but I'm afraid to say that it was a complete waste of money.

In this instance, Sage's text lacks value because it contradicts the reader's autobiographical perspectives. R.H. concurs: "I guess most of us have some bad memories of childhood (I certainly do), but most of us grow up and realise that at least some people had our best interests at heart." This reader appeals to cultural memory to discredit Sage's version of 1950s life in Britain.

Readers position themselves as close or comparable to the perceived autobiographical author as a way of authenticating their own review and ultimately their own experiences. For example, R.S., reviewing Ashworth's *Once in a House on Fire*, describes his/her empathy for the narrative: "I found it shocking how much of it was familiar to me from the lives of people I grew up with." Similarly, R.W. writes, "I was moved to tears by this book—as was my mother, who experienced a similar childhood." Their suggestion of familiarity, their emotional responses, and references to their own experiences allow these readers to speak authoritatively and to speculate upon the meanings of the narrative. R.T. writes specifically about the textual incidents that she relates to and, in doing so, discloses precise details of her own life to parallel Ashworth's: "There were so many parts in it that I could identify with. When Andrea went to the Indian shop and tried to buy the most fashionable school uniform she could using the DSS vouchers I was almost in tears. I was that girl only ten years earlier." It is the reader's autobiographical disclosures that drive her claims to familiarity and closeness to the autobiography and autobiographer.

Another role that is assumed by Amazon.com readers of autobiographies of childhood is that of witness. As suggested earlier in this chapter, a witness responds to testimony; the witness is the "addressee." The witness plays a crucial role in this narrative transaction. Witnesses must recognize and feel the pain of the person giving the testimony, and comprehend the ways that they are implicated in this trauma (Felman and Laub 58). As Rosamund Dalziell suggests, "An encounter with shame in a text, whether as reader or listener, may lead one to recall and interrogate personal memories of shame and, where these are no longer too painful and isolating, to break the silence and speak of them with others" (8). In relation to *Once in a House on Fire*, readers who adopt the stance of witness acknowledge that they have not experienced a life similar to Ashworth's but have developed an empathetic relationship with this autobiography-as-testimony. For example, R.L. writes, "Andrea Ashworth was born in 1969, the same year as myself, and although I experienced nothing of her physical abuse at the hands of drunken stepfathers, her incredible attention to detail evoked many of my own experiences of adolescence that I had forgotten." The witness is encouraged to reflect on his or her own life as relational to the life that he or she is reading about. As Parker argues, "We often sense that the reading public is supposed to supply what [the autobiographer's] past didn't. The hope is that the words of the memoir will draw the readers' eyes in an act of empathic understanding" (499). Similar examples of witnessing can be found in responses to McBride's *The Color of Water*:

> To me, reading this book is an experience. I pull it out and re-read it every year. It encourages me to face hardships, to count my blessings and to recognize that all of us are put on earth for a reason. Thank you, James McBride, for a book that has become a cornerstone in my life. (R.F.)

> Words cannot express the positive impact that his story has had on me. . . . When I got to the part about James's mother (who had hundreds of reasons to give up many times in her life) was enrolling in college, at age 65, to help others, I had to pause and send everyone involved a

congratulatory mental-telepathy message of appreciation for all of their hard work, tenacity, abilities, and compassion for each other and the folks in their communities. . . . It's enough to encourage and uplift an entire nation, if not planet. Stunning! (R.Y.)

These witnesses assert the importance of these texts as consciousness-raisers, urging other readers to follow their lead and read these autobiographies of childhood. Similarly, of Dave Pelzer's *A Child Called "It,"* R.M. writes:

A Child Called "It" by Dave Pelzer is a memoir I read about 8 years ago. I could not put this harrowing book down. Pelzer is a child abuse survivor. He recounts the physical and mental abuse he suffered from the hands of his alcoholic and deeply troubled mother. This book brought me to tears and just broke my heart. I highly recommend this unsettling but important book.

Witnesses may be engaged in the process of "witnessing the self" (Felman and Laub 58) and be required to reflect on their own privilege within the context of the life that they are reading about, as the following readers do of Ashworth's autobiography:

When my mother recommended this book to me I wasn't really sure as I am only 13 but the first page had me hooked and I couldn't put the book down. Although my life compared to that of Andrea is very tame the book made me feel extremely lucky having had such a pleasant upbringing. . . . It made me feel very sad for Andrea (R.E.)

As an 18-year-old I could identify with some of her teenaged problems but also realised that compared to her I have been extremely fortunate in my life so far. If you want to appreciate what you have got, read this book. (R.A.)[4]

These customer comments reflect the ways in which readers implicitly and explicitly engage in a process of mirror talk.

The other side of this argument is that customer reviews limit the meanings of, and assert preferred readings for, these autobiographies in much the same way as professional reviewers do. In terms of style and subject, customer reviews speak to an assumed readership. Though heterogeneous, these reviews are performances that include certain voices and mute others.

Just as there are conventions for professional review writing, clear standards are emerging for customer reviews of autobiographies on Amazon. com. These conventions involve escalating autobiographical responses from readers. Readers are being co-opted into these autobiographical responses, which may work to disempower the readers and commodify their autobiographical responses. As Sidonie Smith argues, "Autobiographical storytelling becomes one means through which people in the West believe themselves to be 'selves'" ("Performativity" 109). Thus, autobiographical disclosure may be a requirement rather than a choice. Paul Gray suggests that "there are some 267 million stories in the naked U.S., all of them yearning to be told and sold" (106). Many of these are now appearing on Amazon.com in the form of responses to autobiographies. The elaborate processes of encouraging readers' autobiographical responses may serve convenient commercial ends as much as anything else.

Reading the Child

When readers—whether professional or recreational—select an autobiography of childhood from the crowded bookshop shelves or congested online selling portal, they begin to engage with the child's life depicted within. Their engagement is inevitably affected by both the broader politics of childhood and their own experiences of childhoods. This fusion results in particular engagements emerging from the readership—engagements that principally revolve around, and thus privilege, empathy and sympathy.

To read a (well-chosen) autobiography of childhood is to have selected a text that has sociological value beyond the individual. The resilient survivor-author has offered his or her text to the reader as a testimony and has asked the reader to witness this testimony through the act of reading. If the text is well received by the reader, the author's testimony is sanctioned—accepted as true but, more significantly, accepted as culturally valuable, educative, or morally instructive. The reader mediates between the author's story and his or her own to find either novelty—a text that the reader will learn from—or to find relationality, where the reader accepts his or her own relationship with the life depicted.

The reader has room to move within such criticism, but—as I have suggested in this chapter—when it comes to reading autobiographies of childhood, professional and recreational readers seem to interpret according to very narrow and predictable templates. As I have argued in this and previous chapters, this is most probably a consequence of the ethical responsibilities that trauma writing and life writing about childhood consecutively summon. When it comes to trauma and the child, readers commonly feel ethically bound to particular modes of witnessing—to approaching the text in ways that demonstrate their intellectual and emotional commitment, and even gratitude, in receiving this narrative. When readers do criticize autobiographies of childhood, they tend to do so by questioning the veracity of the story. There is much, much more we as readers might say about these texts. By giving greater attention to issues of craft (the ways in which stories of childhood are told) and ethics (the explicit efforts made by authors to attend to the ethics of autobiographical storytelling), we will come to learn a great deal more about the textual relationships imagined and realized by autobiographies of childhood. In an age where reviews are becoming thinner and less professional—this is a mandate for scholars.

CONCLUSION

WRITING CHILDHOOD IN THE
TWENTY-FIRST CENTURY

This is an important time to be working on autobiographies of childhood. At the turn of the millennium, a number of autobiographies have emerged to challenge and consolidate dominant ways of thinking about childhood in the twentieth century. In Australia, Stolen Generations testimonies have produced a revolution in the way many Australians think about their own childhoods during the post–World War II period of assimilation. In the United States and United Kingdom, narratives of childhood poverty and abuse have caused readers to reflect on class and gender inequalities in the so-called postwar golden age. These autobiographies have produced a new interest in and attention to the figure of the child in contemporary culture.

When autobiographers write about their childhoods, they are invariably influenced by a variety of forces that enable and limit their storytelling. Autobiographies of childhood are produced, circulated, and received within cultural contexts that place particular expectations on these texts. I have identified a number of contexts for interpreting autobiographies of childhood at the millennium turn, most particularly the institutional contexts and cultural milieu from which these texts emerge. Reading autobiographies of childhood within these contexts has allowed for a discussion of these autobiographies within a range of paradigms: as memory practice, as discourse on childhood, as literature, and/or as an overtly political "call to action."

The movement toward particular forms of autobiographical writing about childhood has significant implications for autobiographical writing in general. The autobiographies in this study have emerged in a variety of forms, with particular trends emerging strongly: autobiographies of childhood as nostalgic explorations of social, family, and personal histories; a space to explore the development of the writer; a genre for considering the symbolic role of the child figure in adult consciousness. But the most significant development within autobiographies of childhood written in the 1990s and 2000s has been the rise (and rise) of traumatic autobiographies of childhood—most commonly written by first-time writers. Several of these autobiographies use conversational language as a vehicle for their narratives, thus challenging established literary forms, or are defiantly didactic in addressing readers in a call to action. Traumatic narratives are often overtly fragmented and multivocal and often declare memory loss. These life narratives commonly test the boundaries of autobiography and cultural memory. As a consequence, their authors may be celebrated for their courage or, conversely, embroiled in controversies over authenticity.

I have explored the tension that exists between autobiographies of childhood written in the nostalgic and traumatic memory modes. Nostalgic and traumatic texts about childhood stem from, and engage with, contemporary cultural flash points or moments of social crises affecting childhood. The representation of childhood within autobiographies demonstrates autobiography's capacity as both an instrument of cultural memory and a weapon of counter-memory. Autobiographies of childhood are involved in a cyclical process of consolidating dominant histories and myths of childhood even as they present challenges to these dominant modes.

Autobiographies of childhood are an important site for the negotiation and expression of childhood identities. In presenting a plurality of childhood experiences, accomplishments, traumas, and relationships, the autobiographies discussed in this study broaden the possibilities for narrating childhood for future autobiographers, largely through asserting and claiming new identities for childhoods lived between the 1920s and 1980s.

But as with all public declarations of self and identity, the autobiography of childhood is a limited form that invariably idealizes certain identities and not others. Readers have come to expect certain identity performances from autobiographies of childhood. As Michael Lambek and Paul Antze argue, "Reinscribing personal stories into these public discourses often obscures their richness and moral complexity" (xxiv). In the act of writing a traumatic autobiography of childhood, an author confirms recovery from abuse. The presence of an author's biographical summary, typically on the front sleeve or back page of the autobiography, functions as a statement affirming the author's survival and subsequent accomplishments. As I suggested, the recovered, resilient, and forgiving author is vehemently celebrated within book reception to the extent that almost no other identities are available. Despite the emergence of new voices within traumatic autobiography, limits have nevertheless been set upon these texts. These limits have paradoxically silenced certain voices more than others (perhaps in much the same way as the voices within these traumatic autobiographies of childhood were previously silenced).

Notwithstanding the limits that autobiography imposes upon traumatic remembering in the present, it is important to recognize that autobiography has been a consistent catalyst for the emergence of marginalized voices. Autobiographers continue to represent the unrepresentable. Autobiography can be an effective mechanism for traumatic disclosure if it challenges "conventional speaking arrangements, arrangements in which women and children are not authoritative" (Martín Alcoff and Gray-Rosendale 204). In light of these observations it will be intriguing to witness what traumatic autobiographies of childhoods emerge in the next ten years.

This project has highlighted the need for further research into autobiographical writing about childhood. For example, in unveiling the range of autobiographical writing about childhood by adults, it reveals an absence of published autobiography written by children or young adults. Future studies might investigate where and how autobiographical writings by young people have featured in both mainstream and alternative autobiographical genres. How many young people engage in forms of autobiography, what is their most common means of access, and how has their involvement changed autobiography? What concerns do young people raise when writing autobiographically? Increased critical attention to these writings can facilitate the incorporation of youth voices into traditional discourses of knowledge. Such research would be of significant interest to autobiography scholars and to media and cultural studies scholars, as well as those studying the sociology of youth. I want to use this conclusion to begin a brief conversation on the possibility of research in this area.

MyLife: Ethics and Technologies of Young People's Life Writing

On February 20, 2007, the body of a fifteen-year-old girl was found on the beach at Horseshoe Bay, South Australia. In the days that followed, the local city newspaper discovered that the deceased girl, Carly Ryan, had a page on MySpace—a phenomenally popular social networking Web site, particularly popular among adolescents, who use the site to socialize and share information such as photos, music, videos, and diaries. MySpace users engage in a form of life writing—telling stories about their lives, documenting and authenticating their lives in the public domain.[1]

The newspaper ran articles for the following week constructing a life for the girl who had died, using information gained from her MySpace site. The not so subtle subtext of most of these articles was a possible link between the girl's death and her engagement with MySpace. MySpace is depicted as a hazardous technology—contravening the boundaries of private and public life and presenting adolescents with opportunities to offer transgressive or otherwise undesirable representations of their lives.

Despite, and perhaps because of, the negative publicity received by social networking sites, hundreds of thousands of people are presenting their life narratives every day via Internet technologies. Life writing in the twenty-first century has been indelibly marked by do-it-yourself cyber-narratives. Social networking, for example, has redefined the ways in which, and the means by which, everyday people present their life narratives. However, I am particularly interested in looking at social networking sites as a site for young people to circulate their lives and/or have their lives received by others. Facebook and MySpace are largely vehicles for the circulation of young people's life narratives, and despite the sites' assurances of privacy and security, the narratives of young adults are available for public consumption in unprecedented ways. Young life writers are potentially rendered vulnerable by their age and inexperience as life writers. They are writing in domains controlled by large corporations and according to templates that sanction particular norms for life-writing practice.

Instead of echoing the backlash against social networking and young people's life writing, I want to argue that this life-writing phenomenon presents a unique opportunity to acknowledge and mark territory for young people's life writing—an undertheorized life-writing form—and to explore the ethics of writing and receiving these texts as autobiographical narratives.

When I refer to "young people" I am largely referring to adolescents—people between thirteen and eighteen years of age. However, the discussion will resonate more broadly (for example, to those under the age of thirteen and young people over the age of eighteen). Traditionally, mainstream children's life narratives, like children's literature and culture, have been, to quote Henry Jenkins, "written by adults, illustrated by adults, edited by adults, marketed by adults, purchased by adults, and often read by adults" (*Children's Culture Reader* 23). And within culture more broadly, as Henry A. Giroux contends, experiences of youth are rarely narrated by the young. He writes:

> Prohibited from speaking as moral and political agents, youth becomes an empty category inhabited by the desires, fantasies and interests of the adult world. This is not to suggest that youth don't speak; they are

simply restricted from speaking in those spheres where public conversation shapes social policy and refused the power to make knowledge consequential with respect to their own collective needs. (24)

However, self-representation is, as Paul John Eakin argues, something that most humans have an "underlying, even unconscious narrative urge" to do (*How Our Lives* 139). However marginalized from mainstream cultures of speaking, young people have been engaging in alternative modes of life writing for many years—from artwork, photography, and written diaries through to independent media production such as perzines and documentaries.[2] And as Anna Poletti suggests, examples of young people's life writing can also be seen in do-it-yourself (DIY) counter-cultural activities such as graffiti, independent music, community-event organizing, and political and cultural activism—which commonly critique the commercialization of youth cultures (185).

The advent of mobile and Internet technologies has broadened the scope of young people's life narratives dramatically. According to Lee Rainie, 87 percent of twelve- to seventeen-year-olds in the United States use the Internet, and 57 percent of these users engage in public creative output—ranging from artwork, audio and video, photographs, and creative writing. Life writing has become instant and broadly accessible for young people—particularly those from the so-called middle classes who have access to Internet technologies in the home. And life writing has fast become the boom product resulting from this access. In online spaces, young life writers have been able to bypass traditional modes of publishing and self-publish aspects of their life narratives through writing, photographs, and music, to give just a few examples.

The most significant development to affect young people's engagement with life-writing practice has been the rise of "Web 2.0" and the growth of social technology: computer-mediated communication environments that have enabled young people to share aspects of their life in an unprecedented way—through blogs, wikis, instant messaging, e-mail, photo-sharing sites such as Flickr and Slide, media-sharing and production sites such as YouTube, and social networking Web sites such as MySpace, Friendster, Facebook, and Yahoo! 360°. Sites such as Bebo and myYearbook have been specifically designed for high school students. The popularity of these sites is forever shifting; a site that is popular one year can easily be replaced by the next big thing in the following year. However, what has remained constant in recent years has been the propensity of young people to engage in interactive new media outlets. The industries behind these technologies have actively courted young demographics—appealing to their skills and knowledge, consumption habits, and consumer potential.

Commentators have offered boredom and narcissism as explanations for the popularity of social networking sites. However, the appeal of these sites cannot be explained so narrowly. They provide outlets for activism—spaces to offer opinions and spaces to (potentially) be heard. For example, a MySpace site called "Freethinking Teens" offers a nonreligious space for discussion. Another MySpace site, the "Teen Choice Action Team," is a pro-choice site for teens to lend their support to reproductive debates. Similarly, Facebook groups such as "Teens Against Suicide" and "Teens Against Drunk Driving" offer spaces for discussion and disclosure. Social networking sites create opportunities for young people to connect with people who share similar interests, and through this to negotiate and validate their identities. For example, sites such as "Teen Lit" on MySpace provide an outlet for writers and readers to meet and discuss a range of issues relating to the production and reception of literature.

But perhaps most significantly, and as I mentioned previously, these sites allow young people to exert some control over both media production, and through this, the production of their own images and life narratives. For instance, YouTube hosts "video blogs" (or "vblogs") which allow online diarists to showcase their daily lives to a potential mass audience. For example, Kevjumba's "I Hate the SAT" video has (to date) been viewed just under half a million times, has received over five thousand comments, and has solicited sixteen "video responses." This is surely a decent audience for life writing from the margins.

To focus this discussion a little more, I want to isolate MySpace as a representative social networking technology, and discuss some specific examples and controversies, before concluding with a more general discussion of these spaces as sites for facilitating life writing. MySpace was launched in January 2004. Within two years it had almost fifty million members (Kornblum, "Teens Hang Out at MySpace"). The reasons for having a MySpace site are multitudinous and varied. For some, MySpace is a place to promote their music; for others, it is a place to showcase their photographs or poetry. For many, it is about networking: maintaining contact with existing friends and making new friends.

MySpace profiles contain two standard front page entries that allow for the construction of a very basic life narrative: "About Me" and "Who I'd Like to Meet." Profiles also contain an "Interests" section and a "Details" section where users can fill in more information about themselves. Users can also write a blog, which is linked to the front page of their site, and they can upload images.

One of the most important markers on MySpace is the "friends" links. The process of adding new friends to your links (these friends might be actual friends you know or cyber-friends) is called "friending." Having a large number of friends is a status symbol in the virtual world as much as it is in the real world. It is proof of "getting a life," of authenticating your own life experiences through participation in everyday culture (Smith and Watson, *Getting a Life* 2–3). This is especially pertinent for youth cultures because, as previously mentioned, the societies from which these texts emerge are largely ambivalent about their existence and validity.

Safe Spaces or Vulnerable Subjects?

Despite all that has been gained by young people on sites such as MySpace, the negative publicity fare outweighs the positive. A number of studies concerning teenagers' use of MySpace suggest that teenagers are "at risk" when engaging in social networking—for example, having their personal information accessed or used without their permission, being contacted by people they do not know, being exposed to online material they do not wish to see, or engaging with people they do not know (Netsmartz). MySpace prohibits those under the age of fourteen from having a page. However, it is relatively easy for a person to lie about his or her age. And if MySpace proves to be too restrictive, there are numerous other sites to create profiles on. MySpace attempts to educate its users about online safety. It also monitors users' pages and removes photographs that contain nudity. However, monitoring millions of sites has proven challenging, and prohibited material inevitably slips through (Kornblum, "Adults Question MySpace's Safety").

A number of high-profile controversies have adversely affected MySpace's reputation. In the U.K., teenager Rachael Bell had an open party invitation listed on her MySpace site. More than two hundred gate crashers caused £25,000 worth of damage to her family's home. Then there was the U.S. teenager Katherine Lester, who ran away to the West Bank to be with a man she met on MySpace (she was recovered in Jordan and sent home before she reached her final destination). And I have previously mentioned the case of murdered South Australian teenager Carly Ryan, whose MySpace site lead the police to suspects and ultimately to make an arrest. In this instance, Ryan's MySpace site provided evidence in the same way a diary or letters might have in murder cases twenty years ago. However, media reports provocatively implicated MySpace in her murder; to quote one indicative example:

A web of secret internet message boards could be crucial to solving the suspected murder of South Australian teenager Carly Ryan. . . . [These message boards] provide an insight to Adelaide's bizarre teenage "goth" and "emo" world, some sites showing graphic images involving bondage, suicide and drug use. (Littlely, Salter, and Wheatley)

There is a strong perception that participation in sites such as MySpace, and more particularly life-narrative disclosures it solicits, exposes young people to harm. They become the "vulnerable subjects" (to again use G. Thomas Couser's term) of their own life-narrative texts, unknowing of the consequences of their self-representations, and will potentially later regret what they have written or shown to the public. However, these concerns are remarkably similar to those commonly faced by people publishing life narratives in mainstream domains. For instance, as suggested in earlier chapters, autobiographers such as Kathryn Harrison have, as Paul John Eakin notes, been accused of engaging in too much self-disclosure and are thus open to accusations of sensationalism and/or bad taste (*Ethics* 3). However, the difference that remains is the contrasting age of these respective life writers.

Web sites such as WiredSafety have been established to protect children using the Internet, and in recent years their focus has shifted strongly to monitoring social networking sites.[3] WiredSafety is directed at parents, providing information on how to best educate and protect children from "cyber predators" and "cyber bullies." While I do not doubt the need for such Web sites and the good work they do, the overwhelming tone of WiredSafety is that parents should, as a proactive, precautionary measure, be anxious about their children's use of social networking sites. There is also a strong emphasis on teaching parents how to police children's use of sites such as MySpace. For example, I quote from WiredSafety's "Internet 101" page on the topic:[4]

So what do you, as a parent, do? First you need to find out if your child has a page on one of these sites. The best way to find out if your child has a profile on this or another similar site is to ask them. If you're not sure that your child is being honest with you, you can search MySpace.com (or the other sites) using their e-mail address, or by searching for their school. (You click on "search" and enter their email address or full name in the appropriate search box.)

> If you find that your child has a profile on the Web site, you should
> review it. It's amazing how much you can learn about your child by
> reading their profiles. Does it contain personal information, such as their
> full name, address or phone numbers? Has your child posted photos? Are
> they photos of themselves or someone else? Are they sharing poems they
> write or provocative comments about themselves or others?
>
> If you want the profile removed (you must remove your child's profile
> if they are under age), first ask your child to remove it themselves. If
> that doesn't work, MySpace.com has a section explaining how to remove
> a page. If you find someone who is underage, you can report it there
> as well.

The site promotes "nannyware"—software that allows parents to monitor
their children's Internet usage, to the point of being able to read what they
post.[5] The primary concerns that adults seem to have about teenagers' use of
MySpace relate to use of profanity, sexually explicit discussions, provocative
photographs, and the amount of personal information divulged. Ironically,
these qualities are all stapes of normal teenage behavior—and have long been
fundamental elements of adult life-narrative practice![6]

These concerns remain the focus of discussions about MySpace despite a
plethora of studies suggesting that most teenagers use MySpace responsibly.
Kate Gross reports a U.S. study in which 40 percent of those teenage users
of MySpace surveyed made their profiles available only to friends. Of those
who had public profiles, 90 percent did not use their full name in their profile
(8). Other studies suggest that teenagers do not share the concerns of their
parents and teachers regarding their online safety (NCMEC).

Adolescents engaging in risky behavior is not a new phenomenon, nor are
adult concerns and attempts to monitor and curb these activities. However,
as I suggested earlier, online technologies present unparalleled opportunities
for autonomous creative activity. This is seldom the focus of discussions
about MySpace; hence I want to focus on, and conclude this discussion with,
an exploration of MySpace as a site for young people to become life-writing
practitioners. I am particularly interested in the ethical issues that surround
the production and reception of these narratives.

Writing and Witnessing: Technology and the
Ethics of Young People's Life Writing

If MySpace and the like have become the primary sites for young people
to write autobiographically, then what are the key impediments to adults

witnessing and sanctioning these narratives as autobiography? Despite their obvious prescriptiveness (for instance, in the narratives they sanction), these sites exist as innovative new-media sites for the construction and/or representation of young lives. However, there is a manufactured culture of fear surrounding sites like MySpace and the narratives they solicit, which highlights their dangers to childhood innocence. Or, conversely, their narratives are represented as trivial and banal—not worthy of serious attention.

As a consequence, when critical, scholarly attention is given to these cultural practices, it is often met with resistance by young life writers who see this attention as yet another form of surveillance or social control.[7]

For Henry Jenkins, concerns about sites such as MySpace reflect contemporary adult anxieties about the digital revolution. The "wide-eyed child as subject to the corruptions of cybersex and porn websites" is "opportunistically evoked" in this debate. Jenkins writes, "The innocent child carries the rhetorical force of such arguments; we are constantly urged to take action to protect our children." But is such "protection" merely impeding both the production of adolescent life narratives and our ability to comprehend these texts as life narratives? Jenkins and others have argued for a more complex understanding of children's cultural lives—as both producers and receivers of culture, as social and political agents (*Children's Culture Reader* 2–3).

Similarly, Jon Katz shifts the focus away from discussions of how we might best protect children from cyberspace toward discussions of how we might better empower their participation. He writes: "Children need help in becoming civic-minded citizens of the digital age, figuring out how to use the machinery in the service of some broader social purposes. . . . But more than anything else, children need to have their culture affirmed" (4).[8] Children's life writing presents us with an opportunity to do just this—to witness children constructing their own lives, images, and cultures.

In his discussion of the ethics of life writing, Eakin argues that "an ethics of life writing is properly concerned with checking its potential for harm, displacing what has been recognized traditionally as its potential for good" (*Ethics* 4). The life-writing practices I have described in this paper are predominantly ethical; however, community responses to them have been largely unethical. Thus the question, then—and perhaps the mandate that remains—is: How can we better negotiate the complex relationship that exists between adults and children as producers and recipients of children's life writing?

Writing Childhood in the Twenty-first Century

In an article for the U.K. *Observer* newspaper in 2001, Kathryn Hughes wrote, "There are signs . . . that memoir's hold on the marketplace is over. Publishers are no longer commissioning it, believing readers to be bored by tales of 'my glandular fever hell'" ("Remembering Imagination"). Hughes made similar statements in an article in 1999 ("I Have Seen"). Despite the plethora of critics willing autobiography into the past, it remains a dynamic force in the present. New forms of autobiography emerge each day in print, on the Web, and, as Smith and Watson suggest, in everyday life. The emergence of different narratives and identities within autobiography mirrors the possibilities for identity formation in broader society. Autobiographical writings about childhood exist within a web of autobiographical intertexts, influencing and being influenced by the range of selves on display.

These texts reveal the types of cultural memory work that autobiography is engaged in at this cultural moment. They demonstrate the limits and possibilities for writing about the child self autobiographically. But, perhaps more significantly, these autobiographies highlight the role that autobiographical writings of childhood play as responders to, and agents in, the broader cultural shaping of childhood.

NOTES

INTRODUCTION: CONSTRUCTING CHILDHOOD, CONTESTING CHILDHOOD

1. Although the United States has signed the convention, it has not ratified it, as it is perceived (in some circles) to be in conflict with the rights of parents. Also, the state of Texas currently allows child offenders to receive the death penalty. President Barack Obama has promised to address this.

2. See Antze and Lambek; Bal; and Hamilton 9–32 for discussions of cultural memory.

3. For example, the U.K.'s National Society for the Prevention of Cruelty to Children (NSPCC) and National Association for People Abused in Childhood (NAPAC)—welfare agencies that work with survivors of child abuse—provide annotated lists of autobiographies of childhood on their Web sites. The Web site of an Australian government department, the Department of Education and Community Services, contains references to autobiographies of childhood on its "Addressing Bullying," "Addressing Child Abuse," and "Addressing Domestic Violence" sections.

4. Sanders writes that these autobiographies of childhoods were "often shaped, consciously or unconsciously, by a sense of what the subject was to become" (202).

5. The bildungsroman became "the most influential genre of the nineteenth century" and heavily influenced autobiographies of childhood produced in the nineteenth and twentieth centuries. S. Smith and Watson, *Reading Autobiography* 101–102.

6. See Coe, *When the Grass Was Taller*; Hooten, *Stories of Herself When Young*; Mc-Cooey, *Artful Histories*. McCooey argues, "What literary critics usually mean by literary autobiography is a form of writing which demonstrates the aesthetic and technical control that the 'higher' forms of literature do," whereas in fact literary autobiography "can accommodate a whole spectrum of style and technique" (3). Many of the autobiographies I have selected would not be classified as literary autobiography because of their overt didacticism or therapeutic references. Autobiographies authored by writers who have previously published fictional works (for example, Diski, Drewe, and Keneally) would probably be interpreted as literary autobiography. However, the contemporary autobiography of childhood is not dominated by famous authors.

7. For McCooey the child is inaccessible through memory and is thus necessarily mythical, part of the adult's imagination. Though located in history childhood is necessarily "beyond history, since childhood is beyond time" ("Australian Autobiographies" 132).

8. See especially Adelman et al.; Begley and Moss; Bing; Blais; Gray; Horvitz ; Hughes, "I Have Seen the Past"; Hughes, "Remembering Imagination"; Jones "It's Better to Tell"; Kirtz; Rust; P. Smith.

9. Alison James, Chris Jenks, and Alan Prout discuss the particular type of attention being directed at childhood: "Once childhood was a feature of parental (or maybe just maternal) discourse, the currency of educators and the sole theoretical property of developmental psychology. Now with an intensity perhaps unprecedented, childhood has become popularized, politicized, scrutinized and analysed in a series of interlocking spaces in which the traditional confidence and certainty about childhood and children's social status are being radically undermined" (3).

10. Roger Neustadter explores "patterns and distinctions that can be discerned in contemporary narratives of childhood" (236). He isolates "heaven," "hell" and "purgatory" as recurring motifs in contemporary autobiographies of childhood such as McCourt's *Angela's Ashes* and Karr's *The Liars' Club*. Though he makes astute and convincing observations about these patterns, Neustadter does not ultimately account for why these patterns might be occurring within contemporary autobiographies of childhood. He questions why certain childhoods are being "remembered" now but does not consider the role cultural memory plays in this remembering, nor does he discuss the ways in which more general cultural constructions of childhood might have an impact on the available spaces for autobiographical representations.

CHAPTER 1 — CREATING CHILDHOOD:
AUTOBIOGRAPHY AND CULTURAL MEMORY

1. For further discussion (and debate) on the function and legitimacy of memory in autobiography see Bal vii–xvii; S. Smith and Watson 16–24; and Lambek and Antze xi–xxix.

2. The term "cultural memory," though distinct, shares a relationship with "collective memory," "social memory," "public memory," and "national memory." These different conceptualizations of memory are astutely summarized by Paula Hamilton, whose arguments I condense here. Traditionally the predominant modes of public memory have been "official memory" or "historical memory"—authorized discourses that shape the ways a society "remembers" (12). Some examples of official policies governing childhood would include government regulations on health, welfare, and education. The past century, however, has witnessed an increasing recognition of memory as a fluid, social process. The interest of historians in oral history from the 1960s onward was one of the primary triggers for this thinking. Oral history promoted the idea that the past was not fixed; historical sources were created in the present, and "so became aware of the 'retrospective and fluid' character of memory" (14).

3. *Cherry*, though a bestseller and praised by critics, did not achieve the same success as *The Liars' Club*. Where *The Liars' Club* was assumed to represent an anomalous childhood (a theory that was later debunked by an outpouring of traumatic childhoods via autobiography), *Cherry* was thought to be analogous—a representative autobiography of adolescence.

4. Consider also the nostalgic autobiography by Gilda O'Neill, *My East End*, a collection of oral histories that construct life in London's East End from its founding to the late twentieth century. *My East End* promotes the idea that there was a golden age in post–World War II Britain, which was the time when the narrator was born. Postwar childhoods are romanticized and are juxtaposed with contemporary childhoods to assert their superiority. O'Neill's narrator cites one of the oral histories she has gathered: "My childhood was happy. We were not surrounded by a lot of children with wonderful toys making us envious [and] there were no big stores filled with unobtainable goodies. . . . [Instead] we made our own amusement. We had marbles, some clay and others more valuable, called glarnies, made of glass, which we put a value on depending on size" (100). O'Neill's narrator describes children today as "pasty-faced little mouse potatoes glued to their computers" (307), revealing how her constructions of golden-age childhoods are dependent on these tropes of contemporary childhood. Scranton discusses this myth: "Children and young people have always posed problems for the adults in their lives yet there remains the much-promoted and oft-quoted myth, usually based on childhood reminiscences of the defining adults, that there was once a 'golden age' of compliance and discipline in which authority prevailed and every child knew its place. The idea that childhood deviance, youth lawlessness and anti-authority attitudes have escalated and are indicative of a broader moral decline within a previously stable and conforming social order is enduring. Each generation progressing through parenthood and into middle-age cannot remember a time when children were so ill-disciplined and so dismissive of their elders" ("Whose 'Childhood'?" 164). Nostalgic representations of British childhood, such as those in *My East End*, are fashioned by demonizing contemporary childhood and drawing on the notions of crisis outlined by Jenks and Scraton in chapter 1.

5. Sage's narrator explains, "As a tribute to topical teenaged angst, the headmistress arranged a make-up lesson by a lady from Ponds. Face paint was strictly forbidden in school, but it was understood that as nice, normal girls we were already dreaming of marrying men like Dad and needed to give off the right signals when we weren't in uniform" (202).

6. See Gilding, *Australian Families*; Kociumbas. Gilding summarizes the history of the Australian child. On occasion he turns to autobiographical narratives, by authors such as Donald Horne and Clive James, to provide further verification of the histories being explored. Moreover, in her historical anthology of Australian childhoods, Kociumbas utilizes autobiographies of childhood as historical resources. This again suggests the cross-fertilization between autobiographical knowledge and historical writing, the

propensity for autobiographies to be considered historical texts, and the tendency for autobiographical writing to perpetuate official memory.

7. Blainey first used this term in his Latham Memorial Lecture, which he delivered in Sydney in 1993. The "Black Armband View" of history was a rival to the traditional way in which Australian history was taught (which he refers to as the "Three-Cheers View of History"). This traditional view considers Australian history as largely a success (10).

8. The potency of memory idealizing the mid-twentieth century has provided the catalyst for a range of counter-memories—shaped as feminist, postcolonial, and queer theories—to emerge strongly from the margins. Autobiography has been involved consistently in projects of counter-memory to "mediate and modify difficult or tabooed moments of the past—moments that nonetheless impinge, sometimes fatally, on the present" (Bal ix). For instance, cultural memory has surfaced strongly within autobiography as a vehicle for restoring Holocaust memories (xi).

9. *The Leaving of Liverpool* is a two-part miniseries screened on the ABC (Australia) in 1994. It is concerned with the migrant/orphan immigration program conducted during the 1950s that saw orphans from postwar England, Ireland, Scotland, and Wales being sent to Australia and Canada.

10. Whitlock writes:

> In the winter of 1997 Australians were immersed in an ocean of testimony. It came in the form of the Report of the National Inquiry into the separation from their families and communities of Aboriginal and Torres Strait Islander children. This Report from the Australian Human Rights and Equal Opportunity Commission (HREOC) is called Bringing Them Home. It records that 'between one in three and one in ten Indigenous children were forcibly removed from their families and communities' from 1910 to 1970 (Wilson 37). The Commission listened to 535 personal stories of forcible removal, and had access to another thousand or so in written form. The Commissioners travelled throughout the country gathering testimonies, listening and reading. In writing the Report they retained as far as possible the actual words as they heard them, and so first-person testimonies are placed alongside third-person reporting and analysis throughout. ("In the Second Person" 198)

The report is the bestselling government publication ever, and the HREOC Web site "has facilitated the transit of these stories across a wide international readership" (198).

11. Attwood writes, "In these years the stolen generations became, in Pierre Nora's terms, a *lieux de mémoire* [*sic*]—a site of memory—a place (in various senses of that word) which, as a result of the convergence or condensation of various histories, embodies a collective memory that has become central to Aboriginal identity in settled Australia" (199). The cultural forms in which these narratives were documented also reflected a move toward more inclusive ways of recording and receiving history: "Whereas the stolen generations narrative of the early 1980s had been created as the result of collaboration between informants and historians and involved a conjunction

of memory- and history-work, now the accounts were more the product of memory and other discursive and textual practices, and they were becoming increasingly symbolic in nature" (200).

12. There are numerous examples throughout *Shadow Child* where the narrator overtly labels the Welfare as ignorant, deconstructing their official knowledge via personal narrative. For example, when Mrs. Kelly sexually abuses her, the adult narrator reflects, "The hospital doctors must have believed the story my foster mother told them: no one—no one at all—asked me what had happened to me. Maybe they did not care enough to even bother to ask; I guess my foster mother was right, no one cared what really happened to kids like us" (21). The adult narrator wonders why no adult welfare provider considered that she was being abused when she was taken to the hospital with a broken arm: "As I grew older, I often thought about that incident. I used to wonder: why did not a single doctor or nurse notice that I had no bruise or scratch on my arm where I had supposedly hit the window sill? Why did the Welfare officer not take the trouble to examine me either? If just one of them had taken a good look, they could have seen the real cause: child abuse" (60).

13. Kay Schaffer summarizes Indigenous life writing in Australia:

The Aboriginal life story is a recent phenomenon in Australia. Aboriginal life stories suddenly entered the book market in the 1980s as texts that did not quite fit the genres of formal auto/biography, history, memoir or fiction. They have become a forum for indigenous people to speak on their own behalf, thus reversing two hundred years of being spoken about, and for, by anthropologists, historians, linguists, missionaries, artists, poets, novelists, and film-makers. Since that time these life stories have performed an educative role for indigenous and non-indigenous readers alike, providing a cumulative challenge to national stereotypes that had previously gained authority through canonical national histories and fictions. (69)

14. Attwood cites Peter Read's "naming" the "removal of children," which created an historical event, replacing previous namings such as "adopted" or "fostered" (189–190).

15. Meehan writes: "Debra [her editor] requested I send the disk of the manuscript but this was not as easy as it sounds: I had only taught myself to use a computer in the previous two years and the hard disk had multiple copies of various chapters. It took me months to go through them all to find the final version. I got so frustrated that I wouldn't turn the computer on for weeks at a time" (303).

CHAPTER 2 — CONSUMING CHILDHOOD:
BUYING AND SELLING THE AUTOBIOGRAPHICAL CHILD

1. According to Terry O'Connor, "They laugh in the book publishing industry when someone says 'You can't judge a book by its cover.' They know that the exact opposite is true, that book covers have to say, 'Buy me' as well as give an indication of what the book is about." Kirsten Abbott, editor of Adult Books at Penguin Australia, suggests

that publishers work on the presumption that it takes consumers, from when they select a book from a shelf, an average of four seconds to decide whether or not they want to buy it (pers. comm.).

2. Autobiographies are prominently displayed in bookshops (actual and virtual). Despite the fluid, often contested boundaries of autobiography and fiction, bookstores consistently provide a separate section for autobiographical writing (usually titled "Biography" or "Nonfiction"), which is customarily positioned alongside "History."

3. Holland argues that photographs mediate between "personal memory and social history, between public myth and personal unconscious" ("History, Memory" 1).

4. Holland is referring specifically to family photographs. However, I find her arguments appropriate for the discussion of childhood photographs.

5. These covers are predominantly paperback editions. This is a significant and deliberate selection, given that these are the less expensive editions most available to consumers. Original hardback editions of autobiographies such as Drewe's *The Shark Net* and Sage's *Bad Blood* do not include autobiographical photographs on the covers. First editions, such as of *The Shark Net*, are marketed at professional readers. The paperback version, containing a picture of a child playing on a Perth beach, is marketed more widely as an autobiography of childhood.

6. Holland astutely refers to family albums as "infrastructure[s] of popular memory" ("History, Memory" 13).

7. To appropriate Bourdieu's term ("Social Definition" 166).

8. This is a point I return to in chapter 7 of this book, which focuses on readers.

9. Another key element in the physical presentation of autobiographies of childhood is the "jacket copy," or promotional or publisher's "blurb"—a short quote usually found on the front or back cover of the autobiography—most commonly penned by a fellow autobiographer or book reviewer. Like cover photographs, these blurbs are highly visible meta-textual elements that suggest preferred or authoritative readings for the autobiography before the text itself is read. Blurbs work at the moment of choice. They classify the narrative, appeal to the reader, and define the kind of reading experience the book can deliver. Like cover photographs, blurbs are important for the marketing of literature. Kirsten Abbott proposes that although the jacket copy is an essential marketing tool for all books, it is *the* main selling tool for autobiography (pers. comm.). This is an interesting proposition: why would a genre and plot description be more important in marketing autobiography than fiction? Abbott suggests that the blurb must give enough information to draw readers into wanting to read the text. Despite the interventions of postmodern scholars, the popular assumption remains that fiction may have multiple, ambiguous meanings, whereas autobiography's (singular) meaning is made apparent and transparent.

10. Abbott suggests that book covers of autobiographies tend to be selected by the author and approved by the publisher (pers. comm.).

11. Jenks explains that a desire for nostalgia is apparent at various levels of contemporary culture: "whereas children used to cling to us, through modernity, for guidance into their/our 'futures,' now we, through late modernity, cling to them for 'nostalgic' groundings, because such change is both intolerable and disorientating for us" (108).

12. A recent autobiography of childhood by Alexandra Fuller, *Don't Let's Go to the Dogs Tonight*, also published by Picador, has a very similar cover image.

13. In her book *Pictures of Innocence*, Higonnet explores the extent to which pictures of childhood "guard the cherished ideal of childhood innocence, yet . . . contain within them the potential to undo that ideal" (7).

CHAPTER 3 — AUTHORING CHILDHOOD:
THE ROAD TO RECOVERY AND REDEMPTION

1. For further discussion of reading post-Oprah, see Douglas, " 'Your Book Changed My Life.' "

2. Barthes warned against extreme critical prioritization of authorial intention, arguing that "a text is not a line of words releasing a single 'theological' meaning (the 'message' of the Author-God) but a multi-dimensional space in which a variety of writings, none of them original, blend and clash" (146). Though the current status of authorship is not suffering from the extreme authorial status that concerned Barthes, allowances for authorial intention and biography alongside a variety of other influences may be a reason for the (perhaps subtle) reemergence of the author.

3. It is worth noting that this issue almost never surfaces with biographies, which are rarely marketed as the work of a particular author. Only when some question about truth or method arises does the biographer tend to become a media issue.

4. As Sherman notes, "The number of available celebrity authors, well-known literary writers and up-and-coming names continues to grow along with bookseller interest in sponsoring store readings" (26).

5. The second and third autobiographies, *'Tis: A Memoir* (1999) and *Teacher Man* (2005), were not as well received as *Angela's Ashes*, nor was McCourt's brother Malachy's memoir *A Monk Swimming*. Frank McCourt also penned a children's book, *Angela and the Baby Jesus* (2007).

6. Karr and Harrison provide review blurbs for the book jacket of particular editions of *Angela's Ashes*.

7. I agree with Claire Armitstead, who notes that the success of *Angela's Ashes* was driven, at least in part, by America's sentimental attachment to its Irish roots.

8. See Jones, "Hard Luck, Good Tales"; Kakutani. Intriguingly, Kakutani criticized McCourt's sequel *'Tis* on the ground that it is much "angrier" than *Angela's Ashes*. Kakutani writes: "Whereas that 'epic of woe' was remarkable for its lack of bitterness and self-pity, *'Tis* is largely animated by the feelings of resentment and envy that the young McCourt experienced in trying to overcome his family's legacy of poverty and

deprivation. Given the difficulties he faced, it's hard to begrudge him such emotions; it's just that this sour tone of complaint does not make for particularly engaging or sympathetic reading."

9. The appeal of this mythology can be traced back to fairy tales such as "Cinderella." It has been a popular trope in literature—famous exemplars include Charles Dickens's *Great Expectations* and Charlotte Brontë's *Jane Eyre*. More recently, the continued popularity of game shows and the rise of "reality television" function to condition everyday people to be aspirational—to believe that anything is possible and that our lives can be bettered through a mix of hard work, self-belief, and opportunity.

10. In an interview with Dave Weich, McCourt recounts that upon sailing into New York, "I was in heaven. I was sailing right into heaven."

11. For further discussion on survivor narratives, see Haaken, *Pillar of Salt*; Felman and Laub.

12. See Gray for a discussion of the rise of celebrity autobiographical authors such as Frank McCourt and Kathryn Harrison. Margaret Maupin suggests that the presence of an author at a book signing can mean thousands more books sold (Symons 30).

13. See Begley and Moss, who write, "Beware a woman scorned—especially if she is clutching a publishing contract."

14. See, for example, Wiltshire Rape Support Line.

15. For detailed discussions of scriptotherapy and the therapeutic uses of life writing, see Henke; Hunt.

16. Autobiographies of childhood are commonly criticized on this front too. The assumption of universality of experience, and the use of generalizations, for instance, has been viewed as overly reductive and limiting. For example, see Levy. In his discussion of *Angela's Ashes*, Levy writes:

> [McCourt's childhood is] described in terms of universals or abstract general ideas which apply equally to all individuals in the same category. For example, the particular 'miserable childhood' recounted is presented as an example of a general type: 'the miserable Irish Catholic childhood' (p. 11). In fact, throughout the work, personal experience is expressed in terms of universals or general types—terms that is, of repeatability and constant nature, in the series of individuals to which they apply. Thus, the singularity of personal experience is rendered in terms of generality. (260)

17. Though, as Susan Engel suggests, children write about their lives every day, "in school newspapers, holiday scrapbooks, diaries, letters, postcards," this writing is commonly facilitated by adults, such as teachers and parents, and very rarely is it published in mainstream public forums (205). Two exceptions are childhood wartime diaries—the internationally renowned diary of Anne Frank, *The Diary of a Young Girl* (1947) and more recently *Zlata's Diary: A Child's Life in Sarajevo* (1993) by Zlata Filipovic. Zines, blogs, and social networking sites such as Facebook and MySpace have opened up opportunities for the autobiographical acts of young people. It will be interesting to see,

considering the ever-changing spaces within autobiography, if any inroads are made to publish child and adolescent autobiographers in the near future. This is a point I take up in the conclusion.

18. Such a tendency can be traced back to earlier critical periods. With reference to nineteenth-century literature, Boris Tomasevskij writes that "we suffered through a period when the writer was necessarily considered a 'good person'" (53), and Foucault argues that "modern criticism uses methods similar to those that Christian exegesis employed when trying to prove the value of a text by its author's saintliness" ("What Is an Author?"150). The tendency to use an author's apparent "goodness" for publicity or critical ends is therefore not a new phenomenon. I am suggesting that this tendency has a distinct relevance to understanding the success of autobiographies in terms of their authorship.

CHAPTER 4 — SCRIPTS FOR REMEMBERING: CHILDHOODS AND NOSTALGIA

1. The McCourt brothers certainly engage in nostalgic remembering. However, since the United States has become *such* a fruitful site for the emergence of traumatic memories of childhood, "linked in its ascendancy to the therapy-driven, culture of confession" (Gilmore, *Limits* 2), this mode has come to dominate the genre, leaving little space for "happy" or nostalgic texts.

2. Such narratives remain prominent within Australian cultural production. See, for example, Elder.

3. A number of autobiography theorists have explored the usefulness of Bakhtin's theory of dialogism for studies of autobiographical narratives. See Brockmeir and Carbaugh 7; Egan, *Mirror Talk* 23–26; and S. Smith, *Poetics of Women's Autobiography* 50.

4. This is the subtitle of this autobiography.

5. See Hattenstone; Cummins. Interestingly, Simon Hattenstone, writing in the *Guardian*, suggests that many Manchester City fans reviled the book because it was factually inaccurate and labeled Shindler an opportunist who was riding the success of Nick Hornby's autobiographical novel *Fever Pitch*. Kev Cummins reveals that upon asking Shindler why his autobiography was called *Manchester United Ruined My Life* rather than *Manchester City . . .* , Shindler replied that his publishers suggested that using "Manchester United" in the title would prove more profitable. Cummins finds the book inauthentic and bemoans the inclusion of Shindler's personal life.

6. Contemporary Australia and its preoccupations offer a further key to understanding the ways in which these nostalgic narratives of childhood function as active cultural texts. As Steinwand suggests, "Nations make use of nostalgia in the construction of national identity. The myths of any nation appeal to the national nostalgic and encourage identification with such nostalgic images as the nation's 'founding fathers' or some 'golden age,' or decisive events in its history and the culture of the people" (11).

CHAPTER 5 — SCRIPTS FOR REMEMBERING:
TRAUMATIC CHILDHOODS

1. See Freud, "Aetiology of Hysteria"; Hacking, *Rewriting the Soul*. Hacking argues that trauma acquired meaning between 1874 and 1886 in France, where it represented "a wound to the soul," a spiritual, psychic, or mental injury (4). For the first time, through the work of pre-Freudian theorists such as Jean-Martin Charcot and Pierre Janet, trauma was linked to memory rather than only to the body. Though many believe that Freud's work on hysteria in the 1890s is the earliest use of the term "trauma," according to Hacking, Freud merely deployed "what had become current" (4).

2. The extent to which children are able to write of trauma during childhood is an important issue deserving of attention in future research. For example, see Martín Alcoff and Gray-Rosendale. As they argue, children are largely presumed to be poor witnesses or not able to give credible testimony (203). I take up the issue of child authorship of autobiography in the conclusion, but many issues in relation to child-authored autobiography are yet to be explored.

3. The primary aim of the "survivors' movement" is to encourage and facilitate survivors' disclosures of trauma in private and public contexts (Martín Alcoff and Gray-Rosendale 199). See also Apgar; Gilmore, *Limits of Autobiography*; S. Smith and Watson, "Situating Subjectivity" 40.

4. Some useful discussions of autobiographical narratives of abuse can be found in the work of Martín Alcoff and Gray-Rosendale and of Apgar.

5. For examples of such criticism see Hughes, "I Have Seen the Past and It Works" and "Remembering Imagination"; Jones, "It's Better to Tell All"; Treneman; Wolcott.

6. Frost summarizes this literary event:

> Kathryn Harrison's memoir *The Kiss* appeared in 1997 at the peak of a publishing trend that has been called alternatively 'the memoir craze' and 'the memoir plague.' *The Kiss* followed, and in some ways was the culmination of, [U.S.] memoirs of extremity such as Susanna Kaysen's *Girl, Interrupted*, Lucy Grealy's *Diary of a Face*, Michael Ryan's *Secret Life* and James Ellroy's *My Dark Places*. But Harrison's subject matter—the author's four-year affair with her father, beginning when she was twenty—seemed to surpass them all. (51)

7. Glynis George discusses how sensationalized depictions of trauma work against the aims of survivor discourse: "Public confessions by traumatized citizens are commonplace in media accounts of current social problems. The focus on individual experiences of child sexual abuse satiates tastes for public drama, implicating a cast of characters whose apparent goodness and evil simplify complex relations and cultural ambivalence towards the institutions of family and state" (46). Martín Alcoff and Gray-Rosendale offer this summary:

> The media often use the presence of survivors for shock value and to pander to a sadistic voyeurism among viewers, focusing on the details of the violations, with

close-ups of survivors' anguished expressions. They often eroticize the depictions of survivors and of sexual violence to titillate and expand their audiences. Survivor discourse has also been used in some cases by the psychiatric establishment to construct victim- and woman-blaming explanatory theories, such as the argument that some women have a 'victim personality.' (200).

8. Scheper-Hughes and Stein argue that although welfare professionals have been grappling with child abuse for many decades, it was only following its "discovery" by medical professionals in the United States in the 1960s that the general public started to express concern (178).

9. Andrews, Gould, and Corry cite seven Australian studies of child sexual abuse. According to the authors, gaining statistical information on the prevalence of child sexual abuse is legally and ethically difficult. Furthermore, only a minority of cases are reported to parents, and fewer are reported to authorities. Their findings are as follows:

> The adjusted prevalence estimate in males was 5.1% and in females 27.5%, which corresponds with rates in comparable countries. The rates for contact plus penetrative abuse were two-thirds of these (ie, 3.6% in males and 17.9% in females). The onset of abuse occurs at a mean age of 10 years, with most starting before age 12. The abuser is a family member in about 40% of cases, and is known to the child in 75% of cases. The abuser is usually male, mean age 32 years. Child sexual abuse is more frequent in families beset by other adversity, and it is difficult to determine the cause of any increased rate of mental disorders in the presence of an aggregation of risk factors.

The authors suggest that these statistics are comparable to studies completed in other countries (458–459).

10. For discussions of narrative therapy, see White and Epston.

11. *Finding Fish* was made into a film (*Antwone Fisher*, directed by and starring Denzel Washington) in 2002.

12. For example, Kathleen O'Malley's *Childhood Interrupted* recounts her abusive childhood at the hands of the Sisters of Mercy in an industrial school in Ireland. In *The God Squad*, Paddy Doyle describes the abuse he suffered during his eleven years in an industrial school, following the death of his parents when he was a small child. A quick search on any literary database reveals a plethora of similarly styled autobiographies of childhood coming out of Ireland.

13. For example, the narrator of *Out of Darkness* includes details of how his nieces, upon reading his manuscript, suggested that it gave them a "better insight" into their father's (Knight's brother's) problems, because he had been unable to discuss them with his family (190).

14. Jennifer Freyd uses the concept "knowledge isolation" to suggest the ways in which the conscious mind suppresses certain aspects of the abuse experience while other aspects can be recalled. For Freyd, this sort of response is a post-traumatic coping mechanism.

15. Maria Flook, reviewing *Skating to Antarctica*, refers to this shift as "annoying in its oddness, but we soon see how Diski wishes to separate herself from the Jennifer entrapped in childhood" ("Cold Comfort").

16. Martín Alcoff and Gray-Rosendale explain:

> At various times and in different locations [child abuse] has been absolutely prohibited, categorized as mad or untrue, or rendered inconceivable: presuming objects (such as a rapist father) that were not statable and therefore could not exist within the dominant discourses. The speech of incest survivors has been especially restricted on the grounds that it is too disgusting and disturbing to the listeners' constructed sensibilities. . . . Incest survivors have also been constructed as mad: "hysterical" women who are unable to distinguish reality from their own imaginations. (203)

Janice Haaken has written extensively on this issue.

CHAPTER 6 — ETHICS: WRITING ABOUT CHILD ABUSE, WRITING ABOUT ABUSIVE PARENTS

1. Burroughs's contemporary comic life writer David Sedaris has been accused of similar ethical indiscretions against family members.

2. Pat Jordan writes:

> I spoke with one of Pelzer's younger brothers, Stephen, 40, who was stricken with Bell's palsy as a child and whose speech is slightly slurred. Stephen denies his mother abused David or burned him or forced him to eat dog feces. "Please!'" he says. "That never happened." As a witness to the stabbing incident, Stephen says: "I saw mom cutting food when David grabbed her arm and got a small cut from the knife. There wasn't even any blood, yet he screamed, 'Mommy stabbed me!'"
>
> Stephen says David wasn't ostracized from the family, but that "he was very close to me and Robert," the oldest brother. "'We were 'The Three Musketeers.' But David had to be the center of attention. He was a hyper, spoiled brat.'"
>
> Pelzer's grandmother, Ruth Cole, 92, remembers him as a "disruptive kid, only interested in himself, with big ideas of grandeur." She says. "His books should be in the fiction section."

3. Barbour is speaking generally about autobiography, rather than traumatic texts. Clearly traumatic texts add an entirely different dimension to the ethics of representing (abusive) parents. There is not a great deal of scholarship in this area, so I hope that my work here makes a contribution to theorizing in the field.

4. In her review of Rosalie Fraser's *Shadow Child: A Memoir of the Stolen Generations*, Jan Mayman applauds the forgiveness that Fraser's autobiography displays. Mayman writes: "Fraser was four years old when her foster mother raped her with a knitting needle during one bout of drunken madness; yet she has forgiven this monstrous woman: [she quotes Fraser] 'I realise how sick she was . . . I still put flowers on her grave.'"

CHAPTER 7 — THE ETHICS OF READING:
WITNESSING TRAUMATIC CHILDHOODS

1. I am drawing here on Rita Felski's "On Confession"; much of the traumatic auto-biography I discuss can be considered confessional writing.

2. For example, Adelman et al.; Armitstead; Begley and Moss; Bing; French; Gray; Herman.

3. To retain a level of anonymity, I have referenced these Amazon "customer reviews" using randomly allocated initials to demarcate between these comments.

4. Rosamund Dalziell writes that reading Indigenous autobiographies "added to my consciousness of Aboriginal disadvantage in contrast with my own privilege. . . . I am impelled to some form of response and action" (4).

CONCLUSION: WRITING CHILDHOOD
IN THE TWENTY-FIRST CENTURY

1. I have previously argued, in "Blurbing Biographical," that online modes of self-representation such as personal Web pages and blogs are considered part of the "new wave" of everyday autobiographical representations that have become prevalent in the twenty-first century, a point echoed by Elizabeth Podnieks (124). As Podnieks argues, "The technological innovations offered by the internet stimulate, enhance and multiply the means for self-expression, but they do not inherently change the motivations for life writing, which have arguably always been to communicate and connect not only with our own disparate selves but also with those of others" (125).

2. Zines are

> self published, low-budget publications produced predominately by people be-tween the ages of fifteen and thirty-five. While the publications can take any form, they are usually booklets A5 or A6 in size, black and white photocopied, and hand bound with staples, string or sewing. Zines often include handcrafted elements distinguishing each copy, such as hand colouring or painting, craft materials such as ribbons and fabrics, post-it notes, handwriting, original photographs, or cut out images from magazines and books. They vary in length from two to fifty pages, and can be edited by a group or single person. (Poletti 184–185)

Perzines, or "personal zines," are autobiographical zines that represent some aspect of the author's life narrative. Arguably, many zines are autobiographical, but perzines are overtly so.

3. High school teachers have been known to peruse their students' MySpace sites to look for evidence of deviant behaviors. And many high schools in the United States have banned students from accessing MySpace on campus. In 2006 Republican congressman Michael G. Fitzpatrick of Pennsylvania attempted to introduce in the House of Representatives a bill that would require any school or library that received government funding to block access to any Web site that "allows users to create web pages or profiles that provide information about themselves and are available to other users, and

offers a mechanism for communication with other users, such as a forum, chat room, e-mail, or instant messenger." Known as the Deleting Online Predators Act, it would also make these sites available only to people age eighteen and older (Fletcher 24).

4. The page is headed "Blog Sites, Profile Sites, Diary Sites or Social-Networking Sites: Parry Addresses Parental Concerns." "Parry" is Parry Aftab, an Internet privacy and security lawyer, who is WiredSafety's executive director.

5. Parry writes:

> There is software you can install that will record what your kids say and post online. There is even one that will e-mail you reports at work. The ones I like best are made by Spectorsoft, and can be found at software4parents.com or spectorsoft. com. But don't use them just to spy on your kids. Treat them like a security video camera in the corner of a bank. No one views the tapes unless and until there is a break-in. Do the same here. Check the program reports if something goes wrong. It will collect whatever you need for evidence and to help your child if something goes wrong.

Despite Parry's discouraging parents from "spying" on their children, it is highly likely that some parents would use this technology to this end.

6. Of course, as Podnieks notes, "sexual revelations from the flirtatious to the pornographic have blushed the pages of diaries throughout history" (137–138); online life writing continues this trend.

7. Cary Bazalgette and David Buckingham note that within sociological research, youth cultures are subject to intense (and increasing) scrutiny (4). Henry Jenkins writes, "Sociological critics focus on the 'deviance' and 'destructiveness' of youth cultures, their 'irresponsibility,' or the rituals of their subcultural 'resistance' " (*Children's Culture Reader* 2).

There is also a question of the ethics of scholars deconstructing these texts in an academic environment. This is perhaps a topic for further research.

8. In "From YouTube to YouNiversity," Jenkins proposes a mandate for educators to embrace these technologies and allow students to use them in practical ways in their education programs.

WORKS CITED

Abbott, Kirsten. "Publication and Promotion of Autobiography." E-mail to the author. 28 Mar. 2001.

ACT Department of Education and Community Services (DECS). 21 Dec. 2005. <http://www.det.act.gov.au>.

Adams, Timothy Dow. *Light Writing and Life Writing*. Chapel Hill: U of North Carolina P, 2000.

Adelman, Michelle, et al. "Thanks for the Memoirs: There Has Never Been a Better Time to Write the Story of Your Life." *Time* 12 Apr. 1999: 100A–104A.

Amazon.com. "Customer Reviews" for Andrea Ashworth, *Once in a House on Fire*; James McBride, *The Color of Water: A Black Man's Tribute to His White Mother*; Dave Pelzer, *A Child Called "It."* 21 June 2008. <http://www.amazon.com>.

Andrews, Gavin, Bronwyn Gould, and Justine Corry. "Child Sexual Abuse Revisited." *eMJA* 176.10 (2002): 458–459.

Angela's Ashes. Dir. Alan Parker. Universal, 1999.

Antwone Fisher. Dir. Denzel Washington. Fox Searchlight, 2002.

Antze, Paul, and Michael Lambek, eds. *Tense Past: Cultural Essays in Trauma and Memory*. New York: Routledge, 1996.

Apgar, Sonia C. "Fighting Back on Paper and in Real Life: Sexual Abuse Narratives and the Creation of Safe Space." *Creating Safe Space: Violence and Women's Writing*. Ed. Tomoko Kuribayashi and Julie Tharp. New York: SUNY P, 1998. 47–58.

Armitstead, Claire. "The Rise and Rise of Memoir." *Guardian* 27 Jan. 2001. 18 July 2008 <http://books.guardian.co.uk/departments/biography/story/0,,428779,00.html>.

Ashworth, Andrea. Interview with BBCi. n.d. 8 Nov. 2002 <http://www.bbc.co.uk/health/hh/intero2.shtml>.

———. Interview with Douglas Eby. n.d. 18 Nov. 2001 <http://www.creativityand-women.com/article1025.html>.

———. Interview with Louise Jameson. n.d. 8 Nov. 2002 <http://www.open2.net/ever-wondered1/image/topic3.htm>.

———. Interview. "Writing from Life: Exploring Contemporary Writing about Childhood." 18 Nov. 2001 <http://www.englishandmedia.co.uk>.

———. *Once in a House on Fire*. 1998. London: Picador, 1999.

———. "When I Was a Little Girl." *Guardian Unlimited* 22 Nov. 2000. 18 Nov. 2001 <http://www.guardian.co.uk/child/story/0,7369,401276,00.html>.

Attwood, Bain. " 'Learning About the Truth': The Stolen Generations Narrative." *Telling Stories: Indigenous History and Memory in Australia and New Zealand*. Ed. Bain Attwood and Fiona Magowan. Crows Nest, NSW: Allen and Unwin, 2001. 183–212.

Bakhtin, Mikhail M. *The Dialogic Imagination: Four Essays*. Ed. Michael Holquist. Trans. Caryl Emerson and Michael Holquist. Austin: U of Texas P, 1981.

Bal, Mieke. Introduction. *Acts of Memory: Cultural Recall in the Present*. Ed. Mieke Bal, Jonathan Crewe, and Leo Spitzer. Hanover: UP of New England, 1999. vii–xvii.

Ball, Karyn. "Introduction: Trauma and Its Institutional Destinies." *Cultural Critique* 46 (Autumn 2000): 1–44.

Barbour, John D. "Judging and Not Judging Parents." *The Ethics of Life Writing*. Ed. Paul John Eakin. Ithaca: Cornell UP, 2004. 73–98.

Barthes, Roland. *Image-Music-Text*. Trans. and ed. Stephen Heath. London: Fontana, 1977. 142–148.

Baudrillard, Jean. *The Consumer Society: Myths and Structures*. London: Sage, 1998.

———. "The Dark Continent of Childhood." *Screened Out*. Trans. Chris Turner. London: Verso, 2002. 102–106.

Bazalgette, Cary, and David Buckingham. "Introduction: The Invisible Audience." *In Front of the Children: Screen Entertainment and Young Audiences*. Ed. Cary Bazalgette and David Buckingham. London: BFI, 1995. 4–14.

Beah, Ishmael. *A Long Way Gone: Memoirs of a Boy Soldier*. New York: Farrar, Straus and Giroux, 2007.

Beard, Jo Ann. *The Boys of My Youth*. New York: Back Bay Books, 1999.

Beard, Mary. "A Vicarage Tea-Party." Rev. of *Bad Blood*, by Lorna Sage. *TLS Times Literary Supplement* 1 Sept. 2000: 36.

Begley, Adam, and Stephen Moss. "A Stab in the Hardback." *Guardian Unlimited* 15 Feb. 1999. 8 Nov. 1999 <http://www.guardian.co.uk/Archive/Article/0,4273,3822291,00.html>.

Berg, Leila. *Flickerbook*. 1997. London: Granta, 1998.

Berlant, Lauren. "The Subject of True Feeling: Pain, Privacy, and Politics." *Cultural Pluralism, Identity Politics, and the Law*. Ed. Austin Sarat and Thomas R. Kearns. Ann Arbor: U of Michigan P, 1999. 48–84.

Bing, Jonathan. "Mass-Marketing Memoirs: Publishing's Memoir Mania." *Writer's Digest* Oct. 1997: 48–49.

Bird, Carmel. "Murder, Myth and Memoir." Rev. of *The Shark Net*, by Robert Drewe. *Australian Book Review* Apr. 2000: 7–8.

Bissinger, Buzz. "Ruthless with Scissors." *Vanity Fair* Jan 2007. 1 Feb 2008 <http://www.vanityfair.com/fame/features/2007/01/burroughs200701?currentPage=>.

Blainey, Geoffrey. "Drawing Up a Balance Sheet of Our History." *Quadrant* 37 (July–August 1993): 10–15.

Blais, Madeline. "So You're Planning to Write Your Memoirs." *Nieman Reports* 51 (Fall 1997): 80–84.

Born into Brothels: Calcutta's Red Light Kids. Dir. Zana Briski and Ross Kaufman. THINKfilm, 2005.

Bourdieu, Pierre. *Distinction: A Social Critique of the Judgement of Taste.* Cambridge: Harvard UP, 1984.

———. "The Social Definition of Photography." *Visual Culture: The Reader.* Ed. Jessica Evans and Stuart Hall. London: Sage, 1999. 162–80.

Boyle, John. *Galloway Street: Growing Up Irish in Scotland.* London: Doubleday, 2001.

Boym, Svetlana. *The Future of Nostalgia.* New York: Basic Books, 2001.

Bragg, Rick. *All Over but the Shoutin.'* New York: Vintage, 1998.

Briscoe, Constance. *Ugly: The True Story of a Loveless Childhood.* London: Hodder and Stoughton, 2006.

Brockmeier, Jens, and Donal Carbaugh, eds. *Narrative and Identity: Studies in Autobiography, Self and Culture.* Amsterdam: John Benjamins, 2001.

Brodzki, Bella. "Mothers, Displacement, and Language." *Women, Autobiography, Theory: A Reader.* Ed. Sidonie Smith and Julia Watson. Madison: U of Wisconsin P, 1998. 156–159.

Brown, Marilyn R., ed. *Picturing Children: Constructions of Childhood between Rousseau and Freud.* Aldershot: Ashgate, 2002.

Bruner, Jerome. "The Autobiographical Process." *The Culture of Autobiography: Constructions of Self-Representation.* Ed. Robert Folkenflik. Stanford: Stanford UP, 1993. 38–56.

Burroughs, Augusten. *Dry.* New York: Picador, 2004.

———. Interview with Andrew Denton. *Enough Rope* episode 75 (television program transcript). 2 May 2005. 10 May 2008 <http://www.abc.net.au/tv/enoughrope/transcripts/s1358565.htm>.

———. Interview with Jane Sullivan. *Sydney Morning Herald* 11 June 2005. 10 June 2008 <http://www.theage.com.au/news/books/running-with-augusten/2005/06/10/1118347580758.html>.

———. *Possible Side Effects.* New York: St. Martin's, 2006.

———. *Running with Scissors: A Memoir.* Sydney: Hachette, 2007.

———. *A Wolf at the Table.* Sydney: Picador, 2008.

Cannadine, David. *Ornamentalism: How the British Saw Their Empire.* Oxford: Oxford UP, 2001.

Caruth, Cathy. *Trauma: Explorations in Memory.* Baltimore: Johns Hopkins UP, 1995.

———. *Unclaimed Experience: Trauma, Narrative, and History.* Baltimore: Johns Hopkins UP, 1996.

Coe, Richard N. "Portrait of the Artist as a Young Australian: Childhood, Literature, and Myth." *Southerly* 41.2 (1981): 126–162.

———. "Reminiscence of Childhood: An Approach to a Comparative Mythology." *Proceedings of the Leeds Philosophical and Literary Society* 19.6 (1984): 1–95.

———. *When the Grass Was Taller: Autobiography and the Experience of Childhood.* New Haven: Yale UP, 1984.

Coetzee, J. M. *Boyhood: Scenes from Provincial Life.* London: Secker and Warburg, 1997.

Collins, Andrew. *Where Did It All Go Right? Growing Up Normal in the 70s*. London: Ebury, 2004.

———. *Wherediditallgoright.com*. n.d. 24 July 2008 <http://www.wherediditallgoright. com/>.

Corsaro, William A. *The Sociology of Childhood*. Thousand Oaks: Pine Forge Press, 1997.

Couser, G. Thomas. "Authority in Autobiography." *a/b: Auto/Biography Studies* 10.1 (1995): 34–49.

———. *Vulnerable Subjects: Ethics and Life Writing*. Ithaca, NY: Cornell UP, 2004.

Croxton, Sally. "The Tale of Two Families." *Newcastle Herald* 11 May 2000: 5.

Cummins, Kev. Rev. of *Manchester United Ruined My Life*, by Colin Shindler. *The Manchester City Supporters Homepage*. n.d. 22 Nov. 2002 <http://www.uit.no/mancity/ reviews/ruined.html>.

Cuthbert, Denise. "Holding the Baby: Questions Arising from Research into the Experiences of Non-Aboriginal Adoptive and Foster Mothers of Aboriginal Children." *Journal of Australian Studies* 59 (1998): 39–52.

Dalziell, Rosamund. *Shameful Autobiographies: Shame in Contemporary Australian Autobiographies and Culture*. Melbourne: Melbourne UP, 1999.

Davies, Rebecca J. Rev. of *The Shark Net*, by Robert Drewe. *Lancet* 356.9237 (2000): 1282.

Davies, Sara. *Running from the Devil*. London: John Blake, 2006.

Davis, Howard, and Marc Bourhill. " 'Crisis': The Demonization of Children and Young People." *"Childhood" in "Crisis"?* Ed. Phil Scraton. London: UCL Press, 1997. 28–57.

Davis, Rocio G. *Begin Here: Reading Asian North American Autobiographies of Childhood*. Honolulu: University of Hawaii Press, 2007.

Diski, Jenny. *Skating to Antarctica*. 1997. London: Granta Books, 1998.

Douglas, Kate. "Blurbing Biographical: Authorship and Autobiography." *Biography: An Interdisciplinary Quarterly* 24.4 (2001): 806–826.

———. "Intergenerational Mediations: Writing about Abused and Abusive Mothers." *Textual Mothers, Maternal Texts: Representations of Mothering in Contemporary Women's Literature: Fiction, Poetry and Life Writing*. Ed. Andrea O'Reilly and Elizabeth Podnieks. Waterloo, ON: Wilfred Laurier Press, 2009.

———. "The Universal Autobiographer: The Politics of Normative Readings." *Journal of Australian Studies* 72 (2002): 173–179.

———. " 'Your Book Changed My Life': Everyday Literary Criticism and Oprah's Book Club." *The Oprah Affect: Critical Essays on Oprah's Book Club*. Ed. Cecilia Konchar Farr and Jaime Harker. New York: SUNY Press, 2008.

Dow, Gwyn, and June Factor, eds. *Australian Childhood: An Anthology*. Ringwood: McPhee Gribble, 1991.

Doyle, Paddy. *The God Squad*. London: Transworld, 2002.

Drewe, Robert. Interview with Ramona Koval. *Australian Book Review* Apr. 2000: 9–10.

———. *The Shark Net*. 2000. Ringwood: Penguin, 2001.

Eakin, Paul John. "Breaking Rules: The Consequences of Self-Narration." *Biography: An Interdisciplinary Quarterly* 24.1 (2001): 113–127.

————, ed. *The Ethics of Life Writing*. Ithaca, NY: Cornell UP, 2004.

————. *How Our Lives Become Stories*. Ithaca, NY: Cornell UP, 1999.

————. "Introduction: Mapping the Ethics of Life Writing." *The Ethics of Life Writing*. Ed. Paul John Eakin. Ithaca, NY: Cornell UP, 2004.

————. "The Referential Aesthetic of Autobiography." *Studies in the Literary Imagination* 23.2 (1990): 129–144.

Edel, Leon. *Writing Lives: Principia Biographica*. New York: Norton, 1984.

Egan, Susanna. "Changing Faces of Heroism: Some Questions Raised by Contemporary Autobiography." *Biography: An Interdisciplinary Quarterly* 10.1 (1987): 20–38.

————. *Mirror Talk: Genres of Crisis in Contemporary Autobiography*. Chapel Hill: U of North Carolina P, 1999.

————. *Patterns of Experience in Autobiography*. Chapel Hill: U of North Carolina P, 1984.

Egan, Susanna, and Gabriele Helms. "Autobiography and Changing Identities." *Biography: An Interdisciplinary Quarterly* 24.1 (2001): ix–xx.

Elder, Bruce. "When Men Were Bonzer and Women Were Sheilas." Extract from *Remembering When . . . Reflections on a Changing Australia*. *Sunday Mail* 30 Mar. 2003: 47–49.

Ellis, Cath. "A Strange Case of Double Vision: Reading Carmel Bird's *The Stolen Children: Their Stories*." *Overland* 158 (Autumn 2000): 75–79.

Engel, Susan. "Children's Life-Writing." *Encyclopedia of Life Writing*. Ed. Margaretta Jolly. London: Fitzroy Dearborn, 2001. 204–206.

Erben, Michael. "Britain: 20th-Century Auto/biography." *Encyclopedia of Life Writing*. Ed. Margaretta Jolly. London: Fitzroy Dearborn, 2001. 141–142.

Fairhurst, Duncan. *Our Little Secret: A Father's Abuse, a Son's Life Destroyed*. London: Hodder & Stoughton, 2007.

Farrell, Kirby. *Post-traumatic Culture: Injury and Interpretation in the Nineties*. Baltimore: Johns Hopkins UP, 1998.

Felman, Shoshana, and Dori Laub. *Testimony: Crises of Witnessing in Literature, Psychoanalysis, and History*. New York: Routledge, 1992.

Felski, Rita. "On Confession." *Women, Autobiography, Theory: A Reader*. Ed. Sidonie Smith and Julia Watson. Madison: U of Wisconsin P, 1998. 83–95.

Fernand, Deirdre. Interview with Constance Briscoe. *Sunday Times* 15 Jan 2006. 27 May 2006 <http://www.timesonline.co.uk/article/0,,2092–1985687,00.html>.

Fisher, Antwone Quenton. *Finding Fish: A Memoir*. New York: HarperCollins, 2001.

Fletcher, Geoffrey H. "Power Up, Don't Power Down." *T.H.E. (Technological Horizons in Education) Journal* 33.14 (Sept. 2006): 24–25.

Flook, Maria. "Cold Comfort." Rev. of *Skating to Antarctica*, by Jenny Diski. *New York Times Book Review* 16 Aug. 1998: 4.

————. *My Sister Life*. New York: Pantheon, 1998.

Ford, Donna. *The Step Child: A True Story*. London: Vermilion, 2006.

Foucault, Michel. *Discipline and Punish: The Birth of the Prison*. Trans. Alan Sheridan. New York: Random House, 1977.

————. *Ethics, Subjectivity and Truth*, vol. 1. Ed. Paul Rainbow. Trans. Robert Hurley et al. New York: New Press, 1997.

————. *The History of Sexuality*, vol. 1. Transl. Robert Hurley. New York: Random House, 1978.

————. "What Is an Author?" *Textual Strategies: Perspectives in Post-Structuralist Criticism*. Ed. Josue Harari. London: Methuen, 1979. 141–160.

Fraser, Rosalie. *Shadow Child: A Memoir of the Stolen Generation*. Maryborough, Vic.: Hale and Iremonger, 1998.

Free Thinking Teens (MySpace site). 15 June 2007. <http://www.myspace.com/freethink ingteens>.

Freeman, Traci. "Celebrity Autobiography." *Encyclopedia of Life Writing*. Ed. Margaretta Jolly. London: Fitzroy Dearborn, 2001. 188–190.

French, Sean. "If Readers Sometimes Find It Hard to Respect the Boundaries between Fact and Fiction, It May Be Because Authors Have Deliberately Blurred Them." *New Statesman* 10 Apr. 1998: 23.

Freud, Sigmund. "The Aetiology of Hysteria." *The Freud Reader*. Ed. Peter Gay. New York: Norton, 1989. 96–110.

————. *Beyond the Pleasure Principle*. 1920. Ed. and trans. James Strachey. London: Hogarth Press, 1955.

————. *Jokes and Their Relation to the Unconscious*. 1905. Ed. and trans. James Strachey. New York: Norton, 1989.

————. "Mourning and Melancholia." *The Freud Reader*. Ed. Peter Gay. New York: Norton, 1989. 584–588.

Freyd, Jennifer. *Betrayal Trauma: The Logic of Forgetting Childhood Abuse*. Cambridge: Harvard UP, 1996.

Frost, Laura. "After Lot's Daughters: Kathryn Harrison and the Making of Memory." *a/b: Auto/Biography Studies* 14.1 (1999): 51–70.

Fuller, Alexandra. *Don't Let's Go to the Dogs Tonight*. 2002. London: Picador, 2003.

George, Glynis. "Contested Meanings and Controversial Memories: Narratives of Sexual Abuse in Western Newfoundland." *Tense Past: Cultural Essays in Trauma and Memory*. Ed. Paul Antze and Michael Lambek. New York: Routledge, 1996. 45–64.

Gerster, Robin. "Memoir from a Vanished Sydney." Rev. of *A Saucepan in the Sky*, by Brian Nicholls. *Australian Book Review* Oct. 2001: 26–27.

Gilding, Michael. *Australian Families: A Comparative Perspective*. South Melbourne: Longman, 1997.

————. *The Making and Breaking of the Australian Family*. North Sydney: Allen and Unwin, 1991.

Gilmore, Leigh. *Autobiographics: A Feminist Theory of Women's Self-Representation*. Ithaca, NY: Cornell UP, 1994.

————. "Limit-Cases: Trauma, Self-Representation, and the Jurisdictions of Identity." *Biography: An Interdisciplinary Quarterly* 24.1 (2001): 128–139.

————. *The Limits of Autobiography: Trauma and Testimony*. Ithaca, NY: Cornell UP, 2001.

———. "Trauma and Life Writing." *Encyclopedia of Life Writing*. Ed. Margaretta Jolly. London: Fitzroy Dearborn, 2001. 885–887.

———. "What Do We Teach When We Teach Trauma?" *Teaching Life Writing Texts*. Ed. Miriam Fuchs and Craig Howes. New York: Modern Language Association of America, Options for Teaching Series, 2007.

Giroux, Henry A. "Stealing Innocence: The Politics of Child Beauty Pageants." *The Children's Culture Reader*. Ed. Henry Jenkins. New York: NYU Press, 1998. 265–282.

———. "Teenage Sexuality, Body Politics and the Pedagogy of Display." *Youth Culture and Identity in a Postmodern World*. Ed. Jonathan S. Epstein. Oxford: Blackwell, 1998. 24–53.

Goldson, Barry. " 'Childhood': An Introduction to Historical and Theoretical Analyses." *"Childhood" in "Crisis"?* Ed. Phil Scraton. London: UCL Press, 1997. 1–27.

Gould, Mark. "Unfinished Business." *Guardian* 28 Sept 2005. 19 May 2009 <http://www.guardian.co.uk/society/2005/sep/28/childrensservices.guardiansocietysupplement>.

Gray, Paul. "Real-Life Misery: Read All about It! Confessionals and Memoirs Spur Book Sales." *Time* 21 Apr. 1997: 106.

Gregory, Julie. *Sickened*. New York: Bantam, 2004.

Gross, Kate. "Most Teens Use MySpace Responsibly." *Youth Studies Australia* 26.1 (March 2007): 8.

Haaken. Janice. *Pillar of Salt: Gender, Memory, and the Perils of Looking Back*. New Brunswick, NJ: Rutgers University Press, 1998.

———. "Sexual Abuse, Recovered Memory, and Therapeutic Practice: A Feminist-Psychoanalytic Perspective." *Social Text* 41 (1994): 115–145.

Hacking, Ian. "The Making and Molding of Child Abuse." *Critical Inquiry* 17.1 (1991): 253–288.

———. *Rewriting the Soul: Multiple Personality and the Sciences of Memory*. Princeton, NJ: Princeton UP, 1995.

Hall, Alan, and Michael Leidig. *Girl in the Cellar: The Natascha Kampusch Story*. London: Sceptre, 2006.

Hamilton, Paula. "The Knife Edge: Debates about Memory and History." *Memory and History in Twentieth-Century Australia*. Ed. Kate Darian-Smith and Paula Hamilton. Oxford: OUP, 1994. 9–32.

Harrison, Kathryn. *The Kiss*. London: Fourth Estate, 1997.

Hattenstone, Simon. "Utter Balls." *Guardian Unlimited* 30 June 2001. 8 Nov. 2002 <http://books.guardian.co.uk/Print/0,3858,4212891,00.html>.

Healy, Chris. *From the Ruins of Colonialism: History as Social Memory*. Cambridge: Cambridge UP, 1997.

Henderson, Meg. *Finding Peggy*. London: Corgi Books, 1994.

Henke, Suzette. *Shattered Subjects: Trauma and Testimony in Women's Life-Writing*. New York: St. Martin's, 1999.

Herman, David. "Autobiography, Allegory and the Construction of Self." *British Journal of Aesthetics* 35.4 (1995): 351–360.

———. "The Culture of Narcissism." *New Statesman* May 1997: 124–127.

Higonnet, Anne. *Pictures of Innocence: The History and Crisis of Ideal Childhood.* London: Thomas and Hudson, 1998.

Hirsch, Marianne. *Family Frames: Photography, Narrative, and Postmemory.* Cambridge: Harvard UP, 1997.

Hodgkin, Katharine, and Susannah Radstone. "Introduction: Contested Pasts." *Contested Pasts: The Politics of Memory.* Ed. Katharine Hodgkin and Susannah Radstone. London: Routledge, 2003. 1–21.

Holland, Patricia. "History, Memory and the Family Album." *Family Snaps: The Meanings of Domestic Photography.* Ed. Jo Spence and Patricia Holland. London: Virago, 1991. 1–14.

———. *What Is a Child? Popular Images of Childhood.* London: Virago, 1992.

Hooten, Joy. "Australia: 20th-Century Life Writing." *Encyclopedia of Life Writing.* Ed. Margaretta Jolly. London: Fitzroy Dearborn, 2001. 203–204.

———. *Stories of Herself When Young: Autobiographies of Childhood by Australian Women.* Oxford: Oxford UP, 1990.

Horvitz, Leslie Alan. "Private Lives . . . Public Laundry." *Insight on the News* 23 June 1997: 36–37.

Hughes, Kathryn. "I Have Seen the Past and It Works." *Guardian Unlimited* 11 July 1999. 11 Nov. 1999 <http://www.guardian.co.uk/Archive/Article/0,4273,3882243,00.html>.

———. "Loving Lorna." *New Statesman* 17 Sept. 2001: 54.

———. "Remembering Imagination: Have We Had Enough of Memoir?" *Observer* (online ed.) 19 Aug. 2001. 17 Nov. 2001 <http://www.observer.co.uk/review/story/0,6903,538944,00.html>.

Hunt, Celia. *Therapeutic Dimensions of Autobiography in Creative Writing.* London: Jessica Kingsley, 2000.

Inglis, Amirah. *Amirah: An Un-Australian Childhood.* Melbourne: Heinmann, 1983.

Jackson, Kevin. "Blurbs 101." *New Yorker* 4 Oct. 1999: 56–58.

James, Alison, Chris Jenks, and Alan Prout. *Theorizing Childhood.* New York: Teachers College Press, 1998.

Jameson, Fredric. "Nostalgia for the Present." *South Atlantic Quarterly* 88.2 (1989): 527–560.

Jenks, Chris. *Childhood.* London: Routledge, 1996.

Jenkins, Henry, ed. *The Children's Culture Reader.* New York: NYU Press, 1998.

———. "From YouTube to YouNiversity." *Chronicle of Higher Education* 53.24 (16 Feb. 2007): B9.

Jolly, Margaretta, ed. *Encyclopedia of Life Writing.* London: Fitzroy Dearborn, 2001.

Jones, Malcolm. "Hard Luck, Good Tales: A Splendid Memoir of a Ghastly Irish Childhood." *Newsweek* 2 Sept 1996. 12 June 2008. <http://www.newsweek.com/id/102743>.

———. "It's Better to Tell All than to Tell It Well." *Newsweek* 27 July 1998: 59.

Jones, Mary Paumier. "Once in a House on Fire." Rev. of *Once in a House on Fire*, by Andrea Ashworth. *Library Journal* 123.10 (1998): 118.

Jordan, Pat. "Dysfunction for Dollars." *New York Times* 28 July 2002. 20 June 2008 <http://query.nytimes.com/gst/fullpage.html?res=9404E4DE1538F93BA15754C0A96 49C8B63>.

Kakutani, Michiko. "For an Outsider, It's Mostly Sour Grapes in the Land of Milk and

Honey." Rev. of 'Tis: a Memoir, by Frank McCourt. New York Times 14 Sept. 1999. 12 June 2008 <http://www.nytimes.com/books/99/09/12/daily/091499mccourt-book-review.html>.

———. "Generous Memories of a Poor Painful Childhood." Rev. of Angela's Ashes, by Frank McCourt. New York Times 17 Sept. 1996. 12 June 2008 <http://query.nytimes.com/gst/fullpage.html?res=9C04E3DA133AF934A2575AC0A960958260>.

Kaplan, E. Ann. Trauma Culture: The Politics of Terror and Loss in Media and Literature. New Brunswick, NJ: Rutgers University Press, 2005.

Karr, Mary. Cherry. London: Picador, 2000.

———. "The Family Sideshow." Penguin Reading Guide for The Liars' Club. 14 July 2008 <http://us.penguingroup.com/static/rguides/us/liars_club.html>.

———. "How I Told My Friends I Was Writing about My Childhood and What They Said in Return." Slate 14 July 2008 <http://www.slate.com/id/2162744/>.

———. The Liars' Club: A Memoir. London: Picador, 1995.

Katz, John. Virtuous Reality. New York: Random House, 1997.

Keneally, Thomas. Homebush Boy: A Memoir. Port Melbourne, Vic.: William Heinemann Australia, 1995.

Kennedy, Rosanne. "The Affective Work of Stolen Generations Testimony: From the Archives to the Classroom." Biography 27.1 (Winter 2004): 48–77.

Kevjumba. "I Hate the SAT." 15 June 2007 <http://www.youtube.com/watch?v=Pt3d2NJJj3s>.

Kirtz, Bill. "Out of the Mouths Of . . ." Quill Apr. 1998: 8–10.

"A Kiss and Sell Affair." Financial Times 15 Aug. 1999. 9 Nov. 1999 <http://www.globalarchive.ft.com/search/FTJSPController.htm>.

Klein, Kerwin Lee. "On the Emergence of Memory in Historical Discourse." Representations 69 (2000): 127–150.

Kline, Stephen. "The Making of Children's Culture." The Children's Culture Reader. Ed. Henry Jenkins. New York: NYU Press, 1998. 95–109.

Knight, Ivor. Out of Darkness. Fremantle: Fremantle Art Centre Press, 1998.

Kociumbas, Jan, ed. Australian Childhood: A History. Sydney: Allen and Unwin, 1997.

Kornblum, Janet. "Parents Question MySpace's Safety." USA Today 8 Jan. 2006. 14 June 2007 <http://www.usatoday.com/tech/news/2006–01–08-myspace-sidebar_x.htm?loc=interstitialskip>.

———. "Teens Hang Out at MySpace." USA Today 8 Jan. 2006. 14 June 2007 <http://www.usatoday.com/tech/news/2006–01–08-myspace-teens_x.htm>.

Koval, Ramona. Interview with Robert Drewe. Australian Book Review Apr. 2000: 8–10.

Kraus, Paul. "Stealing All but Hope." Saturday Magazine: Newcastle Herald 10 June 2000: 8.

Kuhn, Annette. "Remembrance." Family Snaps: The Meanings of Domestic Photography. Ed. Jo Spence and Patricia Holland. London: Virago, 1991. 17–25.

Kurtz, Jane. "Memoirs and the Teenage Reader." Booklist 15 Sept. 1999: 250.

Lacan, Jacques. The Four Fundamental Concepts of Psychoanalysis. Trans. Alan Sheridan. New York: Norton, 1981.

Lambek, Michael, and Paul Antze. "Introduction: Forecasting Memory." *Tense Past: Cultural Essays in Trauma and Memory*. Ed. Paul Antze and Michael Lambek. New York: Routledge, 1996. xi–xxxviii.

Lauck, Jennifer. *Blackbird: A Childhood Lost and Found*. London: Little, Brown, 2000.

Lego, Suzanne. Rev. of *Angela's Ashes*, by Frank McCourt. *Perspectives in Psychiatric Care* 33.3 (July–Sept. 1997): 41–43.

Lejeune, Philippe. *On Autobiography*. Trans. Katherine Leary. Ed. Paul John Eakin. Minneapolis: U of Minneapolis P, 1989.

Levy, Eric P. "The Predicament of Individuality in *Angela's Ashes*." *Irish University Review: A Journal of Irish Studies* 32.2 (Autumn–Winter 2002): 259–274.

Littlely, Brian, Chris Salter, and Kim Wheatley. "Web Hunt for Teen Murder Clues." *News.com.au*. 23 Feb. 2007. 14 June 2007 <http://www.news.com.au/story/0,23599,21271997–2,00.html>.

Loane, Sally. "Forget Politics, Lowitja, and Write the Story of Your Stolen Childhood." *Sydney Morning Herald* 10 Dec. 2001. 12 Dec. 2001 <http://www.smh.com.au/news/0102/26/text/features4.html>.

Loftus, Elizabeth, and Katherine Ketcham. *The Myth of Repressed Memory: False Memories and Allegations of Sexual Abuse*. New York: St. Martin's Press, 1994.

Loose, Julian. "Stranger than Fiction." *Guardian Unlimited* 28 July 2001. 29 Apr. 2003 <http://books.guardian.co.uk/departments/biography/story/ 0,6000,528505,00.html>.

McCooey, David. *Artful Histories: Modern Australian Autobiography*. Cambridge: Cambridge UP, 1996.

———. "Australian Autobiographies of Childhood: Beginning and Myth." *Southerly: A Review of Australian Literature* 55.1 (1995): 132–145.

McCourt, Frank. *Angela's Ashes*. London: HarperCollins, 1996.

———. Interview with Dave Weich. *Powells.com*. n.d. 19 July 2008 <http://www.powells.com/authors/mccourt.html>.

———. Interview with Jay Macdonald. *BookPage*. n.d. 19 July 2008 <http://www.bookpage.com/0512bp/frank_mccourt.html>.

———. *'Tis: A Memoir*. London: Flamingo, 1999.

McCourt, Malachy. *A Monk Swimming: A Memoir*. 1998. Sydney: Picador, 1999.

McKay, Nellie Y. "The Girls Who Became Women: Childhood Memories in the Autobiographies of Harriet Jacobs, Mary Church Terrell and Anne Moody." *Tradition and the Talents of Women*. Ed. Florence Howe. Urbana: U of Illinois P, 1991. 105–124.

McPhee, Hilary. "Other People's Stories." *Australian's Review of Books* 13 Oct. 1999: 3–4.

Mantel, Hilary. *Giving Up the Ghost*. London: HarperCollins, 2003.

Martín Alcoff, Linda, and Laura Gray-Rosendale. "Survivor Discourse: Transgression of Recuperation?" *Getting a Life: Everyday Uses of Autobiography*. Ed. Sidonie Smith and Julia Watson. Minneapolis: U of Minnesota P, 1996. 198–225.

Mayman, Jan. "Stepping out of a Childhood Shadow." Rev. of *Shadow Child*, by Rosalie Fraser. *Age* 30 Oct. 1998. 1 Sept. 2001 <http://theage.com.au/daily/981030/news/news20.html>.

Meehan, Donna. *It Is No Secret: The Story of a Stolen Child*. Sydney: Random House, 2000.

Meeke, Kieran. Interview with Constance Briscoe. *Metro.co.uk*. 30 Jan 2006. 27 May 2006 <http://www.metro.co.uk/fame/interviews/article.html?in_article_id=496&in_page_id=11 >.

Mehegan, David. " 'Scissors' Case Cuts Deep in Literary World." *Boston Globe* 15 August 2005. 15 July 2008 <http://www.boston.com/ae/books/articles/2005/08/17/scissors_case_cuts_deep_in_book_world/>.

Miller, Nancy K. "Introduction: Extremities; or, Memoirs at the Fin de Siècle." *a/b: Auto/Biography Studies* 14.1 (1999): 1–4.

Miller, Nancy K., and Jason Tougaw. "Introduction: Extremities." *Extremities: Trauma, Testimony, and Community*. Ed. Nancy K. Miller and Jason Tougaw. Urbana: U of Illinois P, 2002. 1–22.

Mitchell, James B. "Popular Autobiography as Historiography: The Reality Effect of Frank McCourt's *Angela's Ashes*." *Biography* 26.4 (Fall 2003): 608–618.

Moore, Judith. *Fat Girl: A True Story*. London: Profile Books, 2005.

Moore, Suzanne. Rev. of *Skating to Antarctica*, by Jenny Diski. *New Statesman* 15 Aug. 1997: 44–45.

Morrison, Blake. "The Importance of Not Being Earnest." *Guardian Unlimited* 12 Jan. 2002. 29 Apr. 2003 <http://books.guardian.co.uk/reviews/biography0,6121, 631144,00html>.

Moss, Barbara Robinette. *Change Me into Zeus's Daughter*. New York: Scribner, 2001.

Mysterious Skin. Dir. Greg Araki. Desperate Pictures, 2004.

National Association for People Abused in Childhood (NAPAC). 21 Dec. 2005 <http://www.napac.org.uk>.

National Center for Missing and Exploited Children. *Teen Internet Safety Study*. March 2006. 13 June 2007 <http://www.netsmartz.org/safety/statistics.htm>.

National Society for the Prevention of Cruelty to Children (NSPCC). 21 Dec. 2005 <http://www.nspcc.org.uk>.

Netsmartz. 14 June 2007 <www.netsmartz.org>.

Neustadter, Roger. "Archetypal Life Scripts in Memoirs of Childhood: Heaven, Hell, and Purgatory." *Auto/Biography* 12 (2004): 236–259.

Ngowi, Rodrique. "Family Settles with 'Scissors' Author." *Bookrags.com*. 30 August 2007. 30 January 2008 <http://www.bookrags.com/news/family-settles-with-scissors-author-moc/>.

Nicholls, Brian. *A Saucepan in the Sky*. Maryborough, Vic.: Hale and Iremonger, 2001.

Nora, Pierre. "Between Memory and History." Representations 26 (1989): 7–25.

O'Connor, Terry. "Why Covers Sell Books." *Courier Mail* 26 Sept. 2001: 35.

Ofshe, Richard, and Ethan Watters. *Making Monsters: False Memories, Psychotherapy, and Sexual Hysteria*. New York: Charles Scribner's Sons, 1994.

Oliver, Kelly. *Witnessing: Beyond Recognition*. Minneapolis: U of Minnesota P, 2001.

O'Malley, Kathleen. *Childhood Interrupted: Growing Up under the Cruel Regime of the Sisters of Mercy*. London: Virago, 2005.

O'Neill, Gilda. *My East End*. 1999. London: Penguin, 2000.

Parker, David. "Counter-Transference in Reading Autobiography: The Case of Kathryn Harrison's *The Kiss*." *Biography: An Interdisciplinary Quarterly* 25.3 (2002): 493–504.

Pelzer, Dave. *A Child Called "It"*. London: Orion, 2001.

———. *Help Yourself: Finding Hope, Courage and Happiness*. New York: Plume, 2001.

———. *The Lost Boy*. Deerfield Beach, FL: HCI, 1997.

———. *A Man Named Dave*. New York: Plume, 2000.

Pelzer, Richard B. *A Teenager's Journey: Overcoming a Childhood of Abuse*. New York: Warner Wellness, 2006.

Podnieks, Elizabeth. " 'Hit Sluts' and 'Page Pimps': On-line Diarists and Their Quest for Cyber-Union." *Life Writing* 1.2 (2004): 123–150.

Poletti, Anna. "Self-Publishing in the Global and Local: Situating Life Writing in Zines." *Biography: An Interdisciplinary Quarterly* 28.1 (Winter 2005): 183–192.

"Poor Pitiful Me." *Weekend Australian Review* 18–19 Jan. 2003: R8.

Rainie, Lee. "Life Online: Teens and Technology and the World to Come." Speech to the annual conference of the Public Library Association. 23 March 2006. 13 June 2007 <http://www.pewinternet.org/ppt/Teens%20and%20technology.pdf>.

Riemer, Andrew. *Inside Outside*. Pymble, NSW: Angus and Robertson, 1992.

Roberts, Michèle. *Food, Sex, and God: On Inspiration and Writing*. London: Virago, 1998.

Robinson, Nicola. "Writing Lives." *Australian Bookseller and Publisher* Sept. 1997: 33–36.

Rodriguez, Richard. *Hunger of Memory: The Education of Richard Rodriguez*. New York: Bantam, 1983.

Running with Scissors. Dir. Ryan Murphy. Plan B, 2006.

Rust, Michael. "Read about Why I Love Me and How Much I've Suffered." *Insight on the News* 2 June 1997: 19.

Sage, Lorna. *Bad Blood: A Memoir*. 2000. London: Fourth Estate, 2001.

———. "Living on Writing." *Grub Street and the Ivory Tower: Literary Journalism and Literary Scholarship from Fielding to the Internet*. Ed. Jeremy Treglown and Bridget Bennett. Oxford: Clarendon Press, 1998. 262–276.

Sanders, Valerie. "Childhood and Life Writing." *Encyclopedia of Life Writing*. Ed. Margaretta Jolly. London: Fitzroy Dearborn, 2001. 203–204.

Saunders, Kate. "Their Winning Ways." Rev. of *Ugly*, by Constance Briscoe. *TimesOnline* 29 Jan 2006. 27 April 2006 <http://www.timesonline.co.uk/article/0,,23113–2008077,00.html>.

Schaffer, Kay. "Australia: Indigenous Life Writing." *Encyclopedia of Life Writing*. Ed. Margaretta Jolly. London: Fitzroy Dearborn, 2001. 69–70.

Scheper-Hughes, Nancy, and Howard F. Stein. "Child Abuse and the Unconscious in American Popular Culture." *The Children's Culture Reader*. Ed. Henry Jenkins. New York: NYU Press, 1998. 178–195.

Scott, Elizabeth. "A Passage Home" *Alive Magazine* Feb 2001. 1 Sept. 2001 http://www.alivemagazine.com.au/alive/articles/2001/feb/coverstory.html.

Scraton, Phil. "Preface." *"Childhood" in "Crisis"?* Ed. Phil Scraton. London: UCL Press, 1997. vii-xiv.

———. "Whose 'Childhood'? What 'Crisis'?" *"Childhood" in "Crisis"?* Ed. Phil Scraton. London: UCL Press, 1997. 163–186.

Seltzer, Mark. "Wound Culture: Trauma in the Pathological Public Sphere." *October* 80 (Spring 1997): 3–26.

Sexton, David. "Paperback of the Week." Rev. of *Bad Blood*, by Lorna Sage. *London Evening Standard* 26 June 2001. 27 Sept. 2001 <http://www.eveningstandard.co.uk/ entertainment/stayingin/articles/905405>.

Shayler, Kate. *The Long Way Home: The Story of a Homes Kid.* 1999. Sydney: Random House, 2001.

Sherman, Steve. "Booksellers Vie for Places on Author Tours: Publishers Are Demanding Creative Proposals, Proven Track Records." *Publishers Weekly* 243.17: 26.

Shiells, Joanne. "Ordinary People, Extraordinary Lives." *Australian Bookseller and Publisher* Oct. 1999: 26–30.

Shindler, Colin. *Manchester United Ruined My Life.* London: Headline, 1998.

Slater, Lauren. *Lying: A Metaphorical Memoir.* New York: Penguin, 2001.

Slaughter, Carolyn. *Before the Knife: Memories of an African Childhood.* London: Black Swan, 2002.

Smith, Patrick. "What Memoir Forgets." *Nation* 27 July 1998: 30–36.

Smith, Sidonie. "Autobiographical Manifestos." *Women, Autobiography, Theory: A Reader.* Ed. Sidonie Smith and Julia Watson. Madison: U of Wisconsin P, 1998. 433–40.

———. "Performativity, Autobiographical Practice, Resistance." *Women, Autobiography, Theory: A Reader.* Ed. Sidonie Smith and Julia Watson. Madison: U of Wisconsin P, 1998. 108–15.

———. *A Poetics of Women's Autobiography: Marginality and the Fictions of Self-Representation.* Bloomington: Indiana UP, 1987.

Smith, Sidonie, and Kay Schaffer. *Human Rights and Narrated Lives: The Ethics of Recognition.* New York, Palgrave, 2004.

Smith, Sidonie, and Julia Watson, eds. *Getting a Life: Everyday Uses of Autobiography.* Minneapolis: U of Minnesota P, 1996.

———. *Reading Autobiography: a Guide for Interpreting Life Narratives.* Minneapolis: U of Minnesota P, 2001.

———. "Situating Subjectivity in Women's Autobiographical Practices." *Women, Autobiography, Theory: A Reader.* Ed. Sidonie Smith and Julia Watson. Madison: U of Wisconsin P, 1998. 3–52.

Smith, Thomas R. "Introduction: Autobiography in Fresh Contexts." *a/b: Auto/Biography Studies* 13.1 (Spring 1998): 1–5.

Spence, Jo, and Patricia Holland, eds. *Family Snaps: The Meanings of Domestic Photography.* London: Virago, 1991.

Spufford, Francis. "The Wish for White." Rev. of *Skating to Antarctica*, by Jenny Diski. *TLS Times Literary Supplement* 25 July 1997: 11–12.

Steedman, Carolyn. "Enforced Narratives: Stories of Another Self." *Feminism and Autobiography: Texts, Theories, Methods.* Ed. Tess Cosslett, Celia Lury, and Penny Summerfield. London: Routledge, 2000. 25–39.

————. *Landscape for a Good Woman*. London: Virago, 1986.

————. "Stories." *Women, Autobiography, Theory: A Reader*. Ed. Sidonie Smith and Julia Watson. Madison: U of Wisconsin P, 1998. 243–54.

Steinwand, Jonathan. "The Future of Nostalgia in Friedrich Schlegel's Gender Theory: Casting German Aesthetics Beyond Ancient Greece and Modern Europe." *Narratives of Nostalgia, Gender, and Nationalism*. Ed. Jean Pickering and Suzanne Kehde. New York: NYU Press, 1997. 9–29.

Stuever, Hank. "Growing Up Truly Absurd." *Washington Post* 30 July 2002. 1 July 2008 <http://www.washingtonpost.com/ac2/wp-dyn?pagename=article&node=&content Id=A19023-2002Ju129>.

Sturken, Marita. "The Remembering of Forgetting: Recovered Memory and the Question of Experience." *Social Text* 57 (1999): 103–125.

————. "The Wall, the Screen, and the Image: The Vietnam Veterans Memorial." *Representations* 35 (1991): 119.

Sturrock, John. "Theory versus Autobiography." *The Culture of Autobiography: Constructions of Self- Representation*. Ed. Robert Folkenflik. Stanford: Stanford UP, 1993. 21–37.

Symons, Allene. "Around the Panels: Celebrity Authors, Author Celebrities." *Publishers Weekly* 244.32: 30.

Teen Choice Action Team (MySpace site). 15 June 2007 <http://profile.myspace.com/index.cfm?fuseaction=user.viewprofile&friendid=157008726>.

Teen Lit (MySpace site). 15 June 2007 <http://groups.myspace.com/teenlit>.

Terdiman, Richard. *Present Past: Modernity and the Memory Crisis*. Ithaca, NY: Cornell UP, 1993.

Terry, Jennifer, and Jacqueline Urla. *Deviant Bodies: Critical Perspectives on Difference in Science and Popular Culture*. Bloomington: Indiana UP, 1996.

Thorogood, Julia. "Story Packs a Punch." Rev. of *Once in a House on Fire*, by Andrea Ashworth. *Times Educational Supplement* 17 Apr. 1998: 9.

Tompkins, Jane. "Me and My Shadow." *Feminisms: An Anthology of Literary Theory and Criticism*. Ed. Robyn R. Warhol and Dianne Price Herndi. New Brunswick, NJ: Rutgers UP, 1997. 1103–1116.

Tomasevskij, Boris. "Literature and Biography." *Readings in Russian Poetics: Formalist and Structuralist Views*. Ed. Ladislav Matejka and Krystyna Pomorska. Cambridge: MIT Press, 1971. 46–55.

Treneman, Ann. "When Did You Last See Your Panda?" *Independent* 8 Feb. 1998. 12 Dec. 1999 <http://www.independent.co.uk/archives/reviews/mccourtgenart080298.shtml>.

Up! (Series) Dir. Michael Apted. Granada Television, 1999.

United Nations Convention on the Rights of the Child. 4 Jan 2008 <http://www.unicef.org/crc/>.

"We Like to Watch." *Time* 26 June 2000: 56.

Wells, Kevin. *Goodbye Dearest Holly*. London: Psychology News Press, 2005.

West, Carol. "Once in a House on Fire." Rev. of *Once in a House on Fire*, by Andrea Ashworth. *New York Times Book Review* 12 July 1998: 21.

White, Michael, and David Epston. *Narrative Means to Therapeutic Ends*. New York: Norton, 1990.

White, Michael. *Maps of Narrative Practice*. New York: Norton, 2007.

Whitfield, Charles L. *Memory and Abuse: Remembering and Healing the Effects of Trauma*. Deerfield Beach, FL: Health Communications, 2002.

Whitlock, Gillian, ed. *Autographs: Contemporary Australian Autobiography*. St. Lucia: U of Queensland P, 1995.

————. "Disciplining the Child: Recent British Academic Memoir." Unpublished essay, 2002.

————. "From Biography to Autobiography." *The Cambridge Companion to Australian Literature*. Ed. Elizabeth Webby. Cambridge: Cambridge UP, 2000. 232–257.

————. "In the Second Person: Narrative Transactions in Stolen Generations Testimony." *Biography: An Interdisciplinary Quarterly* 24.1 (Winter 2001): 197–214.

————. *Soft Weapons: Autobiography in Transit*. Chicago: U of Chicago P, 2007.

————. "Why Then a Writer of Memoirs Is a Better Thing than an Historian." Unpublished essay, 2002.

Wiltshire Rape Support Line. 9 June 2003 <http://www.rapeline.org.uk/helpline2e.htm>.

WiredSafety. 14 June 2007. <http://wiredsafety.org/internet101/blogs.html>.

Wimsatt, W. K. "The Intentional Fallacy." *The Verbal Icon: Studies in the Meaning of Poetry*. Lexington: U of Kentucky P, 1967. 3–20.

Wolcott, James. Rev. of *The Kiss*, by Kathryn Harrison. *New Republic* 31 March 1997: 32–37.

Woodward, Richard. "Reading in the Dark: Has American Lit Crit Burned Out?" *Village Voice Literary Supplement* Oct. 1999. 31 May 2000 <http://www.villagevoice.com/vls/164/woodward.shtml>.

Zailckas, Koren. *Smashed: Growing Up a Drunk Girl*. London: Ebury, 2006.

INDEX

Page numbers in italics refer to illustrations.

Abbott, Kirsten, 185–186n.1, 186nn.9–10
abductions, of and by children, 4. *See also* Stolen Generations
Aborigines, *see* Indigenous Australians
accessibility: of author, 162; of autobiography, 162. *See also* knowability
Adams, Timothy Dow, 59
addiction, Western campaigns against, 49
adolescence, prolonged, 49. *See also* young people's life writing; youth cultures
adolescent self, as radical pacesetter, 33
adult: as author of childhood autobiographies (*see* author); children failed by, 134–135, 136; desire for and investment in children, 48; as empathetic good citizen, 61; normative expectations and parental responses, 48–49; production of children's life narratives of, 173
adult–child binary, 6
advertisements: depictions of children in, 45–47, 60; nostalgic, 23
Aftab, Parry, 194nn.4–5
"After Lot's Daughters: Kathryn Harrison and the Making of Memory" (Frost), 156
agency, child's: in autobiography, 188–189n.17, 190n.2; lack of, 31, 43, 45, 122, 173
"agony-overload," 157
alcoholism, parental, 31–32
All Over but the Shoutin' (Bragg), 106
Amazon.com reviews, 156, 163–168

Amirah: An Un-Australian Childhood (Inglis), 35
Angela and the Baby Jesus (McCourt), 187n.5
Angela's Ashes (McCourt), 9, 10, 16, 68, 69–70, 72–75, 85, 182n.10, 187nn.6–8, 188n.16
anger, autobiographer's, 187–188n.8; and exposure of trauma's perpetrator, 147, 148; of limited value in childhood autobiographies, 137
Anne Frank: The Diary of a Young Girl (Frank), 188n.17
Antwone Fisher (film), 191n.11. *See also* Fisher, Antwone
Antze, Paul, 20, 24, 38, 97, 108, 171
Apgar, Sonya C., 110
Apted, Michael, 2
Araki, Gregg, 107
Armitstead, Claire, 187n.7
Ashworth, Andrea, 5, 68, 70, 75–82, 158, 161
Attwood, Bain, 6, 34, 39, 185n.14
Auntie Rita (Morgan), 11
Australia: advocacy for, though autobiography, 39–40; "black Armband" vs. "Three-Cheers" views of history, 184n.7; child abuse statistical profile, 191n.9; and metonymic childhood autobiographies, 41; postwar immigrants, 34–35, 100; Stolen Generations (*see* Stolen Generations). *See also* Indigenous Australians; Stolen Generations
"Australian Autobiographies" (McCooey), 10
Australian Human Rights and Equal Opportunity Commission (HREOC) report, 184n.10

ABOUT THE AUTHOR

Dr. Kate Douglas is a Senior Lecturer in the Department of English, Creative Writing, and Australian Studies at Flinders University (South Australia). She is the editor of *Trauma Texts* (with Professor Gillian Whitlock) (Routledge, 2009).